# T. F. Torrance in Recollection and Reappraisal

# T. F. Torrance in Recollection and Reappraisal

Bruce Ritchie

*Foreword by Robert T. Walker*

PICKWICK *Publications* · Eugene, Oregon

T. F. TORRANCE IN RECOLLECTION AND REAPPRAISAL

Copyright © 2021 Bruce Ritchie. All rights reserved. Except for brief quotations in critical publications or reviews, no part of this book may be reproduced in any manner without prior written permission from the publisher. Write: Permissions, Wipf and Stock Publishers, 199 W. 8th Ave., Suite 3, Eugene, OR 97401.

Pickwick Publications
An Imprint of Wipf and Stock Publishers
199 W. 8th Ave., Suite 3
Eugene, OR 97401

www.wipfandstock.com

PAPERBACK ISBN: 978-1-7252-7643-7
HARDCOVER ISBN: 978-1-7252-7642-0
EBOOK ISBN: 978-1-7252-7644-4

*Cataloguing-in-Publication data:*

Names: Ritchie, Bruce, author. | Walker, Robert T., foreword writer

Title: T. F. Torrance in recollection and reappraisal / Bruce Ritchie.

Description: Eugene, OR: Pickwick Publications, 2021 | Includes bibliographical references and index.

Identifiers: ISBN 978-1-7252-7643-7 (paperback) | ISBN 978-1-7252-7642-0 (hardcover) | ISBN 978-1-7252-7644-4 (ebook)

Subjects: LCSH: Torrance, Thomas F. (Thomas Forsyth), 1913–2007 | Jesus Christ—Person and offices | Theology, Doctrinal—History—20th century

Classification: BT40 R58 2021 (print) | BT40 (ebook)

01/14/21

For my dear wife Grace,
with love.

*We are not to think of the humiliation and exaltation of Christ simply as two events following one after the other, but as both involved in appropriate measure at the same time all through the incarnate life of Christ.*

—T. F. TORRANCE, *ATONEMENT*

# Contents

*Foreword by Robert T. Walker* | ix
*Acknowledgements* | xiii
*Abbreviations* | xiv
*Introduction* | xv

**PART ONE: RECOLLECTION** | 1
Chapter 1: Theological Teacher | 3
Chapter 2: Theological College | 10
Chapter 3: Theological Course | 24

**PART TWO: METHODOLOGY** | 39
Chapter 4: Theological Science | 41
Chapter 5: Theological Depth | 54
Chapter 6: Theological Knowledge | 62
Chapter 7: Theological Concepts | 83

**PART THREE: CHRISTOLOGY** | 93
Chapter 8: "Man of Israel, Lord God" | 95
Chapter 9: Jesus as Teacher | 100
Chapter 10: Jesus as Agent | 125
Chapter 11: Jesus as Savior: Calvary | 148
Chapter 12: Jesus as Savior: Bethlehem | 161

Part Four: Reappraisal | 173
Chapter 13: Christology in Reverse | 175
Chapter 14: Christology and Time | 186
Chapter 15: Christology and History | 198
Chapter 16: Christology and Gospel | 209

*Appendix 1: The Dogmatics Course* | 217
*Appendix 2: The Dogmatics Exams* | 226
*Appendix 3: The Firbush Conferences* | 242
*Appendix 4: The Historical/Theological Exegesis
 of 2 Corinthians 5:21* | 248

*Bibliography* | 269
*Index* | 275

# Foreword

BRUCE RITCHIE IS ONE of the last generation to have studied under T. F. Torrance at New College, and this is a fascinating account, by one of Torrance's ablest students, of what it was like to have been taught by him and of the intense intellectual stimulus which this generated. Coming, as Ritchie did, from an evangelical perspective influenced by the Westminster tradition, this book is his account of the questions posed by the encounter between the tradition in which he had been nurtured and what he now met at New College in 1973. It is a vivid and enthralling story of the clash as he experienced it, and of his struggles to come to terms with the very real similarities, but also differences, between them. Torrance was clearly evangelical, thoroughly Christological, and Trinitarian, but how could the two approaches be held together, if at all, or were the differences irreconcilable?

Written in the form of an autobiographical account detailing all he was now having to think through, the book is an absorbing story of a journey of theological discovery and development; but it is very much more than that on at least three fronts. First, in recounting step by step Torrance's teaching, setting it alongside the evangelical Westminster tradition, the book is a careful examination of the two in dialogue as it were. Throughout, it endeavors to sympathetically assess the strengths of each and explore the extent to which they can be complementary if not held together. Second, the book also serves as a wonderful introduction to Torrance's theology in general, particularly for evangelicals and those of the Westminster tradition. Third, the book introduces significant new material about Torrance, hitherto not widely available, which will add to its appeal and be of particular interest to those already familiar with Torrance.

The new material derives from the fact that the book is a firsthand account, reconstructed from copious, meticulous notes, fashioned during his studies and aided by a still vivid memory, recording Ritchie's experience and feelings at the time. It was clearly a momentous, deeply formative period for him, just as it was and had been for many others. Of particular interest here, in addition to the teaching, are the various appendices. Two of the appendices detail the whole structure of the three year course in Christian Dogmatics: in terms of year, lecture topics and lecturer, sequence, prescribed and supplementary reading, seminar topics and set texts, essay topics and suggested reading, yearly exams, and the six, three-hour final honours exams with the full lists of their questions. The detail is extra-ordinary, even down to the precise date of each lecture or seminar, and the initials of the lecturer. Together, both content and detail make the book unique, but also very timely and priceless in the sense that this is remarkable, first-hand material which, with the passing of the generations, would soon have been lost for ever. It is certainly unlikely that anyone other than Ritchie would have all the information at hand, let alone be able to assemble it the way he has.

The uniqueness of this book also stems from Ritchie being both accomplished church historian and theologian, able to combine the rigours and skill of both disciplines along with the pastor's skill of engaging and effective communication to a congregation through a lifetime of preaching. That combination of skills is seen to good effect in the book's content, structure, and style. The sixteen chapters, despite the depth of their content, are mostly only ten pages on average and read like a novel in their lively, fluid style, with only two stretching to twenty pages on account of their complexity and subject matter.

After a career in the Church of Scotland ministry (1977–2013) spanning three parishes, the far south-west (Galloway), the middle (Crieff), and the north (Dingwall), interspersed just before the last by a spell teaching Systematic Theology in Malawi (2001–2006) and gaining a PhD on Robert Moffat, the nineteenth-century Scottish missionary to southern Africa, Ritchie began lecturing in "Scottish Church History" and "Understanding Worship" at the Highland Theological College in Dingwall (2007). Since retiral from full-time ministry in 2013, he has been able to devote more time to his lectureship and turn his hand to major writing subjects dear to his heart, including the history and theology of St Columba of Iona and the theological legacy of Thomas F. Torrance.

In this book, Ritchie uses the three final chapters to elaborate on possibilities he detects in Torrance's theology for bridging some of the divisions in Scottish theology. He takes concepts and statements central to

Torrance and suggests how they can be developed to achieve a rapprochement between the differing ways in which Torrance and the Westminster tradition see the incarnation and atonement. These chapters are the most challenging conceptually in the book, as well as the most controversial. Some may argue they stretch Torrance's logic beyond where Torrance himself would go, at least in the way Ritchie has termed and phrased his conclusions; but, as expected, the chapters are beautifully crafted, carefully and astutely argued, and deserve the deepest consideration.

After the publication of his magisterial work on *Columba: The Faith of an Island Soldier* (2019), Dr. Ritchie has now followed it with a masterful book on Thomas F. Torrance.

**Robert T. Walker**

# Acknowledgements

THANKS ARE DUE TO all who have encouraged and stimulated me in this project. Such a list could go back to my student days at New College, but, more recently, I have been particularly motivated by the study group which met at Andrew McGowan's manse in Inverness, and by the group which, at time of writing, still gathers for regular conferences at Firbush, Loch Tay. There is one person who ought to be mentioned by name. That is Robert (Bob) Walker, whose enthusiasm and joy in theology is infectious, and whose comments I have appreciated tremendously. Thanks also to my publishers, Wipf & Stock, for their involvement and guidance.

# Abbreviations

| | |
|---|---|
| *ANCF* | Ante-Nicene Christian Fathers |
| *CD* | Barth, Karl. *Church Dogmatics.* Translated by G. T. Thomson et al. Edinburgh: T. & T. Clark, 1936–77. |
| *DSCHT* | *The Dictionary of Scottish Church History and Theology.* Edited by Nigel M. de S. Cameron. Edinburgh: T. & T. Clark, 1993. |
| *NCF* | Nicene Christian Fathers |
| *SBET* | *Scottish Bulletin of Evangelical Theology.* |
| *SJT* | *Scottish Journal of Theology* |
| *WCF* | *Westminster Confession of Faith* |
| *WTS* | Westminster Theological Seminary |

# Introduction

OVER THE YEARS, TWO theological streams have fed my Christian faith. One is the Reformed conservative-evangelical tradition, with roots in the Federal Calvinism of the *Westminster Confession of Faith*. This was introduced to me by John Riddell, my parish minister in Jedburgh, himself influenced by James Philip of Holyrood Abbey Church in Edinburgh, and by Willie Still of Gilcomston South Church in Aberdeen. The other is the teaching of Thomas F. Torrance at New College, of the University of Edinburgh. Sometimes these two theological currents are tempestuous and opposing floodwaters, creating violent turbulence wherever they clash. Sometimes they dovetail and harmonize more agreeably. But I value each of them. This book is an exploration of some aspects of theology, mainly from Torrance's perspective but ever aware of questions posed by that other rich theological tradition.

It is easy to drown in the ocean of Torrance literature now available. There is a vast corpus of material written both by him and about him.[1] Books, articles, websites, internet forums, Facebook groups, conferences and conference papers, increase week by week. However, whilst this book has the normal expected references to important published works, I have based it principally on my direct experience of the lectures which Torrance gave us at New College, especially in the never to be forgotten autumn term of 1973, which was my first in the Faculty of Divinity. Hence, the main sources for this book are my own notes, scribbled down in class as the lectures were delivered. These are the USP of the present volume. Thankfully, my appreciation of what Torrance taught us has deepened over the years, and so this work combines what I and my classmates first heard

---

1. Extensive lists of Torrance's published works are given by McGrath, *T. F. Torrance: An Intellectual Biography*, 247–633; and the online T. F. Torrance website, *Participatio*.

in these lectures—or at least thought we heard—with later reflection. All being well, readers will detect where one ends and the other starts!

The lecture notes were hand-written, and with a neatness of penmanship which has vanished after typing on a computer keyboard for so long. The 200-page student-notepads, at that time used by nearly everyone at college, were blocks of narrow-lined A4 writing paper, with prepared holes, ready for insertion into ring-binders. These were purchased from *Thin's* bookshop on Edinburgh's South Bridge, or from *Bauermeister's* on George IV Bridge. *Thin's* was a long-established Edinburgh institution, established in 1848, with an extensive theology section in its basement, stocking both new and second-hand books. Its theological bias reflected the interests of its founder James Thin, who, in the late nineteenth century was a prominent member of the United Presbyterian Church, serving on its hymnody committee for some years. Since the 1970s, *Thin's* has mutated into *Blackwell's*. *Bauermeister's* is no more. In my student days, there were at least fifteen second-hand bookshops with theology sections, all within easy reach of New College. On many a midweek afternoon, I toured these treasure troves, both north and south of Princes' Street. The most extensive was *Thin's,* but the well-known publisher T. & T. Clark in George Street also boasted a good selection in its lower floor. One afternoon, my fellow-browser at T. & T. Clark was Tom Torrance himself. He spotted a set of Quasten's *Patrology*, and murmured, "I must get these for my son Iain." T. & T. Clark were also helpful in that they were delighted to provide new dust-jackets, free of charge, for my copies of Barth's *Church Dogmatics*, many of which I picked up second-hand.

Returning to the lecture-notes, most of them are dated, though not all. However, all the pages are consecutively numbered, making it clear when, in the series, a particular lecture was delivered. These personal, hand-written, lecture notes continue until the Spring term of early 1975 in the second year of our studies. That was when Tom Torrance delivered his lectures on soteriology. For that module he issued to the class full printed handouts for each lecture, before going through them in detail in class, adding comments and explanations. Hence, I have no hand-written notes for these lectures apart from observations written in the margins of the handouts themselves. This explains the fewer references to personal notes in chapters of this book touching upon soteriology. However, these class-handouts were almost identical to documents pulled together by Bob Walker and published as Torrance's *Atonement* book. A list of class handouts appears in Appendix 1. What I have found intriguing, in

*Introduction*

re-reading the lecture notes and the class handouts, are the annotations which I inserted. These often reveal questions which occurred when revising for exams.

What I have tried to present in this book is a sense of the evolving process of understanding—and of misunderstanding—which we experienced as Torrance's students, as we attempted to digest his ideas for the first time. He challenged us with new ways of thinking. It took time to work out what he was saying. And it took time to see the consequences of what he said. In some areas, that process was only completed years after we left New College. My hope is that this volume may convey something of the tussle which went on in our minds as we sat in lecture room and seminar class listening to our professor. That is what I want this book to be. It is not meant to be a neat, edited-cut, version of Torrance's theology, skipping over the perplexities, the questions, the wrong turnings, the blind alleys, and the suspect thinking, which we dallied with on the way to the destination. Though Torrance was never comfortable with the notion of Process Theology, he may have been appreciative of the theological process which his students went through!

Appendix 1 gives insight into the structure of the course in Christian Dogmatics at New College, as molded by Torrance himself. This appendix reproduces reading lists, seminar details, and the titles of many of the printed handouts which came our way. Appendix 2 reproduces the exam papers in Dogmatics which we had to sit. These exam questions reveal with precise clarity the issues which Torrance wanted his students to address.

This book focusses, in particular, on key aspects of Torrance's methodology and Christology. But do these have a natural link? Are they comfortable bed-fellows? I think so. And the reason why they go together is because one of Torrance's foundational thoughts was that *being* and *act* need to be linked, and should not be separated in a radical disjunction of *form* and *content*. Therefore, a central concern of this book revolves around Torrance's understanding of the relationship between incarnation and atonement. In order to grasp his approach to that particular issue, his methodological convictions concerning the unity of being and act, form and content, become of prime importance.

At the same time, our exploration of Torrance's thinking on incarnation and atonement will take us beyond what he stated explicitly, to implications which we believe are necessary consequences of his position. Specifically, we shall explore the notion that Calvary is the presupposition of Bethlehem, that Bethlehem is the presupposition of Calvary, and that what undergirds the mutual dependence of one on the other, and makes everything possible, is in fact the cross of Calvary and the first Easter. Hence, in a similar way to how Torrance argued that everything in God's covenant relationship with Israel was, "dependent upon the one great sacrifice on the day of atonement when the covenant was renewed for the year,"[2] we shall affirm that everything in God's covenant relationship with his people in Christ is dependent upon the cross. Everything is rooted in the cross. Absolutely everything. What this means, quite incredibly, is that, in a very real sense, the incarnation itself takes place through the portal of the cross. But, more of this later.

One further point of introduction. And this concerns methodology in particular. Of vital importance to Torrance was the notion of intuitive knowledge in which an enquirer apprehends the "wholeness" of something, thus gaining a knowledge beyond what can be inferred deductively from individual scraps of data which may be accessed through formal experimental procedures.[3] What this meant for Torrance was that, when a scholar—or any believer—grasps, however imperfectly, the overall logic and grammar of Christian theology, then the way in which he or she reads the Word of God is thoroughly changed; and his or her understanding of the possibilities of God's actions in human history—actions to which Scripture so powerfully witnesses—is radically transformed. The converse is also true: if there is no understanding or appreciation or grasp of the divine reality which alone provides the rationale and logic of Scripture, then, quite simply, Scripture cannot be read aright, and all our theology is compromised. All being well, this will become clearer as we proceed.

---

2. Cf. Torrance, *Atonement*, 16, 39–40.
3. Cf. Torrance, *Theological Science*, 239–41.

— *Part One* —

# Recollection

— *Chapter 1* —

# Theological Teacher

OF ALL TWENTIETH-CENTURY SCOTTISH theologians, Thomas Forsyth Torrance has had, and continues to have, the greatest academic impact on a global scale.[1] Others have gained international reputations, and James Denney, John MacLeod, P. T. Forsyth, Donald and John Baillie, Hugh Ross Mackintosh, Ronald Gregor Smith, William Barclay, Donald MacLeod, Sinclair Ferguson, to name but a few, loom large. However, Torrance is the scholar who is studied most worldwide; and, as the twenty-first century unfolds, interest in all aspects of his theology is increasing.

## A Brief Biography

Thomas Forsyth Torrance was born in 1913 in western China of missionary parents. He had two brothers and three sisters. His brothers, James B. Torrance and David W. Torrance, also feature in this book, although, wherever the name Torrance occurs without explanation, it is T. F. Torrance whom it denotes. References to James and David are made clear in context. Concerning TFT, as he was known by generations of students, most of his early education was in China before the family returned to Scotland where he completed his schooling at Bellshill Academy, Glasgow. He then progressed to the Universities of Edinburgh and Basel. At Edinburgh he graduated MA in philosophy, before studying for his BD under H. R. Mackintosh and other teachers at New College. In class, Torrance told us that reading, and re-reading, Mackintosh's *Types*

1. For biographical details see: Torrance, *Gospel, Church and Ministry*, 25–73; Noble, "Torrance, Thomas Forsyth," 823–24; McGrath, *T. F. Torrance: An Intellectual Biography*, 3–107; Torrance, *Reluctant Minister*, vi, 1–20.

*of Modern Theology* was what provided him with the underpinning for his own thinking.² In Basel he wrote his doctoral thesis on *The Doctrine of Grace in the Apostolic Fathers,* with Karl Barth as supervisor.³ He then had a brief teaching stint at Auburn University in the United States before returning to Scotland.

From 1940 until 1947 Torrance served as parish minister in the rural village of Alyth in Perthshire, though for an important part of the period—1943 to 1945—he was an Army Chaplain during the Second World War. He told us of reading his Greek New Testament daily throughout his Army service. Sometimes his parish experiences came into his lectures. One day he talked about a member of the Alyth congregation who was a shepherd and also a keen reader of theology, especially Calvin's *Institutes*. The shepherd asked him to preach on the doctrine of justification by faith, and a few Sundays later he did so, with his sermon emphasizing that men and women are made right with God purely by divine grace and not by human merit. At the close of the service one of the church elders was in tears, confused, even angry. "Dr. Torrance, do you mean to say that all I've done in my life makes no difference before God!" Taking him aside, Torrance explained patiently the true nature of the divine grace which is in Jesus Christ, and the concomitant truth that the Christian lives a holy life in response to grace, not as a means to earn it.

In 1947 Torrance was called to Beechgrove Church Aberdeen, where H. R. Mackintosh had once been minister. The Aberdeen stay was brief. In 1950 he became Professor of Church History at New College. Then, in 1952, he transferred to the chair of Christian Dogmatics which he occupied for the rest of his professional career. In 1976 he was honored by being elected Moderator of the General Assembly of the Church of Scotland. One of the highlights of our time at New College was being invited, as his final year students, to a Moderator's reception which took place in the Signet Library, off Parliament Square in Edinburgh. We all went along, despite it being in the middle of the exam week for our Finals. It was a magnificent occasion on a brilliantly sunny evening in May. At one point, Torrance stood on a rickety wobbly chair to address the company of invitees, with the Principal Clerk to the General Assembly holding firmly to chair and Moderator together! Among the many guests whom we met that evening were a couple from Alyth who remembered

---

2. Torrance, "Hugh Ross Mackintosh."
3. Torrance, *Doctrine of Grace in the Apostolic Fathers.*

with deep affection the young minister coming to their parish, full of energy and full of enthusiasm.

After retirement from New College in 1979, Tom Torrance remained busy. He wrote intensively. He lectured internationally. Most of all, he was able to spend more time with his wife Margaret. He died in 2007, at the age of ninety-four.

As previously stated, there exists a vast body of Torrance's published works, including articles, reviews, reports, and books. In 1947 he became founding editor of *The Scottish Journal of Theology* along with J. K. S. 'Jacko' Reid. From 1955 he was co-editor of the English translation of Karl Barth's *Church Dogmatics*. The first volume of Barth's work had appeared in English in 1936, through the industry of G. T. Thomson of Edinburgh; but it was Torrance, along with G. W. Bromiley, who was the driving force for the translation of the rest of Barth's *magnum opus*. In the 1960s he and his brother David edited a fresh translation of *Calvin's New Testament Commentaries*, which were published by the St. Andrew Press of the Church of Scotland.

For Torrance, Christian theology had to be rooted in faith. Moreover, it had to take place within the community of the church, the body of Christ. For Torrance, the church was the scientific community which provided the individual theologian with context, and with intelligent cross-examination of what he or she wrote. This meant that he regarded any notion of a person being a freelance theologian as incongruous. As part of his committed churchmanship Torrance chaired doctrinal committees for the Church of Scotland and the wider church; and, in 1958 his Church of Scotland activity produced the influential report, *The Biblical Doctrine of Baptism*.[4] Throughout the 1950s he was involved in international and ecumenical theological work, and it was during these years that his *Faith and Order* books were published. He was an enthusiastic ecumenical thinker. He engaged with Roman Catholic theologians; and he helped to revive connections between the Church of Scotland and the Orthodox churches. Then the 1960s and 1970s saw him developing his thinking on theological method, producing a cascade of important publications; this area of his work is referred to in some detail in subsequent chapters.

Torrance saw himself a theologian of the universal church; not of one branch of it. Nevertheless, one of his abiding concerns was his Scottish Reformed heritage. Consequently, in 1959 he produced *The*

---

4. Church of Scotland, *Biblical Doctrine of Baptism*.

*School of Faith,* which made available new editions of some of the classic Catechisms of the Reformed Church.[5] Almost as important as the selected Catechisms, Torrance wrote a one-hundred-and-twenty-six-page introduction for the *School of Faith* as a robust presentation of his own theological position over against traditional Westminster theology. Years later, in 1996, he published *Scottish Theology from John Knox to John McLeod Campbell,* which further explored the fault lines between his position and that of Federal Calvinism.[6] Torrance's position vis-a-vis the *Westminster Confession of Faith* separated him from many traditional conservative-evangelicals within the Kirk, although in his later years a rapprochement and warmer relationship developed between himself and his more conservative colleagues.

Despite his gigantic publishing output, Torrance's New College classroom lectures on Christology remained unavailable to the wider public until his nephew Bob Walker had them published in two large volumes: *Incarnation: The Person and Life of Christ* (2008), and *Atonement: The Person and Work of Christ* (2009). Torrance intended to publish them himself, but a stroke made this impossible. Before the *Incarnation* and *Atonement* books appeared, Torrance's Christology notes were scattered among his own papers, or in students' binders in the form of the class handouts which we were given in the second year of our studies. When the *Incarnation* and *Atonement* books came on the market they were sought-after worldwide, with study groups springing up to discuss their theology. One such group formed in Inverness in the north of Scotland, in the home of my friend Professor Andrew McGowan of Highland Theological College of the University of the Highlands and Islands. Bob Walker was invited to our first meeting, and he gave an overall view of Torrance's theology. Over the next few years the group met monthly. Inevitably, one of the major issues to emerge from these sessions was the tension between Torrance's understanding of Reformed theology, and how Reformed theology was interpreted within the Westminster and Puritan tradition.

### The Firbush Conferences

In November 2010, following the success of the *Incarnation* and *Atonement* volumes, Bob Walker instituted a Torrance Retreat Conference.

---

5. Torrance, *School of Faith.*
6. Torrance, *Scottish Theology from John Knox to John McLeod Campbell.*

This soon became a twice-yearly event. One held in early summer. The other in late October or early November. These took place at Firbush, an Edinburgh University outdoor center in Perthshire, on the southern shores of Loch Tay.

Firbush has an idyllic location. It is situated on a small promontory, jutting out from a woodland of silver-birch trees which are pale-green in springtime and russet-brown in the autumn. Across the water, on the north side of the loch, Ben Lawers and its neighboring summits dominate the skyline. On a sunny day the loch glistens and sparkles. On a wet day its grey waters blend with grey mist and grey hills, creating a beguiling atmosphere. Firbush has all the accoutrements of any outdoor center: bunkhouse, kayaks, canoes, boots, wet-gear, and the many bits and pieces of equipment which are essential for hill-walking and water sports. In addition, it has a small conference room; and it was this facility which made it a superb location for these retreat conferences.

Around twenty-five to thirty men and women attended each conference, exploring a variety of Torrance-linked issues. What we found was that, whatever the theme for a particular gathering, never far away was Torrance's emphasis on the relationship between incarnation and atonement. These two foci and their interconnection were central in Torrance's thinking as he sought to interpret Christian theology as a cohesive and integrated entity.[7] Torrance argued that, just as modern science had to develop new ways of thinking after the discoveries of James Clerk Maxwell and Albert Einstein, so also must theology. When Torrance looked at modern science, he saw it focusing on dynamic fields in their interrelationships rather than on discrete objects and forces as was the case in traditional Newtonian mechanics. He became convinced that, just as modern science—under pressure from the nature of reality itself—had been compelled by that reality to develop notions of a continuum-of-being, so also theology needed to find a more dynamic and integrated way of understanding its subject-matter. Torrance saw all the actions of God as inter-connected. And he understood all of them to cohere, ultimately, within the person of the Mediator himself. It is in Jesus Christ that incarnation and atonement, being and act, coincide and inter-relate.

At Firbush, as in our study-group in Inverness, the relationship between incarnation and atonement, and the rooting of the work of Christ in the person of Christ, raised a host of questions. Was the

---

7. Cf. Walker (Introduction to Torrance, *Atonement*, xxxv): "At every point Torrance sees the interconnectedness of all Christian doctrine."

approach valid? Was Torrance's interpretation of the relationship between incarnation and atonement biblical? Did Torrance pour too much significance into the person of Christ in his incarnation at Bethlehem? Did he leave any need for an atoning death on Calvary? Was everything achieved simply by God becoming man in Christ? Had Torrance traded Calvary for Bethlehem? Had he, in effect, replaced the Cross with the Birth? Did his exalted view of Christmas and the nature of the incarnation render Easter unnecessary? Allied to these were other questions, especially relating to the type of humanity which the Son of God took to himself in the womb of Mary.

With some of these issues in mind, I presented a paper to the Firbush November 2013 conference entitled: "*Christology in Reverse: A re-evaluation of Torrance's Theology.*" In other Firbush papers, before and after that date, I explored related themes such as: "*Torrance, the Gospel, and Universalism*" (2010); "*The Notion of Human Response in the Theology of T. F. Torrance*" (2016); "*Jesus is Himself the Gospel*" (2018); "*Being a Student of T. F. Torrance*" (2019) and "*Torrance's Theological Method*" (2019). This book has grown from these submissions, especially the 2013 lecture "*Christology in Reverse.*" The argument of that paper, explored in greater detail later in this book, was that although in Christian theology there is a persuasive logic for centering everything in the person of Christ, nevertheless, when we drill deep into the nature of the incarnation, what we discover is that the incarnation itself is *centered in*, and is *dependent upon*, the cross and the resurrection. This means that when we ask the question, "what is it that makes the incarnation what it is?," we discover that it is the decisive event of cross and resurrection which actualizes and make possible the event of incarnation itself. This is the "reversal" of normal thinking as indicated in the title of the lecture "*Christology in Reverse.*"[8] Hence, whereas normally we understand incarnation as preceding atonement both chronologically and ontologically, the thesis of this book is that Calvary is the presupposition of Bethlehem. Of course, it is also true that Bethlehem is the presupposition of Calvary. However, ultimately it is the cross which provides the undergirding reality and foundational logic

---

8. Torrance, *Atonement*, 3, alluded to a related reversal of thinking necessitated by the cross: "[The death of Jesus Christ] entails a complete reversal of our previous attitudes and all of our preconceived ideas. This reversal means that *we cannot think our way into the death of Christ because the continuity of our thinking and striving has been interrupted by it, but we may think our way from it* if we follow the new and living way opened up to us in the crucifixion" (italics Torrance's).

for both. The Son of God was able to be *born* at Bethlehem because sin was *borne* at Calvary. Such a rethinking has, I believe, two major benefits. First, some diverse elements in traditional orthodox Christian theology fit together in a more integrated fashion. Second, some—though by no means all—of the tensions between Torrance and Westminster theology can be resolved.

T. F. Torrance Conferences are held all over the world; but the Firbush conferences have a unique feature, in that they have significant input from the Torrance family itself. Bob Walker, Tom Torrance's nephew and editor of the *Incarnation* and *Atonement* volumes, has been the conference organizer, and usually the presenter of each initial keynote paper. Much of his editing of the *Incarnation* and *Atonement* books took place at Firbush's lochside location. Also attending has been Tom Torrance's youngest brother, David W. Torrance, who, though into his nineties, has presented a paper at almost every gathering. Uniquely, David has been able to illuminate our understanding of his brother's thinking from recollections of family discussions.[9] David's son, also David, has likewise taken part. Another nephew, Alan Torrance, son of Tom's other brother James B. Torrance, has contributed, as has Alan's son Andrew who addressed the issue of modern Christian apologetics in relation to the mind-set of contemporary academia which too readily assumes a methodological naturalism.

Over the years, visiting academics and researchers have included: Baxter Kruger, Andrew McGowan, David Fergusson, Douglas and Caroline Kelly, Tom Noble, Jason Radcliff, Alexandra Stuart-Lee, Vanessa Platek, Joanna MacDonald, Geordie Ziegler, Robin Parry, Jennifer Floether, Sandy Forsythe, Tomas Kodacsy, Angus Morrison among many more. A comprehensive list of Firbush speakers and titles of their papers is given in Appendix 3. Part conference, part retreat, Firbush events are eagerly anticipated by all of us, whether students, ministers, lay churchfolk, or professional theologians. This book aims to continue some of the discussions which I enjoyed both at Firbush and in Inverness. May it contribute to conversations surrounding Torrance's thinking, and to the enrichment of faith which such occasions have made possible.

---

9. Cf. Torrance, *Reluctant Minister*.

— *Chapter 2* —

# Theological College

NEW COLLEGE, EDINBURGH, NOW known as the Divinity School of the University of Edinburgh, was built in 1846 as one of the training seminaries of the recently formed Free Church of Scotland following the Disruption of 1843. In 1900 it became the property of the United Free Church of Scotland; and, in 1935, following the 1929 union of the United Free Church with the Church of Scotland, it was merged with Edinburgh University's already existing Faculty of Divinity. Perched high on the ridge of the Castle rock, above Princes' Street Gardens, and only a stone's throw from Edinburgh Castle itself, New College has a spectacular outlook. The view from its gates over Princes' Street, over the UNESCO Heritage site of Edinburgh New Town, and over the waters of the Firth of Forth to the coastline of Fife and the hills beyond, is stunning.

This was the view enjoyed by John "Rabbi" Duncan who, in the mid-nineteenth century, was Free Church Professor of Hebrew and Oriental languages at the College. But Rabbi Duncan was not only an expert in Semitic tongues. He was also a theologian with an original, and a sometimes mystical, cast of mind. One of Rabbi Duncan's concerns was that Christian theology should link the events of Bethlehem and Calvary far more closely than has sometimes been the case. Though he never disputed that the cross of Calvary is the center of Christian faith, he was concerned that,

> We make far too little of the Incarnation; the Fathers knew much more of the incarnate God. Some of them were oftener at Bethlehem than at Calvary; they had too little of Calvary, but they knew Bethlehem well. They took up the Holy Babe in their arms; they

loved Immanuel, God with us. We [can never be] too often at the cross, but we are too seldom at the cradle; and we know too little of the Word made flesh, of the Holy Child Jesus.[1]

For Rabbi Duncan, Bethlehem represented the incarnation, and Calvary the atonement. Significantly, he believed that the former (Bethlehem) should be understood as far more than simply the necessary chronological precursor of the latter (Calvary). He saw each as bound up in the other; and he regarded each as having meaning only because of the other. Bethlehem and Calvary, incarnation and atonement, belong together.

In the 1970s, and roughly a century after Rabbi Duncan's era, I was one of numerous students, from all parts of the world, who studied theology at New College, many of whom attracted by Tom Torrance's reputation. Each day I took the bus from my student lodgings into Edinburgh city center. I walked up the Mound. I passed through the college gates. I acknowledged John Knox's statue in the inner quadrangle. And then I entered the college proper. Over the next few years, what I found was that Rabbi Duncan's desire to link Bethlehem and Calvary more closely, was also a guiding principle in the approach to Systematic Theology under Tom Torrance's leadership.

At New College, Systematic Theology was called Christian Dogmatics, and was structured as a positive exposition of Christian theology. This complemented the Divinity course which concentrated on philosophical critiques of religious thought. As first-year students we were given a combined module termed General Theology, which had four sessions each week, with splits between Dogmatics and Divinity. Monday, Tuesday, Thursday, and Friday, were teaching days. There were no classes on Wednesdays, which was the day customarily reserved for personal study in the morning, and for University sports in the afternoon for those of an athletic disposition. In these days, New College still operated with the traditional three terms, rather than the two-semester system which, at that point, only Stirling University of the then-eight Scottish Universities had adopted.

In the opening autumn term, the focus in Dogmatics was methodology, with Tom Torrance himself lecturing. Later in the academic year his brother James Torrance gave us introductory lectures in Christology, Pneumatology, and Ecclesiology. These lectures ensured that every student, even if they only read Dogmatics for one year, had an overview of

---

1. Stuart, *Recollections of the Late John Duncan, LL.D.*, 167.

all the major themes of Christian theology. In second and subsequent years Dogmatics and Divinity had their own independent modules. Complementing these, the courses on offer at New College embraced the traditional theological subjects of: New Testament, Old Testament, Church History, and Practical Theology.

## Divinity

The Divinity department was headed by Professor John McIntyre, assisted by D. W. D. (Bill) Shaw, Noel O'Donoghue, Frank Whaling and Elizabeth Maclaren. At the time, John McIntyre was temporary Acting-Principal of the University meaning that we saw little of him, though we did study his detailed circulated notes. Bill Shaw was a lawyer by profession before studying theology, and had been a squash-player of international standard. Bill introduced us to critiques of Christian faith from philosophy, sociology, Marxism, psycho-analysis, process-theology, and other disciplines. Father Noel O'Donoghue was a quiet, reflective, figure, lecturing on prayer, religion and science, and the problem of evil. Frank Whaling came from the Methodist tradition, with his specialty being the relationship of Christian faith to world religions. Frank was also a keen table-tennis player who regularly visited the student common-room for a game.

Elizabeth McLaren had recently joined the teaching-staff, after graduating as an exceptional student. She was to marry Douglas Templeton, one of the New Testament lecturers; and, in future years she acquired an international reputation in progressive theology. Of all the lecturers at New College, Elizabeth gave us the most detailed feedback on our assignments, writing copious comments on our scripts. Her specialty was critiquing faith from the viewpoint of creative writers. She challenged us with questions about God-talk, especially questions posed by modern culture. The very first handout she circulated to the class was dialogue from Samuel Beckett's play "Waiting for Godot." Behind her approach was the question, "Does the divine spirit speak to us through the human spirit?" If so, is it in the arts, and through men and women of creative insight into the human condition, that we learn most of God?

## Dogmatics

The Dogmatics department was located in New College's Ramsay Wing, named after the eighteenth-century Edinburgh poet Alan Ramsay who lived nearby, and whose statue stands in Princes' Street Gardens near the floral-clock. Assisting Tom Torrance were his brother James B. Torrance, the eccentric Canon Roland Walls, and the neat and dapper Alasdair Heron. John Zizoulas from the Orthodox tradition had recently been associated with the faculty but was now based in Glasgow.

⌒

James Torrance was as passionate about theology as his brother; and, as well as teaching various sections of the regular Dogmatics course, James also delivered two exceptional series of lectures for the benefit of honors and post-graduate students. One series, delivered in conjunction with the Church History department, was on Scottish Theology from 1560 until 1843. The other series featured nineteenth-century theology, especially in Germany. James' students soon became familiar with his many sayings. One was that the relationship between God and his people was, "A Covenant not a Contract." Another was, "Love without justice is sentimentality, but justice without love is demonic." One time, James and his wife Mary invited our group to their house for supper. During the evening he talked to us at length about the need to believe in the transforming power of the Gospel. In particular, he spoke about his lecture-tour visits to South Africa and challenging white South Africans about apartheid. He told us that most South Africans, whom he met, knew the system was wrong, but they were terrified of change because of reprisals they feared would follow. He urged them to believe in the Gospel which they professed, and to believe in the liberating power of God, through that Gospel, to effect change miraculously without bloodshed. Believe the Gospel! Live out the Gospel! Put into practice what you know is true in Christ! Trust the Lord whom you follow!

James loved to embellish his lectures with chalk-drawn diagrams. These often focused on illustrating how the trinitarian being of God is involved not only in all of God's own actions, but also in the human response to God's grace. Latterly, James was appointed Professor of Theology at Aberdeen University where he taught until retirement. He published little. But whatever he did put into print, mainly in the form of journal articles or contributory chapters to larger works, was always accessible and highly usable. When I taught the Understanding Worship module at Highland Theological College, I tried to make my students familiar with James' thinking.[2] It gave them a theological underpinning to their understanding of worship through a theology focused around James' emphasis on Christ as the one true worshipper, in which he expounded the implications of the vicarious humanity of Christ in relation to our own response to God.

Canon Roland Walls was a member of *The Community of the Transfiguration* based at Rosslyn Chapel, a few miles south of Edinburgh. Rosslyn Chapel later featured in the screen version of Dan Browne's book *The Da Vinci Code*. Canon Walls' particular interest was ecclesiology, holding a high-view of the church as the bride of Christ. On one occasion, when a student moaned about the church, he retorted sharply, "How dare you insult my mother!" He embraced totally Augustine's dictum that no one can have God as their Father who does not have the church as their mother! Absent-minded as he was, he could be seen regularly walking to New College in his hiking boots, with his shirt-tail flapping half-out of his trousers, and carrying his small battered brief-case. I met him once before being taught by him at New College. It was when he came to speak to our Christian Union meeting on his favorite topic, the Church. He had been his usual entertaining and creative self, though somewhat surprised that someone from his theological tradition had been invited to address an Inter Varsity Fellowship gathering. His life and calling became the subject of John Miller's book, *A Simple Life: Roland Walls and the Community of the Transfiguration,* and Ron Ferguson's publication, *Mole under the Fence: Conversations with Roland Walls.*

Alasdair Heron arrived at the start of our second year. He was entrusted with taking us through the detailed Christology of the Church Fathers, a task which he fulfilled superbly to our permanent benefit. He drilled us well. Years later, when I taught theology at Zomba Theological College in Malawi, I based my own Christology lectures on what Alasdair had taught us so thoroughly.

---

2. Torrance, "Christ in our Place."

Alasdair made an early mark in academic theology. Whilst still a young probationer minister he had an article on the *Filioque* clause accepted and published by the *Scottish Journal of Theology*, with the article making a lasting impact in the field of *Filioque* studies. Two of his important later contributions were his editorial work on a collection of essays on the *Westminster Confession of Faith*, arising from doctrinal discussions in the Church of Scotland; and his brilliantly written *A Century of Protestant Theology*.[3] At New College, a large photograph of Karl Barth with pipe in hand adorned the wall of Alasdair's office. In due course he became Professor of Reformed Theology at the University of Erlangen-Nuremberg in Germany. My last contact with him came when I was teaching in Malawi. I emailed Alasdair about the change Calvin had made from a *Duplex Munus* Christology to a *Triplex Munus* Christology. His reply was generous, extensive, and helpful.

In addition to these full-time staff-members we benefitted from the doctoral student Chris Kaiser, who was tasked with leading our honors seminars on Hilary of Poitier's *On the Trinity*. John Zizoulas returned to deliver a one-off lecture on his favorite topic of personhood and the Trinity. The Australian George Yule was also based at New College for a period, during which he give a short series of lectures on his favorite topic, Martin Luther. Years later, George Yule spent a weekend with us at our country manse in the village of Twynholm in Galloway, preaching on the Sunday.

## Debate

During our era, all the New College departments enjoyed a full complement of lecturers. Professor Alec Cheyne was head of Church History, with his team known affectionately as the "Cheyne Gang"! Professor James Blackie led the Practical Theology department until his sudden death when Duncan Forrester took over. We had two Professor Andersons. There was Professor George W. Anderson of Old Testament, who specialized in the Psalms. And there was Professor Hugh Anderson of New Testament, who specialized in Mark's Gospel.

In the 1970s, divinity faculties were still absorbing the impact of Bishop John Robinson's controversial best-selling book *Honest to God*. One week, a discussion was organized at New College on the question:

---

3. Heron, *Westminster Confession in the Church Today*. Heron, *Century of Protestant Theology*.

"Who is Jesus?" Tom Torrance, Hugh Anderson, and George Anderson, were the three panelists for the event which was held in the upper floor of the students' common-room. My memory of that long-ago evening was that inter-departmental fault-lines emerged quickly, especially between Dogmatics and New Testament. As I remember the occasion, Hugh Anderson argued that, although faith might attribute qualities to Jesus such as Son of God, divinity, etc., as a New Testament scholar he had to approach the question "Who is Jesus?" only from the standpoint of the empirical historical data which scholarship could glean from the New Testament documents and any other relevant sources. His argument was that the scholar gathers data using historico-critical tools; and then, from that fragmented basis, the scholar attempts to reconstruct a picture of Jesus. This approach sought to understand Jesus "from below." However, as Professor Anderson himself conceded, the only picture this can ever create of Jesus is the man, Jesus of Nazareth. Anything else is a statement of faith. Nevertheless, he was convinced that it is only when scholarship focuses on this man, known purely as a man, that we can make sense of the New Testament.

Torrance was diametrically opposed to this approach. During the evening he pursued a line of thinking, familiar to us from class lectures, that liberal theology operates with a radical disjunction between God and his creation, with that radical disjunction affecting all that we try to know and understand. Torrance pointed out that this dualistic approach automatically, and *a priori*, eliminates any possibility of knowing God in himself, and eliminates any possibility of recognizing the living God as being present and active within our space and time. Torrance argued that such an approach simply does not allow God to be God. He insisted that, in fact, the New Testament makes *less* sense, not *more* sense, when we eliminate the supernatural, and when we eliminate understanding Jesus in terms of being truly God and truly man. Torrance maintained that it is only when the inner logic of Scripture governs our thinking, and only when Jesus is understood as truly God and truly man, that the New Testament witness, especially that of the Gospel narratives, coheres in any coherent way and has any rationality. In Torrance's opinion, the liberal contention, that focusing on the man Jesus will simplify things, actually turns out to be the very opposite.[4] The New Testament makes *less* sense,

---

4. Torrance, *Atonement*, 307, was of the opinion that New Testament scholars need to take into account the theology of the New Testament *before* they do their analyses, not *after*: "It is time that most New Testament scholars paid more attention to the work

not *more*, when it is read without the presumption that its central figure is God who became man.

During the evening the debate swung back and forward, with Hugh Anderson and Tom Torrance dominating the discussion. George W. Anderson, of Old Testament, was more an onlooker, though he did provide a moment of wry theological humor. Turning to Torrance, he commented on the fact that there were two Professor Andersons present, and expressed the hope that the theology professor would, "neither confuse their persons, nor divide their substance"! Humor apart, major theological issues underlay the discussion that evening. Similar issues reappear in this book.

## The Classroom Experience

For myself and many others, Tom Torrance's lectures were the highlight of our New College experience. We were keen. We were eager. And what we received from him were stimulating lectures based directly on his most recent work and research. His lectures, even those written for raw first-year students, were not tired discourses which had become dog-eared and listless through wearied and unaltered repetition over the years. On the contrary, they sprang from the work he was dynamically engaged with at that moment.

My seat in the Dogmatics classroom was front-row, on the left, beside my friend Douglas Horne. There I could give maximum concentration. This also happened to be next to the door connecting the classroom and Torrance's study. One January morning, in our second year, my engagement to my future wife Grace was in the *Scotsman* newspaper announcements; and, as Torrance strode into class, he stopped, shook me by the hand, offered congratulations, and spoke of his own marriage to his wife Margaret, "Bruce, I was more nervous at my wedding than I was going into battle as an army chaplain!"

On another occasion, Torrance was in less ebullient mood as we gathered for a seminar session. He seemed, as we came into the room, to be disgruntled. The cause soon became apparent. He had read in the morning's newspaper that the Government were considering taxing unpublished manuscripts when an estate was referred to probate, rather

---

of the theologians which has been going on parallel to that of biblical studies." In other words, the detail can only be understood if first the logic and meaning of the whole has been grasped.

than waiting until the manuscripts were actually published at a later date. Understandably, he considered this to be totally unfair, and shared his frustration with us. "The Government! Taxing unpublished manuscripts! Next they'll want to tax unthought thoughts!" Then he laughed, and launched into the seminar with his usual zest and enthusiasm.

Tom Torrance had a warmth which, though sometimes hidden, was genuine. In his later years, away from the pressures of college responsibilities, he acceded readily to requests from former students who asked him to speak to their elders and congregations. In 1988, he gave a memorable talk on the eldership in the Reformed tradition to my own church office-bearers in Crieff. He was similarly helpful to former doctoral students who themselves had become professors, and who invited him to deliver guest lectures. It was at the request of my former classmate Tom Noble, Professor of Theology at the Nazarene College in Manchester, that Torrance delivered the 1982 Didsbury lectures, later published as *The Mediation of Christ*.

In terms of his overall approach to theology, Torrance rejected the Enlightenment principle that the proper study of man is man. Consequently, he also rejected the common assumption that objective, academic, and scientific theology can only discuss human *ideas* about God rather than affirming what God is actually like. This conviction profoundly affected the way in which he taught. Whereas some theology professors might structure their course by discussing what a range of theological writers have said, for example, on the doctrine of the Trinity, Torrance hardly ever spent time in class discussing what other theologians taught. He saw his task as teaching about *God*, not teaching about human *ideas* about God. As students, we were expected to read other theologians for ourselves. Torrance refused to interpret the core task of theology as reflection on the ideas of others. Instead, the core task of theology was in knowing God himself. God is the primary subject-matter, not the thoughts of theologians. Important scholars in theology, philosophy and science may be mentioned in the by-going, but Torrance's focus was on God's own self-revelation in Jesus Christ as attested in Scripture.

However, if his lectures carried few references to people, they could, and they did, involve extended exegesis of Scripture. I remember, in particular, the depth of biblical exposition undergirding Torrance's lectures on soteriology, especially regarding Jesus as the kinsman-redeemer, the

*Goel*.[5] In Torrance's estimation, much contemporary biblical scholarship had veered wildly in the wrong direction. Because of this, he felt pressed to do his own biblical analysis for his students, much as Barth had had to. At the same time, Barth and Torrance did not always agree. Torrance told us of how, when Barth finally rejected the validity of infant baptism, he flew to Basel to reason with his teacher about what he saw as an abandonment of the principles of grace. But Barth was immoveable; and the fragment volume of *Church Dogmatics* IV/4 is testament to his thinking on the issue.

One thing which did surprise me was that Torrance dismissed the importance of the traditional "Proofs of God," including the classic argument from design. He did not want his students to base their faith or their theology on such a foundation. In his estimation, the only truly valid proof of the reality of God is in actual encounter with God in Jesus Christ. That, and that alone, brings us into a situation where we meet God and hear his Word. However, as a young Christian, I had been greatly helped by Frank Morrison's book *Who Moved the Stone?* with its strong and detailed arguments for the empty tomb and Jesus' resurrection. Consequently, before I understood properly what lay behind Torrance's approach, I was somewhat shocked and disappointed when he stated that "Who moved the Stone?" arguments had little to do with Christian faith. Helpfully, in the class lectures Torrance explained more clearly what he meant. He argued, "any logical proof of God's existence is really cheating," for, in it, we are using human reason which has already "been baptized by grace" and "are therefore presupposing him."[6] Nonetheless, despite setting a low value on the standard "Proofs of God," he did refer enthusiastically to the Second Law of Thermodynamics, pointing out its implication that the Universe, if left to itself (without God), must increase in disorder, whereas what

---

5. Torrance, *Atonement*, 44–47. For Torrance, the *Goel* aspect of atonement lay "behind the unity of his person and his sacrificial act." (*Atonement*, 61). The *Goel* concept, more than any other, pointed to the unity of being and act in the mission of Jesus Christ.

6. Ritchie, Personal Lecture Notes, 5 (25th October, 1973). Cf. Notes, 15 (23rd November, 1973): "God enables us to understand creation [through science] without taking him into consideration; but we come to the point of asking what is a sufficient reason for this state of affairs. We are pushed to the boundary of being and non-being; yet, no line of thought can terminate upon god, although it is driven on and on. This is the problem of contingent existence." Also, Personal Lecture Notes, 14 (Autumn, 1973): "God creates the Universe out of nothing: so, if we argue from the Universe towards God we get into nothing! The spatio-temporal relationship is not reversible. God is spatio-temporally *involved* in the Universe but not *bound* in it."

has actually happened in the emergence of life with its highly complex organic structures, has been a movement in the opposite direction.

What, then, should be the basis for theology? And, how should theology proceed? Torrance pointed out that, in any science, the first question must be about the *nature* of the object of enquiry. In the natural sciences this is a "What?" question. In theology the "What?" question becomes a "Who?" question. This is because in theology we deal with personal being (God), and not with impersonal objects. Therefore, the primary theological question is the question "Who?" But, this question has to be asked within the context of an actual encounter with God. Therefore, we have to start with the *concrete* question, and so any theoretical questions about the existence of God arises afterwards, not before. This is because we are concerned with the living God of Abraham, Isaac, and Jacob, and not with the theoretical God of the philosophers.[7]

Despite his status and reputation, when it came to assignments and exams Torrance was a generous marker. This was because he asked himself what it was that a student was trying to say, even if the expression of their thoughts on paper was not as lucid as it might have been. We reckoned this was also how he read the great theologians of the church, from Athanasius, to Calvin, to Barth. We suspected he gave them credit for insights which they may or may not have inserted consciously into their writings. Certainly, among Torrance's critics there has been the suspicion that he could read more into some theological texts than might be there, and that too readily he saw these as harbingers of his own theology. Could it really be that all of the great Christian thinkers through the centuries were Torrancian at heart? And yet, when his references have been followed up and analyzed, there is evidence, time after time, that what he claimed to detect in the Church Fathers or in the Reformers did have a presence in their works.

And so the Church Fathers, as well as his wet-behind-the-ears students, were interpreted generously. This was rooted in Torrance's overall approach to theological method. His methodology consistently forced him to ask himself: "*What is the reality lying deep within an object? Because, whatever that reality is, it is that which I should be connecting with.*" The spin-off from this approach benefited his students, as he sought to appreciate our thinking beyond our scribbled words; and, as alluded to above, this also affected his reading of theology, as he sought to understand what

---

7. Ritchie, Personal Lecture Notes, 9 (8th November, 1973).

theologians were trying to express, despite their writings being limited by the constraints of their particular culture or historical circumstances. His rubric and guiding principle, applied to major theological treatises and to students' essays alike, was: *"What is the truth lying behind what has been presented to me?"*

He wanted his students to do well. In our final year a new external examiner was appointed for the Dogmatics course. This was Professor Huw P. Owen who taught Systematic Theology at King's College, London. However, when Torrance re-read Owen's book, *The Christian Knowledge of God,* he became anxious that Owen's view of Christian epistemology—how we know things—varied far more from his own thinking than he had appreciated when reading Owen for the first time. Would his students, trained in his methods, suffer because of this? Would their degrees be affected? Because of this concern, Torrance instituted a weekly seminar in which we went through Owen's book with Torrance himself leading the discussion. Some of the academic implications of Owen's differences from Torrance we pick up on later.

## Clarity and Agreement?

The Owen seminars came when we were no longer so naïve theologically. However, in the early weeks, during the autumn term of the first year of our studies, we frequently struggled to follow Torrance's thinking. James Weatherhead, one-time Principal Clerk and Moderator of the Church of Scotland's General Assembly, once jibed: "Professor Torrance's incomprehensibility is legendary." And yet, that verdict was perhaps too harsh. If a student after a lecture, or if a member of the support staff after a College Service, admitted they had difficulty following his train of thought, he was more than willing to sit down and explain matters more simply. At the same time, some students did find him intimidating. When Alasdair Heron's wife studied at New College she struggled with Dogmatics, especially Tom Torrance's lectures, but she was too nervous to approach him directly. Fortunately, another student directed her to James Torrance, who explained carefully and clearly what his brother meant, and with James' help she was set on the right track.[8] There is no doubt that Tom Torrance's lectures were challenging. New terminologies had to be learned. New concepts had to be understood. Even those of us

---

8. Heron, "James Torrance: An Appreciation" (*Participatio*, 2014), first published in the J. B. Torrance *Festschrift*: Hart and Thimell, *Christ in Our Place*.

who came to theology as science graduates found we had to rethink what scientific method was all about.

Needless to say, Tom Torrance was not everyone's favorite. Many conservative-evangelical students, whilst charmed by him as a man, and stimulated by him as a thinker, viewed his theological position with some suspicion. We had been cautioned about Torrance. We had been warned about his neo-orthodoxy and his Barthianism. Even before we met him, questions were in our minds Did he have a right doctrine of Scripture? Did his theology lead to Universalism? As a student from that conservative-evangelical tradition I was a member of the Theological Students' Fellowship, known through its initials as the TSF. At that time, Torrance's car registration plate happened to have the letters TFS. The joke which went around New College was that TFS might be as close as Tom Torrance would ever get to the TSF! Later, I came to appreciate that Torrance had in fact a tremendously high view of Scripture.

On one occasion, towards the end of a lecture, he was pressured by the class to state whether he believed that all men and women are ultimately saved, or whether some are lost for eternity. The class wanted a clear and unequivocal statement. And he appeared to give this when he said: "Yes, there is this terrible, irrational, fact that not all will be saved." But then, and with a mischievous smile, he gathered up his lecture notes, adding, almost as a throwaway comment: "But remember, in the Book of Revelation, it is stated that ultimately hell itself will be thrown into the lake of fire." His allusion was to Revelation 20:14: "*Then death and Hades were thrown into the lake of fire. The lake of fire is the second death.*" Grinning from ear to ear he left the lecture room, leaving us wondering what exactly he meant. In fact, his articles and books make it clear that Torrance was no Universalist in the sense under discussion. For example, in early editions of the *Scottish Journal of Theology* he published a series of articles in which he argued vigorously against Bishop John Robinson who advocated a universalist position.[9] What Torrance taught was that although human rejection of God's grace in Christ is a rational impossibility, nevertheless it can be a terrible actuality. As a state of being, it has a surd-like reality.[10] And, precisely because of its surd-like nature, it

---

9. Robinson, "Universalism: Is It Heretical?"; Torrance, "Universalism or Election?"; Robinson, "Universalism: A Reply," *SJT* 2 (1949). See also Torrance, *When Christ Comes and Comes Again*, 168, and Torrance, *Preaching Christ Today*.

10. At Firbush (November, 2019), Robert Walker pointed out that, in the Book of Revelation, Jesus is described as he *who is*, who was, and is to come (Revelation 1:4,8;

can never be something which we can ever demonstrate to be in logical continuity with the ways of God. Nonetheless, it is a dreadful reality.[11]

From the other theological perspective, liberal theologians had little common ground with Torrance, and he had little with them. The *Times*' obituary for Torrance cited the story of Torrance's confrontation with a German PhD student who had spoken up for Bultmann: Torrance retorted, "You speak with the voice of the anti-Christ; please leave the room!"[12] The same *Times* obituary stated that Torrance refused to regard the works of Bultmann, Bonhoeffer, and Tillich with any seriousness. However, Bonhoeffer's *Cost of Discipleship* was recommended reading for Dogmatics I, and Bonhoeffer's *Christology* was a seminar text for Dogmatics II. The *Times* article was correct in that Torrance placed little value on Bultmann and Tillich—though Tillich's *Systematic Theology* was also in the Dogmatics reading list—but to include Bonhoeffer within the same censure was glaringly inaccurate.

A more obvious enemy was British theological liberalism. When Bishop John Robinson's *Honest to God* became a worldwideide best-seller in the 1960s, Torrance was appalled at the betrayal of faith which he saw the book as promulgating. And so, when Robinson was invited to New College to give a guest-lecture, Robinson was aware of the enormous gulf between his liberalism and Torrance's orthodoxy. As Robinson arrived, he was met by a student who accompanied him into the college. The student said to Robinson that he was now entering the lion's den. Robinson responded with the dismissive remark, "Tom Tiddler's land!" Only then did he realize, somewhat embarrassingly, that Torrance was walking immediately behind!

---

4:8), whereas the beast is described as he *who is-not,* was, and is to come (Revelation 17:8). Walker suggested that the "is-not" of the beast points to the surd-like impossible possibility which characterizes the "state of being" of evil.

11. Cf. Ritchie, Personal Lecture Notes, 17 (Autumn, 1973): "If evil makes a gap between creation and God then this discontinuity makes us unable to properly think of evil logically because evil itself makes all arguments about itself discontinuous . . . We cannot get round evil because the New Testament says that evil is *bottomless* (hence the cry of the cross). A point of discontinuity cannot be circumscribed else it would not be a discontinuity. We usually try to get round a discontinuity by turning it into a good, but this is not enough. We cannot say that evil is only a privation of good for (i) there would be no devil, and (ii) the cross would be a mockery . . . Calvary means that the gap of evil was so bottomless that it could only be crossed by God himself, even at great cost to him. Man is wholly involved in this abyss of evil." Cf. Torrance, *Atonement*, 4.

12. *The Times*, (11th December 2007.)

— *Chapter 3* —

# Theological Course

IN THE 1970S NEARLY all divinity students at Scottish Universities were already University graduates. At that time, theology could only be studied as a second degree, apart from the case of mature-students who missed out on University earlier in their lives. This was because of the long-standing tradition that a church minister's training, like that of a medical doctor or a lawyer, had to involve at least six years of University study. Consequently, virtually everyone in the theology classroom held a degree, with some students exceptionally qualified. Bill Peat, one of our class-mates, had been senior lecturer in physics at Heriot-Watt University where I studied mathematics. Another student, Iain Paul, had been a university lecturer in chemistry. Yet another was Rudolf Dehn, a nuclear scientist at the Dounreay Fast Reactor facility in Caithness before studying for the ministry. Dehn was an amiable and charming man of mature years; and, as a fluent German speaker, he engaged with Barth's works in the original language, much to Torrance's delight.

Despite so many coming to New College armed with degrees in the sciences or the arts, Tom Torrance's lectures pushed everyone to the limit. To begin with, we had to work out his overall purpose in making his many references to science. Was he using science to prove God? Was he arguing that theology had the same evidential basis as the natural sciences? Soon we realized these were not his aims. Instead, his concern was with scientific method, and with establishing theology as a scientific discipline. This was what occupied the electrifying series of lectures he delivered in the autumn of 1973.

Our first Dogmatics class was on Thursday, 11th October, 1973, only a few days after we had gone through registration. Now we were in the classroom awaiting our first lecture from this famous theologian. Torrance was to kick off our whole theology course. The large General Theology first-year class didn't meet in the Ramsay Wing, as its rooms were too small, but in an older part of the college. We waited. He walked in. He placed his notes on the table-lectern. He bowed his head. And he started with the words, "Let us pray." That was impressive! But what did "Let us pray" signify? Was it an expression of individual piety? Was it a carry-over from when New College had been a church college rather than a University Faculty? Or, was he reminding the class that most of us were, after all, training to be ministers of the Gospel? In due course we understood that "Let us pray" meant much more.

## Theology as Vocation

To begin with, Torrance said "Let us pray" because he saw no tension between his calling as a minister of the Christian Gospel and his appointment as a University Professor. All of his academic work was part of his vocation. Consistent with this, when he received the prestigious Templeton Prize in 1978, for work in the field of religion and science, he wore his clerical collar. His primary calling was to be a minister of the Gospel; but, within that calling, he had the special responsibility of exploring, explaining, and establishing, the intellectual foundations of the Gospel within the rigorous scholarly environment of the University.

Torrance's understanding of his professorial role was fully in line with one of the major documents of the Scottish Reformation, the 1578 *Second Book of Discipline*. This referred to four main offices in the Reformed Kirk, namely: Deacon, Elder, Doctor and Minister.[1] Within this arrangement, the office of Doctor involved instructing the faith at the highest level; and it was this role which Torrance sought to fulfil. He saw his task as that of teaching the Evangel in a manner true to the voluntary self-revelation of God in Jesus Christ, as attested in Holy Scripture. And he carried out that task in a manner consistent with his convictions concerning the academic validity of the enterprise.

---

1. *Second Book of Discipline*, 5,2: "[The office of Doctor] is to open up the mind of the Spirit of God in the scriptures simply, without such applications as the minister uses, to the end that the faithful may be instructed, and sound doctrine taught, and that the purity of the gospel be not corrupted through ignorance or evil opinions."

Undergirding everything in his career was a passion for the Gospel, with an intrinsic connection between theology and mission lying at the heart of his work. It was Christ clothed with his Gospel which fired Torrance's academic endeavors. In 1976, when he took the chair as Moderator of the General Assembly of the Church of Scotland, he spoke to the Assembly about the student-missions he had been involved with, relating how he summoned holidaymakers to gospel-meetings by ringing a handbell. Similarly, in the 1950s he welcomed the Tell-Scotland/Billy Graham evangelistic campaigns. Though not always agreeing with every detail of Billy Graham's theology, he recognized Billy Graham as an authentic man of God who also had a genuine, heart-felt, passion for Christ and the Gospel. All of this meant that, when Tom Torrance lectured, his aim was to bring his students into a deeper knowledge of the God of all grace. It was certainly not his aim to titivate their minds with abstract concepts. Because of the passion which Torrance had for mission, it was appropriate that, when New College established a post in his honor, the appointee bore the title "T. F. Torrance Lecturer in Theology and Mission."

**Theology as Study**

Because he regarded his work in the academy as part of his Christian vocation, each of Tom Torrance's lectures opened and closed with prayer. The same was true for his brother James and for a number of other New College staff, including George W. Anderson of Old Testament. However, opening and closing in prayer went beyond piety. The discipline of prayer was also rooted in Torrance's view of theology as a *science*. This is important. It is key to his whole theology. In Torrance's understanding, proper scientific method in any faculty of the University involved allowing the nature of the object to determine the manner in which that object is known. For example, in the mathematical sciences the mode of knowing may be regarded as that of pure logic—though under Gödel's theorem that assertion has to be modified. In the physical sciences the mode of knowing is empirical experimentation, in which we interrogate nature through experiments to force it yield its secrets. In the social and human sciences the mode of knowing is through inter-personal relationship. But, in theological science, which involves knowing God who is transcendent Person, the object of examination (God) is also Lord, and thus not subject to human questioning in the same way as human persons are. Hence, with God, the scientific mode of knowing is worship.

Torrance introduced us to this notion of a hierarchy of knowing on the 18th October, 1973, returning to it in more detail as the weeks passed. My class notes record him saying,

> When we put our questions to God, the tables are reversed, for he has already put his questions to us. He is our creator. We ask questions of nature in an impersonal mode. We ask questions of people in a personal mode. We ask questions of God in a worshipful mode. It is only in an intensely personal and prayerful way that we can know God. Knowledge of God can only be face-to-face with him. Prayer and theology cannot be divorced. To study nature we must be reconciled to it. To study a person, we must be reconciled to them. To study God we must be reconciled to him. Theology can only be studied in an attitude of repentance.[2]

Bill Peat saw a biblical principle in this approach, and, in one of our seminar discussions, quoted the Scripture verse, "We cannot take the Kingdom of God by violence."[3] In other words, in knowing God we are not in the driving-seat, and never can be. On the contrary, knowing God *scientifically* depends upon God's voluntary self-revelation of himself. As Emil Brunner put it, "Through God alone can God be known."[4] Or, as Torrance's teacher, H. R. Mackintosh, stated, "All religious knowledge of God, wherever existing, comes by revelation; otherwise we should be committed to the incredible position that man can know God without his willing to be known."[5]

On this basis, Torrance argued that, within the University context—a context demanding rigorous objective knowledge—knowing God in a *scientific* manner involves knowing God in a way consistent with his nature; but God's nature is such that knowledge of him depends *necessarily* upon God's voluntary self-revelation. Moreover, since God is himself personal being, then any knowledge which he does give of himself will be within a relationship of person to person. Furthermore, because he is God and Lord, then this person-to-person relationship must also—and again, *necessarily*—involve worship and prayer. Hence, it is only within *that* context that truly academic, scientific, objective, theological enquiry

---

2. Ritchie, Personal Lecture Notes (19th October, 1973).
3. Ritchie, Personal Seminar Notes (11th November, 1975).
4. Brunner, *Mediator*, 21.
5. Mackintosh, *Christian Apprehension of God*, 70, cited by Torrance, *Theological Science*, 47n1.

can take place.⁶ Therefore, prayer is not an adornment to academic theology. Instead, prayer is an epistemologically necessary component.

With God we deal with the supreme person. We too are persons, but we are not his equal. He is our Lord. Hence, we can never compel God to reveal himself. Nor can we ever force knowledge out of God. As supreme personal being, God can only be known when he chooses to reveal himself. Hence, in following the principle that to be scientific is to know something in accordance with its nature, we understand that to know God is to know him in his voluntary self-revelation. Consequently, for Torrance, opening in prayer was not pietism. It was part of objective, academic, theology. Indeed, it was a logical necessity if theology were to be the objective, scientific, discipline which it must be in the University. On 18th October, 1973 I jotted down the following as he lectured,

> [In theology] we need a mode of rationality appropriate to the being of God. Hence we must cultivate the appropriate mode. We cannot just transfer one mode of knowing from one field to another. And with only one God we are up against unique difficulties. [There are] no comparisons, no contrasts. Cf. Origen: "We can only know God as God will be known." The object does not only define the mode of *knowing* but also the mode of *verification*, the mode of *demonstration*. A physical world needs a physical question. [But] a proof of God cannot be by the mode of logic (timeless mathematics), or by the mode of physics, but only by the 'mode of God.' In asking questions with a person, we bear in mind that a person has a rational being and is not

---

6. Cf. Barth, *Evangelical Theology*, 148–58. Barth discussed each chapter of his *Evangelical Theology* with his teenage grandson (Zellweger-Barth, *My Father-In-Law: Memories of Karl Barth*, 47). The book grew from lectures delivered in the United States. Barth wrote: "The first and basic act of theological work is prayer. Prayer must, therefore, be the keynote of all that remains to be discussed" (149). Also: "But theological work does not merely begin with prayer and is not merely accompanied by it; [rather] in its totality it is peculiar and characteristic of theology that can be performed only in the act of prayer" (149). Also: "Proper and useful theological work is distinguished by the fact that it takes place in a realm which not only has open windows . . . facing the surrounding life of the church and world, but also and above all has a skylight. That is to say, theological work is opened by heaven and God's work and word, but it is also open *towards* heaven and God's work and word" (150). He continued: "The object of theological work is not some *thing* but some *one* . . . The task of theological work consists in listening to him, this One who speaks through his work" (152). Also: "Every act of theological work must have the character of an offering in which everything is placed before the living God" (155). Finally: "*Veni, Creator Spiritus!* Theological work, therefore, lives by and in the petition for his coming. All its questions, inquiries, reflections, and declarations, can only be forms of this petition" (158).

dumb—unlike nature: hence a different mode [is required]. But with regard to God what is the mode of our questioning? We ask questions of nature in an impersonal mode. We ask questions of people in a personal mode (give and take). We ask questions of God in a worshipful mode. It is only in an intensely personal[7] and worshipful mode that we can know God. Knowledge of God can only be face to face with him. Prayer and theology cannot be divorced.

And so, in Torrance's understanding, the scientific, and objective, and academic, standing of theology was not undermined by the apparently pietistic act of prayer before and after lectures. The very opposite was the case. Theology could *only ever be* a scientific, academic, objective, discipline if carried out within that context. God is not some-*thing* but some-*one*. Therefore, for Torrance, the scientific basis and academic justification for Christian theology as a discipline within the University, lay precisely in our readiness to enter into a relationship with this person, and to respond worshipfully and intellectually to God's voluntary self-revelation in Jesus Christ, as attested in Holy Scripture.

## Dogmatics I

Did we understand all of this immediately? Not at all. As raw first-year students, we respected the fact that our professor prayed before and after each lecture. It was only later we grasped what it implied. However, we did listen attentively to his lectures on theological method. Behind them lay generations of debate on epistemology; and, what we discovered was that Torrance regarded the epistemological methods of the natural sciences as pointing to a solution for many of the problems of epistemology which had bedeviled philosophy and theology for centuries. We return to this later.

In Dogmatics I the reading-list included: Athanasius' *Against the Heathen* and *Concerning the Incarnation*; D. M. Baillie's *God was in Christ*; and Karl Barth's *Dogmatics in Outline* plus a section of his *Church Dogmatics* I/1. Dietrich Bonhoeffer's *Cost of Discipleship* was also recommended, as was Torrance's own book *God and Rationality,* plus his introduction

---

7. For Torrance, personal knowledge was knowledge gained in and through a person to person encounter. Personal knowledge was not code for private, idiosyncratic, knowledge; nor was it code for the post-modern notion that everyone has their own truth. The opposite was intended. It is knowledge belonging to, and affirmed by, an informed community of enquirers.

to *The School of Faith*. In lighter vein he suggested F. J. Sheed's, *Theology and Sanity*! These were the principal texts we were expected to immerse ourselves in. The weekly seminar discussion was on Barth's *Dogmatics in Outline*, which was my introduction to Barth's theology. I was fascinated by the story in its introduction that Barth first delivered the content of the book in the immediate aftermath of World War II, meeting with his audience at seven in the morning within the ruined buildings of the University of Bonn, from which he had been expelled by Hitler in the 1930s.

The first term essay assignment had the title: "*Assess the significance of Matthew 11:27 and Luke 10:22 for the doctrine of the Person of Christ.*" These Matthean and Lukan verses were critical for Torrance: "*All things have been committed to me by my Father. No one knows the Son except the Father, and no one knows the Father except the Son and those to whom the Son chooses to reveal him.*" In working on that assignment many of us started by consulting all the commentaries we could find in the New College library. That was a bad move! What Torrance wanted from us was a theological understanding beyond what most biblical scholars were prepared to provide. And so, it was only when we consulted the Scripture indices of theological works, and when we read how dogmatic theologians built on these verses, that we were on a better track. The core of the essay was establishing that there is no God apart from the God whom we meet in Jesus Christ; that God is known in and through Jesus Christ; that God is known as he chooses to be known; and that God is not under our scrutiny at our pleasure. Torrance's understanding of these critical verses differed significantly from how Adolf von Harnack interpreted them in his famous Berlin lectures of 1899/1900, published in English under the title *What Is Christianity?* Harnack had argued that such verses merely expressed Jesus' self-awareness of having a divine mission; and that they simply pointed to Jesus' growing conviction that he knew God as no one ever knew God before. Harnack was adamant that no deep theological statements regarding the being (ontology) of Christ should be built on them.[8] That was insufficient for Torrance. For him, these remarkable verses indicated that both revelation and reconciliation are based in the oneness of being (*homoousion*) of the Father and the Son.

---

8. Harnack, *What Is Christianity?*, 128.

## Dogmatics II

In our second-year course, Dogmatics II, we had an in-depth, rigorous, examination of Christology and Soteriology. The main set texts were: Anselm's *Cur Deus Homo?* Athanasius' *Concerning the Incarnation*; various sections of Barth's *Church Dogmatics*; Bonhoeffer's *Christology*; Brunner's *The Mediator*; various sections of Calvin's *Institutes*; and John McLeod Campbell's *The Nature of the Atonement*. Added to these were Torrance's *Theology in Reconstruction*, and his *Space, Time and Incarnation*. The weekly seminar texts were Bonhoeffer's little book *Christology*, and Anselm's *Cur Deus Homo?* For those of us intending to do honors in Dogmatics there were further seminars: these were on Hilary of Poitier's *On the Trinity* which were led by Chris Kaiser, and on Athanasius' *Against the Arians*.

On a personal level, Torrance's book, *Theology in Reconstruction*, became hugely important to me. I read it over and over again; and, in the run up to the honors examinations in my final year I studied it in real depth, making copious notes, and writing my own commentary on each chapter. That was the discipline which provided, for me, the theological foundation which I took into the exam hall.

Returning to the second-year course, Dogmatics II. When we came back to New College after the 1974 summer break, we were given a printed handout which stated: "Dogmatics II is devoted to a thorough study of *Christology* and *Soteriology*, in which we come to grips with the central substance of the Christian Gospel, as it centers in the Incarnation and Atonement; but we also try to see organic connection of all dogmatic theology with this 'core.'"[9] This indicated the heart of the matter for Torrance. First, the whole of the Christian Gospel centers on the incarnation and the atonement, *in so far as these are taken together*. Second, all of Christian theology coheres in that core. And our assignments for Dogmatics II were in line with this philosophy. In Dogmatics II we had to complete two standard essays.

The first assignment, in the autumn term, was to analyze section 15 of Barth's *Church Dogmatics*, I/2, entitled "*The Mystery of Revelation.*" In this section we have Barth's exposition of the incarnation under three sub-headings: "The Problem of Christology," "Very God and Very Man," and, "The Miracle of Christmas." The whole section had to be précised into no more than 2,500 words. Coming as it did in the autumn term,

---

9. Torrance, "Dogmatics II" (Class handout).

the exercise was completed in the weeks leading up to Christmas, and it transformed that Christmas for me. When I went home from New College for the winter break my thoughts were full of what I had gleaned, not just from Barth's own thinking, but, through Barth, from the whole history of Christian thought on the incarnation. Everything about Christmas was deepened immeasurably. I recall sitting by the fire, reading Hilary's *On the Trinity* which was to be the seminar text for the next term, but with my head still buzzing with insight after insight which the précis exercise in Barth had opened up.

The second assignment, in the spring term, was to write an essay entitled, "*The Relationship between the Incarnation and the Atonement.*" In the handout describing this exercise—which was to be submitted by Monday, 3rd February, 1975—Torrance emphasized quite clearly what he was looking for. He wrote: "N.B. NOT an essay on the Incarnation and/or the Atonement, but on the RELATION between the Incarnation and the Atonement." The words "not" and "relation" were capitalized. The major prescribed readings were from Brunner, Barth, McLeod Campbell, and Calvin.[10]

Much later, as we reflected on these two exercises, we came to see that the first assignment (the précis), was to prepare us for the second assignment (the essay on the relation between incarnation and atonement). Behind each of them was Torrance's concern that the work of Christ is achieved in the person of Christ.[11] For Torrance, the person of Christ is itself an atoning reality. Thus *being* and *act* are to be understood in their inter-relationship. This lay at the very center of Torrance's thinking. He emphasized repeatedly that in theological science there must be an integration of form and content, being and act. For Torrance, such an integration should be characteristic of all proper scientific work in any discipline; and, when applied to theology, it meant that the work of Christ is achieved *in* the *person* of Christ, and not simply *through* the *actions* of Christ. Hence, the incarnation of the Son of God is not simply a means, or a stage, or a process, or an event, which took place merely to enable Jesus to live on earth, so that, after thirty-three years he might be qualified for Calvary where the "real event" of the atonement could take place. Rather, atonement is achieved in the very person of Jesus Christ. And yet, all of that is true without diluting the centrality of the specific

---

10. Brunner, *Mediator*, 339–535; Barth, *CD* IV/1, 157–357; Campbell, *Nature of the Atonement*; Calvin, *Institutes* 2.12–17.

11. Cf. Torrance, "Vicarious Humanity of Christ."

historical event of Calvary. It was this inter-relationship of incarnation and atonement which Torrance wanted his students to grasp. In order to achieve this, a new way of thinking had to take place; and, for many of us, this would be the theological equivalent of the Copernican Revolution in the natural sciences.[12]

## Dogmatics III, IV, V

In our third year we did nothing but Dogmatics, completing the Dogmatics III, Dogmatics IV, and Dogmatics V courses. Dogmatics III focused on Pneumatology (the doctrine of the Holy Spirit), Ecclesiology (the doctrine of the Church), and the Sacraments. Dogmatics IV covered the History of Christian Thought and incorporated the two special lecture courses given by James Torrance: one on nineteenth-century theology, and the other on Scottish theology. If, as most of us chose, a student submitted a final year dissertation then they did not have to sit the exam in Dogmatics IV, though they were required to attend all of its lectures and seminars.

My dissertation was on, "*Athanasius' doctrine of Union with Christ.*" Before the 1975 summer break I met with Torrance to discuss possible dissertation topics, and he had suggested, "*Union with Christ in the theologies of Athanasius, Augustine, and Calvin.*" During the summer, in the spare time I had available from working on a local Borders farm, helping with the harvest, I started reading all three theologians with that title in mind. I also contacted the Roman Catholic Drygrange Seminary near Melrose, only a dozen miles from where I lived, drove over one evening, and discussed Augustine with one of the Drygrange theology tutors. However, becoming increasingly aware that the topic as it stood was too wide-ranging I had further discussion with Torrance as soon as college resumed, and we agreed that it should be a more in-depth study of Athanasius on his own.

Dogmatics V was a special topic of our own choosing. It was to be self-motivated and self-researched, with frequent short essay submissions to our departmental supervisor, plus a full exam on the topic as part of the series of final examinations in the month of May. My chosen

---

12. Torrance, *Space, Time and Incarnation*, 43, and Torrance, *Theological Science*, 306, employed the expression 'Copernican Revolution' in reference to Kant's philosophy. However, we use it in relation to the alteration of perspective in astronomy when a sun-centered model of the solar system replaced an earth-centered one.

topic was "Theology and Logic." This gave me the opportunity to probe further into Torrance's theological method which I had found so stimulating in first year.

Then came that heady week in May 1976, when we were re-examined on all of the dogmatic theology which we had ever learned at New College. Throughout University I had a rule that I never studied past midday on Saturday. Sunday was completely free. I recall approaching the intense week of honors examinations in that way. I closed my books on Saturday lunchtime. And, on Sunday, after the evening service at James Philip's church, my fiancée Grace and I went for a relaxed walk over the Gullane sand-dunes, feeling carefree, content, relaxed, and rested. On the way back to Edinburgh we stopped in Port Seton for chips! God gave the Sabbath for our blessing! My conviction was that if I didn't already know, understand, and believe, what I was going to write from Monday to Friday, starting at 9.30 on Monday morning, then it was too late anyway. The intense week of final honors examinations also included a paper designated as Dogmatics VI: this involved us writing a single extended essay over three hours from a short list of titles which were only revealed when we entered the exam room. It was a paper we could not revise for. Its purpose was to see to what extent we had actually become theologians!

## Theology and Thinking

Such was our course in Theological Science. In Scotland, the term "theological science" had long been used to describe collectively the whole range of subjects studied in a Faculty of Divinity; but, with Tom Torrance, as with Karl Barth, the term referred more specifically to theological method as an academic, objective, scientific, discipline. This is something we explore more deeply in the next chapter; and it is also something which takes us back to Torrance opening and closing each lecture with prayer. Torrance had a precise definition of what "to be objective" meant. And, for Torrance, "to be objective" meant having our rationality determined by the object and not by our subjectivity. It involved putting the object in control of our knowing of it. It involved resisting the temptation to impose our own structures of thought on the object.

Building on this, Torrance rejected the idea that being "objective" meant maintaining a distance of cold detachment between the enquirer and the object under investigation. Consequently, he also rejected the assumption that, at University level, true scientific theology can only be pursued if the enquirer puts aside his or her faith. For Torrance, such a position was *scientism* not *science*. To his mind, such an approach, in which an academic divests himself or herself of his or her faith-context in order to pursue theology in a supposedly objective manner, was a non-starter. Torrance argued that if a theologian moves outside his or her relationship to God through Jesus Christ, then they are actually engaging in pseudo-science and are adopting a pseudo-objectivity which leads inexorably to a barren dead-end. In other words, we cannot do theology if, at the very outset, we discard the one vital ingredient necessary for a true knowledge of God: namely, allowing the living God, who is the object of our enquiry, to communicate himself to us in the manner of his choosing. True knowledge of God is revealed from the Father, through the Son, in the Holy Spirit, attested in Scripture; and is received by men and women who are surrendered to him in prayer and worship. My erstwhile classmate, Tom Noble, in his article on Torrance in the *Dictionary of Scottish Church History and Theology*, expressed this succinctly, "[For Torrance] true objectivity therefore lies not in a supposed detachment from reality, but in an engagement with reality in which [that reality] is sovereign."[13]

Torrance argued that the whole enterprise of the natural sciences would be distorted at the outset if scientists adopted the supposed "detached objectivity" so beloved of theologians and philosophers who confuse detachment with academic objectivity. In the natural sciences it is the nature of the object which determines the manner in which it is known. And, if this is the case in the natural sciences, so also must it be in theological science. Hence, any true, proper, scientific, and academic, knowledge of God *must* allow the nature of God to determine the mode of our knowledge of him. Hence worship and prayer *must* be at the very center of a specifically scientific approach to theology.

All of this means that the mind needs to think in a way determined by the object (God). But, in order to engage with God in his voluntary self-revelation through his Word, the minds of men and women need to repent. Torrance illustrated this with a story of an internationally renowned concert-pianist who asked a maestro to help him develop his skills even further.[14] After several sessions, the maestro confronted the concert-pianist. He told him bluntly, that to progress then even the muscles of the concert-pianist's hand would have to repent of all they had

13. Noble, "Torrance," 824.

14. Cf. Torrance, *Atonement*, 442–43, where Torrance has more detail. My version comes from the class lecture.

ever been accustomed to. His hands would have to unlearn every habit. They would have to unlearn every familiar action. Only then could he become what he wanted to become. In other words, despite the pianist's existing high skills, what he needed was a radical repentance of tendon, and muscle, involving the very structure of his hands. I remember Torrance leaning on his lectern, clasping and unclasping his fingers as he made his point. For Torrance this illustrated the extent to which the human mind and human habits of thought, however lofty and intellectually powerful they may have become, need to be transformed and redirected by the Word of God.

Torrance's emphasis on the repentance of the mind provoked deep discussion. After one lecture, a group of us walked down Edinburgh's Royal Mile, arguing vigorously whether Torrance was viewing repentance as an *intellectual reorientation* of the mind, rather than as a *moral surrender* of the will. Whatever our concerns, that was certainly not Torrance's intention. It was simply that, within the context of his lecture series on methodology, he had been expounding the nature of repentance as it impacts human thinking in knowing God. Torrance had no intention of denying a necessary moral repentance of the mind, the will, and the affections. But, within the context of the lectures, he was reflecting the New Testament emphasis on the need for the mind to be transformed as men and women come to know God. (Romans 12:1, Colossians 1:19f, etc.) There was no denial on his part that the minds of men and women suffer from more than just a lack of mental agility. As made clear in the *Atonement* lectures, the mind is profoundly affected—morally as well as intellectually—by the brokenness arising from human rebellion against God.[15]

It is precisely because the object itself should dictate the whole process of knowing, that there must be a constant repentance of the mind. Again and again, the enquirer's presuppositions have to be set aside. Again and again, these need to be replaced by the self-revelation of the object in question. This was what lay behind Torrance's illustration of the concert-pianist and the maestro. Every part of the pianist's hands, had to be reshaped, remolded, and retaught, as part of a radical transformation comparable to a new birth. Everything inbuilt by habit. Everything acquired by previous training. Everything introduced by unconscious presupposition. All of these needed repentance and transformation. And this level of reshaping faced every student of theology when engaging

---

15. Cf. Torrance, *Atonement*, 437–47.

with God's self-revelation in Jesus Christ. There were no shortcuts. Only by subjecting themselves to this process, as scientists have to do when faced with nature's own self-revelation, could they engage scientifically in theological work. This thought was captured in my lecture notes for the 19th October, 1973,

> A scientist asks an interrogative question to force information: it is then that we get something that we couldn't argue to, it is something new. [Yet] we cannot ask a question unless we have a framework of knowledge, [and so] sometimes we must change the framework. We ask our first question from within our own framework; the answer makes us alter our original framework slightly; we then ask another question in this new framework, and the cycle goes on.

But how does God's voluntary self-revelation in Jesus Christ, transforming our minds, reshaping our assumptions, work in practice? It was at one of the Firbush conferences that Bob Walker illustrated how Torrance personally applied this core principle of revelation, in which the object (God) communicates himself, restructures our thinking, and remolds our presuppositions.

Walker referred to a series of sermons which Torrance delivered on the book of Revelation when he was parish minister in Alyth. These were later published in book form as *The Apocalypse Today*. Torrance prepared for the sermons by reading the book of Revelation over and over again: not just three or four or five times, but many, many more. And, as he read he prayed. And this reading, and re-reading, and re-reading, steeped in prayer, was a deliberate discipline. It was designed to allow that self-revelation of God in Jesus Christ to impose itself on his thinking, to strip away his existing presuppositions, and to transform his interpretation. And, as he surrendered his mind to the Word of God; and, as he sought to allow the Spirit of God to break, to melt, and to refashion his thinking; he saw himself allowing the object of enquiry (God) to determine what he knew and how he knew it.

This important example can be held in mind for later, when we discuss Torrance's notion of intuitive knowledge. All of this lay behind Torrance's approach to theology. And all of this explains why "Let us pray" was an absolutely necessary preamble to each lecture.

— *Part Two* —

# Methodology

— *Chapter 4* —

# Theological Science

IN CARRYING OUT RESEARCH for this book I rediscovered the boxes in which, years ago, I deposited all of my New College material, including information leaflets, hand-written lecture notes, exam papers, and class handouts. It took time to bring them from storage to the light of day; but, on opening these old and dusty files, I found that the very first sentence I jotted down during Torrance's opening lecture on the 11th October, 1973, was the following,

> We cannot tell *how* to know a thing before we know it: we cannot separate form and subject matter; epistemology cannot exist in relation to a particular discipline in an isolated way.[1]

In that initial lecture, Torrance argued that Western thought since the Enlightenment had gradually divorced form from content. By way of example, he referred to what he viewed as the disintegration of form in the arts, especially twentieth-century art. He illustrated this by describing his visit to an art-gallery in the United States, in which different eras of art were displayed on successive levels of the building. Going back and forward between these floors, he interpreted the changing art styles as evidence of increasing philosophical disintegration, in which form (structure) and content (meaning) dissociate and drift apart. To Torrance, this spoke of form and content, structure and meaning, being torn asunder; and, in his assessment, this ran counter to the best methodologies of the natural sciences in which form and content are grasped as a unity, and in which what an object presents to us on the one hand, and its

---

1. Ritchie, Personal Lecture Notes, 1 (11th October, 1973).

inner meaning on the other, are in harmony and are not disjoined. As he described this to us, he employed one of his favorite phrases: "There must be no *radical disjunction* between form and content."

In the same lecture he explained that in theology he would, "adopt a scientific method of examination." He lamented that much modern theology, which boasted of being academically objective, was in fact not objective enough and hence doomed to collapse. We wondered what he meant by this claim. What did it mean to say that swathes of modern theology were not objective enough? Torrance was, in fact, arguing that modern, liberal, theology lacked proper objectivity because it did not allow the object (God) to determine how it would be known. It did not seek to know God in a manner appropriate to his nature. Above all, it did not allow God to be God; and it had no way of dealing with a living God who creates, becomes incarnate, is immanent to his creation, and intervenes. In Torrance's view, modern theology confused "being academic" with adopting a supposedly neutral and naturalistic stance, and with side-lining the supernatural. He had in mind the type of thinking lying behind John Robinson's book, *Honest to God*, which was taken even further in Robinson's follow-up publication, *But That I Can't Believe!* Robinson argued that if miracles, virgin birth, and other far-fetched supernaturalisms, were eliminated from the church's teaching, then what was left would be more true, more reasonable, more scientific, and more palatable for the modern educated mind. In other words, it would be more "objective." Torrance saw all of this as a disastrously mistaken view of what constitutes objective knowledge.

Torrance regarded the concept of scientific objectivity quite differently. He understood scientific objectivity in terms of disciplining ourselves to think in a way determined by the object, and not by our own presuppositions. He referred frequently to the Greek phrase *kata phusin*—according to the nature of a thing—as a principle used by the Church Fathers. The enquiring mind disciplines itself to think *kata phusin*. Hence, we think rationally if and only if we think in a manner which allows the object to communicate *its* rationality to us, and not when we impose *our* thinking on it. A week later, I scribbled the following in my lecture notes,

> When we think only as we are forced to think (by the object) we think rationally. This 'forcedness' gives freedom. To be not free is to be under the power of irrationality and vice versa. When Soren Kierkegaard talked about a "leap of faith" he did not mean

irrationality: he meant that the reason must be in accordance with the nature of God, and that we must think in a dynamic way in accordance with a living, moving, reality.[2]

In other words, true objectivity occurs when the object determines the *mode* of knowing, as well as the *content* of what we know. In this way form and content are kept together. And so we cannot pre-determine what is rational. It is the object itself which tells us what is rational. In connection with this, Torrance pointed out that John Calvin defined reason as the mind thinking in obedience to reality.[3]

For Torrance, such an approach contrasted absolutely with what he saw as the pseudo-objectivity and pseudo-science beloved of the *Honest to God* school. The pseudo-objectivity of theological liberalism interpreted scientific objectivity to mean that we must exclude from the outset the possibility of miracle, the possibility of incarnation, and the historical validity of any event in the Gospels which depends on supernatural intervention. Only what can be mediated and verified through the senses—plus a modicum of religious instinct and religious experience—is acceptable. Over against this, Torrance argued that we cannot limit, circumscribe, or pre-determine God's freedom to act; nor can we restrict his freedom to communicate himself. Because of this, Torrance insisted that if we are to think in a truly rigorous scientific manner, and not in a pseudo-scientific fashion, then we need to allow our object (God) to make possible a true knowledge of himself. This involves taking the possibility of God's self-revelation seriously; therefore theology only becomes scientific, only becomes objective, only becomes academic, when God's self-revelation is its basis. Thus, for Torrance, as with Barth, a theology based on God's self-revelation was not theological obscurantism. And no theologian should ever be scrambling around apologetically, vainly trying to validate the concept of revelation within a scientific theology. The opposite should be the case. Revelation, as God's voluntary self-communication, is in fact the one essential for scientific theology to function at all, because

---

2. Ritchie, Personal Lecture Notes (19th October, 1973).

3. At Firbush, November, 2019, Bob Walker discussed Torrance's assertion that reason is not a *power* of the mind to determine what is true or false. Instead, reason is a *function* rather than a *power*. Reason is functional: it is our receptive capacity to respond to the rational intelligibility of the universe. It is our capacity of openness to the objective logic of the universe impressing itself upon us. In this way the rational intelligibility of the universe, embedded deep within the Universe itself, becomes the foundation of human rationality.

only a revelation-based theology is capable of allowing the object (God) to determine the form and content of our knowledge.

This means that objectivity should never be confused with adopting a detached, self-styled, neutrality. Andrew Torrance, James Torrance's grandson, speaking at the November 2015 Firbush Conference, stressed this selfsame point, insisting that academic objectivity should not be confused with the adoption of methodological naturalism, which has become the largely unchallenged *de facto* starting-point in much of Western academia.[4] Instead, if God is God, then he is the living God. If that is excluded, then theology has accepted atheistic criteria, and has built atheistic premises, into its very foundations.

## Theology and the Academy

In pursuing this approach, Torrance was aware that he was battling against strong currents of intellectual thinking. Following the Enlightenment, and in line with the mood of the Age of Reason, there had been attempts to make theology more "rational" and more "academically respectable." In the Universities this tended to narrow theology to aspects of scholarly study which even a rationalistic world could accept as being worthy of academic investigation. In time this restricted so-called academic theology to a few outlets: Church History; analysis of biblical texts; reflection on the history of theological thought; and reflection on religious experience. Hence, if at a University the Faculty of Theology taught Church History, biblical textual analysis, discussed what others had written about God, or examined the religious consciousness or the religious experiences of humankind, then these could be categorized as properly scientific and objective disciplines. However, if at a University, the theology professor claimed to teach what God was actually like, or to teach what God had actually done, then that was not academic work: it was preaching, and was more fitted to the church pulpit than to the college lectern. Within this context, a culture developed within academia in which academic theologians shied away from attempting to say what God is in himself, and preferred to discuss human ideas about God, or to reflect on the human response to the God-concept. Hence—and admittedly at this point we paint with a very broad brush—by the close of the nineteenth century the academic study of theology was dominated by Biblical Criticism (as represented by Wellhausen), the History of Dogma

---

4. Andrew Torrance, "Christ and the God of the Gaps," Firbush, November, 2015.

(as represented by Harnack), and the examination of the Religious Consciousness (as represented by Schleiermacher.) Added to this was Applied Christianity, in which Christian beliefs and ethics were related to political and social questions. By and large, this was the theological syllabus, with its accompanying assumptions, which the young Karl Barth was exposed to.

Torrance rejected this understanding of academic theology. He argued that it surrendered straightaway what theology was all about: namely, a true knowledge of God. Over against such a position, Torrance committed himself to establishing theology as scientific, objective, and academic; but proven as such, and recognized as such, from within the school of faith itself. From his own perspective, Torrance believed ardently that theology is a science if, and only if, it is carried out within the framework of faith, prayer, and worship. Consequently, and in direct opposition to widespread academic assumptions, he maintained that true academic objectivity emerges only *within* faith, and not *outside* of faith. He insisted that theological work only has validity, whether in the church or in the academy, when God is allowed to be true to his nature as the living God, and when we listen to this living God as he discloses himself to us.

With this approach functioning as his foundational principle, we, as Torrance's students, found that he applied insights from the methodology of the natural sciences for two main purposes. First: to undermine the secular claim that theology is not a scientific discipline. Second: to demonstrate that theology, rightly pursued, gives real and objective understanding of God as he is in himself.

Torrance knew that Enlightenment thinking had been influenced massively by techniques developed in the physical sciences, and especially by the spectacularly successful empirical method which involved experimentation and gathering data through the senses. However, the critical place of the senses in epistemology was by no means an idea newborn at the Enlightenment. Several hundred years earlier than the Age of Reason, Thomas Aquinas first formulated the dictum: *"There is nothing in the mind which has not first been in the senses."*[5] However, the cultural context was all-important. Aquinas lived in a high-medieval faith-culture. Therefore, for Aquinas, living within that faith-culture of his era, the dictum explained why the existence and nature of God must be able to be

---

5. First formulated by Aquinas in his argument that God can be proved from the natural world: See Aquinas, *De Veritate* q. 2 a. 3 arg. 19. Later employed by others as an argument for empiricism, naturalism, and agnosticism.

inferred from examination of the physical, empirical, natural world, and why proofs of God's existence must be constructible from empirical data. For Aquinas, working within a faith-culture, the conclusion was inescapable. In his thinking, axiom one was: It is obvious that we know God. Axiom two was: All our knowledge comes through the senses. Conclusion: God must be able to be known through the senses.[6]

Centuries later, Enlightenment thinkers—now living in quite a different rationalistic milieu—turned Aquinas' conclusions upside-down. They agreed with him: *"There is nothing in the mind which is not first in the senses."* But, contrary to Aquinas, they argued that this dictum proves God can in fact never be known by the human mind. This is because, since God is spirit and not matter then he cannot be known through the senses (because the senses can only detect the material); and, if God cannot be known empirically through sense-data, then—because there is nothing in the mind which is not first in the senses—he cannot be known at all. Hence theology, especially academic theology, has to limit itself to analyzing human theories about God. Theology has to abandon any attempt to know God directly. Such knowledge is *a priori* impossible.

In intellectual European culture, increasingly molded by Enlightenment thinking, it was this assumption which lay behind the growing view that the only valid academic tasks for a Faculty of Theology were in the fields of Church History, biblical textual analysis, the history of theological thought, or the exploration of the religious consciousness, feelings, and instincts, of humanity. Study of theology at the academy could continue if theologians limited themselves to these disciplines. And so it became assumed that we cannot study God as he is in himself, though we might validly study the religious history, thought, consciousness, feelings, and instincts of humanity. These are amenable to empirical examination, even if God himself is not. Hence, theology may stay in

---

6. Similar reasoning undergirds Roman Catholicism's appeal to natural theology and natural law: nature, if examined deeply enough, yields not only knowledge of itself, but knowledge of God and of God's moral order for the universe. Cf. the definition of Natural Law given by Cardinal A. G. Cicognani to Karl Barth on behalf of Pope Paul VI in a letter dated 11 November, 1968: "As for Christians, revelation does not suppress natural law, which is equally divine, it simply elucidates it, completes it, makes its observance possible through the Holy Spirit, and above all orders it to the supernatural calling of the children of God which remains their sole salvation. This fact, that natural law finds itself thus ordered to salvation, explains why its prescriptions can be the subject of the church's magisterium" (Barth, *Letters of Karl Barth, 1961–1968*, 357–58).

the University as a serious objective, scientific, discipline, provided it is pursued in this fashion. If this approach were adhered to, Theological Faculties could yet endure in a scientific age.

## Barth and Theological Science

Some of these issues were reflected upon by James Torrance, in his lectures on nineteenth-century theology. He taught us how Schleiermacher focused theology in the religious consciousness, especially the feeling of absolute dependence on God. This was Schleiermacher's way of trying to develop a theology which could be described as scientific, though this did not prevent Hegel sneering at Schleiermacher's key-idea, commenting that if feelings of absolute dependence were the foundation of religion, then dogs must be the most religious creatures on earth! Mockery aside, Schleiermacher's methodology, in which the human experience of religion took center-stage as the empirical foundation of theology, found wide acceptance. His notion of "absolute dependence" was regarded by many as satisfying basic scientific criteria, because of its focus on an empirical—and hence analyzable—experience of religion. When Schleiermacher combined all of this with a warm, romanticist pietism, the result was his widely read work *The Christian Faith*. In class, James Torrance summarized the issue: "Schleiermacher's concern is not to say nothing about God; but to say nothing about him which does not relate to us."[7]

The young Karl Barth was attracted to Schleiermacher's thinking, as he was to other aspects of the Liberal Protestantism which flourished in late nineteenth-century Universities. But, when the First World War broke out, Barth was shocked that so many of his admired teachers were enthusiastic about war. Adolf von Harnack, the most prominent of them all, had gone so far as drafting the Kaiser's War Manifesto speech. As Barth thought through the situation, he became increasingly aware that a widespread philosophical view in the late nineteenth century had been that German culture was in tune with the divine Spirit, meaning that Christian faith itself could be discerned from the insights and presuppositions of that culture. But, if that were the case, how could that lead to the rampant war-enthusiasm of August, 1914? Somewhere there was a mismatch. As Torrance pointed out, "It was through his sharp conflict with the *ethic* of his Neo-Protestant teachers that Barth was forced to

---

7. Ritchie, Personal Seminar Notes (11th November, 1975).

question radically all their exegetical, historical, and dogmatic interpretations of the Gospel."[8]

As he worked day-to-day as a pastor in the Swiss village of Safenwil, Barth wrestled with these matters. What he found was that he had to rethink what was it that actually constituted the foundations of his faith. This led him to study Paul's *Letter to the Romans*. And Barth emerged from the study of his Safenwil manse, not only as the author of an explosive and idiosyncratic commentary on the book of Romans (*Der Römerbrief*), but as a man convinced that the central task of theology does not in fact consist in examining human thoughts about God. Nor does it consist in examining the religious consciousness. Nor does it consist in connecting the spirit of a culture with the Spirit of God. Nor has it to do with finding God through a culture which supposedly reflects the impress of the divine Spirit. Instead, the central task of theology is in listening to God's Word concerning God and humanity. In a lecture delivered in 1916, Barth stated, "It is not the right human thoughts about God which form the content of the Bible, but the right divine thoughts about men."[9] This thinking became the basis of Barth's massive *Church Dogmatics,* first developed in his *Göttingen Dogmatics*.

In the *Göttingen Dogmatics* of the 1920s a defiant Barth was already describing his work as "Scientific Theology." And he stated boldly and unapologetically that it was scientific precisely because its objectivity and validity lay in the self-revelation which God has made of himself in Jesus Christ. In taking that stand, Barth went far beyond, "Schleiermacher's view that theology is the science which systematizes the doctrines prevalent in the Christian Church at any one time."[10] For Barth, theology was a science because it speaks of God; or rather, it echoes what God has

---

8. Torrance, *Karl Barth: An Introduction to his Early Theology, 1910–1931,* 74.

9. Barth, "The Strange New World Within the Bible" (1916), in Barth, *Word of God and the Word of Man,* 28–50, especially 43: "It is not the right human thoughts about God which form the content of the Bible, but the right divine thoughts about men," and 44: "The Word of God! The standpoint of God!" Cf. Barth, *The Göttingen Dogmatics, Vol. I,* 8f: "I take over an older dogmatic tradition, and call dogmatics reflection on the Word of God, whereas all those other definitions speak more or less expressly of faith, religion, or the religious consciousness, sometimes with an explicit limitation to present-day faith. The tradition behind them does not date only to Schleiermacher. It goes back by way of Pietism to Protestant orthodoxy. Not to Zwingli and Calvin, one must say."

10. Ritchie, Personal Lecture Notes (11th November, 1975). Cf. Schleiermacher, *Christian Faith,* 88 (§19).

spoken to us! *Deus Dixit*! On this basis Barth argued that the notion of theology as a science should not be restricted to dry-as-dust analysis of biblical texts, or to investigation of religious feelings, or to Church History, or to the history of dogma. Instead, the study of God's self-revelation in Jesus Christ is, in itself, also a science.[11] Indeed theology only becomes a science when the *object* of theological knowledge (God) is the *subject* determining our knowledge of him.[12]

Many of Barth's former teachers, including Harnack, shook their heads in despair, even in anger. Harnack rejected outright any idea that a theology based on revelation could be described as scientific. For Harnack, only technical procedures, such as the historico-critical examination of the New Testament, could be termed scientific.[13] Harnack was diametrically opposed to Barth's position; and Harnack was even prepared to regard the qualities and insights of a highly developed human culture as a basis for theology. This was because of the impress which he believed the divine Spirit to have made upon such a culture; an impress enabling the theologian to read off significant divine characteristics from their expression in the high-points of that culture, in its music, art, science, philosophy, and ethics. Barth rejected this categorically.[14] But, if Harnack viewed Barth as retreating into an outdated traditional orthodoxy, Barth was exciting a new generation of theologians, including Torrance.

## Torrance and Theological Science

By the 1930s Barth had made a significant impact in Scotland. John McConnachie of St John's Church, Dundee, had published two books of

---

11. Cf. Barth, "Faculty of Theology" (1960), in Barth, *Fragments Grave and Gay*, 21–26, especially 23: "The Bible speaks of Jesus Christ—the name is unavoidable since he is the very essence of it. This source of theology (which can also be called Gospel) is also its subject-matter, to which it is tied just as all other branches of knowledge pursued at the University are tied to their subject-matter. Without it, theology could and would quickly dissolve into amateurish excursions into history, philosophy, psychology, and so on."

12. Cf. Torrance, *Karl Barth: An Introduction to his Early Theology, 1910–1931*, 148: "Harnack had failed to see that, while scientific activity is concerned with the pure knowledge of its object, for that very reason the nature of the object must be allowed to prescribe the specific mode of rational activity to be adopted in knowing it."

13. Cf. Rumscheidt, *Revelation and Theology*, 31, 36.

14. Rumscheidt, *Revelation and Theology*, 30, 33, 37. Cf. editor's comments, 57–58.

Barth's theology.¹⁵ And, at New College, H. R. Mackintosh was engaging insightfully with Barth's thinking. For example, in 1930, Mackintosh spoke to the Edinburgh Clerical Society, commending Barth as "a corrective to the broad humanism of the Liberal Protestant school of thought."¹⁶ At the same time, Mackintosh was unsure of some aspects of Barth's theology. And so, when Barth visited Scotland in 1931, his lasting memory of Mackintosh was bidding him farewell at Waverley Railway Station in Edinburgh, with a puzzled Mackintosh wearing a "very solemn face" and quizzing Barth about his view of the reconciling death of Christ.¹⁷ Mackintosh's Highland Presbyterian Calvinist tradition left him still uncertain about this new theology. But, if Mackintosh wondered, many of his students, including Torrance, would embrace Barth's thinking with fewer reservations.

And yet, it would be misleading to give the impression that Torrance was totally dependent on Barth for the notion of theology being a scientific discipline precisely because it is based on the self-revelation of God. The young Torrance was already thinking along these lines quite independently. Nevertheless, Barth's insights, plus Mackintosh's teaching at New College, helped to develop Torrance's view of theology as a science whose objectivity lies in God himself.¹⁸ After Mackintosh died suddenly in June, 1936, his successor was G. T. Thomson who had translated the first part of Barth's *Church Dogmatics* into English. As soon as it was published Torrance bought a copy and read it from beginning to end.¹⁹

---

15. McConnachie, *Significance of Karl Barth*; McConnachie, *Barthian Theology, and the Man of Today*.

16. *The Scotsman* (11th March, 1930).

17. Busch, *Karl Barth: His Life from Letters and Autobiographical Texts*, 205.

18. Cf. Barth, *Göttingen Dogmatics*, 13: "Scientific dogmatics, as distinct from dogma, is the attempt to *discover* (note, not to establish or produce but to discover) these necessary standpoints" (italics added).

19. Barth, *CD* I/1, discussed theology as a science, with the very first section of his *magnum opus* carrying the heading: "The Church, Theology, Science": "As a theological discipline, Dogmatics is the scientific test to which the Christian church puts herself regarding the language about God which is peculiar to her." (1). This slightly ambiguous statement is clarified later in words more closely approximating Torrance's understanding: "The language of the church about God has long been criticized from many quarters, and attempts have been made to correct it. But what must be done here is to criticize and revise it from the standpoint of the essence of the church, of Jesus Christ as her foundation, her end and her content . . . [Philosophers] judge the church's language about God on principles foreign to it, instead of on its own principles, and thus increase instead of diminishing the harm on account of which the church needs

Later, he described his exhilaration at Barth's declaration that the Word of God is not simply statements *about God* but is *God himself* in his revelation; and that Dogmatics is a science whose objectivity lies in that divine self-revelation in Jesus Christ, attested by Scripture.[20]

This understanding of objectivity was important to Torrance. He had read Schleiermacher's *The Christian Faith*, and liked much of what he found there. And yet, even as he studied Schleiermacher's book, he felt instinctively there was something wrong with it. Later he identified this as an intuition that Schleiermacher developed his ideas without having any proper objective foundation for what he wrote, and without rooting the overall structure of his theology in its proper basis, namely the nature of the object of enquiry itself.[21] Schleiermacher's theology was based on observations of the human religious experience. As such, Schleiermacher had a phenomenological approach, and one which Torrance would reject decisively as being rooted in human subjectivity.[22] Over against Schleiermacher, Barth seemed to point to a true objective basis, and therefore to a theology whose form and structure were fully molded by the material content of the subject matter. And so, Barth's writings, allied to Torrance's own developing thinking, became part of the foundation upon which Torrance would build his considerable work on theological science.

It would be three decades after his own student days of the 1930s before Torrance published the bulk of his work on the continuity between theological method and scientific method. When he did, the ideas he expressed were well-travelled and familiar concepts for him. For example, at the close of the 1930s Torrance had a brief teaching stint at Auburn University in the United States, where he made quite a mark; and, when Princeton showed interest in securing his services, Torrance explained to Princeton that if he were appointed he would teach theology as a science, because in science,

---

a critical science" (5). Nevertheless, in these early days, Barth was not convinced that the term "science" could ever sit totally comfortably within theology: "Of the efforts made to assign [theology] a place in the system of sciences, theology must say itself that this is too great—and too small—an honor" (6). In pages 7 and 10, Barth reverted to a more limited notion of theology as a science.

20. Cf. Torrance, "My Interaction with Karl Barth," Lecture at Queen's College, Birmingham, UK (11th February, 1987). Audio version in the Princeton Seminary Media Archive: https://commons.ptsem.edu/id/TFTorrance_1987-02-11.

21. Torrance, "My Interaction with Karl Barth."

22. Torrance, *Space, Time and Incarnation*, 48.

> We think not as we *choose* to think, but as we are *compelled* to think in accordance with the nature of the object, and thus in manners which are governed by the objective grounds on which the science rests.[23]

Princeton wanted Torrance. But the dark clouds gathering over Europe brought him back to Scotland. Nevertheless, the principle of theology as a science was already deeply rooted in his thinking. It was this early insight which lay behind his later series of books published in the 1960s on the theme of the rationality of theology, culminating in *Theological Science* (1969), which grew out of his Hewett Lectures of a decade earlier. In *Theological Science* Torrance argued that a theology based on the self-revelation of God in Jesus Christ is indeed a true science in which we gain authentic objective knowledge of God. However, unlike other sciences in which we are the masters of the process, and in which we can compel the object to reveal itself by subjecting the object to experiment and interrogation, theology is dependent on God, in his freedom, choosing to do so.[24]

This was key for Torrance. In other sciences we are the masters. In other sciences we are in control of how something is known. For example, in the physical sciences we force nature to reveal its mysteries by conducting experiments. In class he described this as the scientist's ability to "torture nature," compelling it to yield its secrets. However, in theological science we are no longer the masters. Instead it is the object of our enquiry (God) who is master and Lord. And so, theology can only ever be a true science when grounded in God's voluntary self-revelation. In theological science the enquirer ceases to be lord and becomes servant. In this epistemological reversal, it is the object of enquiry (God) who becomes the active agent in *our* knowledge *of him*. As Torrance stated in class, an "epistemological inversion" takes place.[25] Nevertheless, the theological

---

23. Cited by McGrath, *T. F. Torrance: An Intellectual Biography*, 57.

24. Cf. Torrance, *Theological Science*, 131: "In all our knowing it is we who know, we observe, we examine, we inquire, but in the presence of God we are in a situation in which he knows, he observes, he examines, he inquires and in which he is 'indissoluble subject.' He is the Lord of our knowing even when it is we who know, so that our knowing is taken under command of the lordship of the Object, the Creator himself." In a footnote Torrance referred to Barth, *CD* I/1, 438; II/1, 21–25.

25. Cf. Ritchie, Personal Lecture Notes, 9B (8th November, 1973): "We ask God: he gives us an answer, but we come to know him in himself, not out of ourselves. 'You know God, *but are known of God*' (Galatians 4:9); 'You did not choose me, but I chose you' (John 15:16); 'Not that we first loved God but he loved us.' (I John 4:19) Our knowing is governed by the object, by God. An epistemological inversion."

process is still unequivocally a scientific methodology. It is so, because it is a procedure in which the human enquirer allows the nature of the object to determine the manner and mode of the investigation. As such, it is the nature of the object, not our human presuppositions, which determines how we know and what we know. Moreover, because knowledge is determined by the object, and not by our conjectures, then it is truly objective; and, in being truly objective it is also properly scientific and academic. Therefore, in the University, theology has no need to be apologetic or embarrassed about its grounding in the voluntary self-revelation of God in Jesus Christ. On the contrary, this is precisely where—and *only* where—theology gains its scientific objectivity and establishes its proper rationality. Undergirding everything is the discovery that God, out of pure grace, has given himself to us; hence our knowing and thinking him reposes, "upon his prior decision or movement in grace to be the object of our knowing and thinking."[26]

This was what Torrance taught us in that memorable series of lectures, delivered in the opening weeks of term one, year one, of our theological studies. God must be allowed to be the living God. God is himself directly involved in revelation and reconciliation. If theologians put this principle aside then they build atheistic premises deep into the foundations of their science.

---

26. Torrance, *Theological Science*, 157.

— *Chapter 5* —

# Theological Depth

IN HIS LECTURES, TORRANCE stated that the Universe is intelligible, and amenable to scientific investigation, precisely because God the creator has granted it its own rationality. He said, "all empirical science depends on nature being created out of nothing, and being *given* a contingent order."[1] More than that, the whole scientific enterprise is given to humanity by God, in order that the Universe may come to a knowledge of itself and may glorify its Creator,

> Man is the being in the Universe whose task it is to enter into intelligible relations with the world, and to enter into its order and harmony. Man is that being within the Universe through which the Universe should come to know itself. Man's function in his scientific work, is to make the Universe come to know itself. Man 'named' the realities around him in Genesis. He is the crown, the priest of creation. It is through man that the creation is made to glorify the Creator.[2]

In class, Torrance went as far as insisting that modern scientific progress had only been possible in a society whose ideas had been molded by the Judeo-Christian concept of God the creator. All of this was delivered within the ideas-packed opening lecture of the 11th October, 1973. He stated, "It was Christianity which taught that God gave the world an inherent order to it, which is the fundamental basis of modern science. This is in contrast to Greek science which was essentially dualistic."[3] In the

---

1. Ritchie, Personal Lecture Notes, 15 (Autumn, 1973).
2. Ritchie, Personal Lecture Notes, 16 (Autumn, 1973).
3. Ritchie, Personal Lecture Notes, 1 (11th October, 1973). Torrance continued:

# Theological Depth

same lecture, Torrance referred to three statements attributed to Albert Einstein: "God does not play dice," "God does not wear his heart on his sleeve," and, "God is deep."[4]

## "God Does Not Play Dice"

This declaration was made by Einstein in response to some interpretations of Heisenberg's Uncertainty Principle. Werner Heisenberg was one of the key pioneers of Quantum Mechanics, and, in his Uncertainty Principle, he asserted a fundamental limit to the precision with which certain pairs of physical properties of a particle can be known at the same time (for example, *both* position *and* momentum).[5] But does such a limit exist because there is an *objective* randomness at the core of physical reality? Or does it exist because there is a *subjective* limit in our ability to know things? In other words, does the uncertainty relate to *ontology* or to *epistemology*? For those who maintained that Heisenberg's Uncertainty Principle indicates an inherent randomness within reality itself, then Einstein's questioning of Heisenberg's principle was viewed as an argument for determinism. Over against this criticism, Torrance held that Einstein simply wanted to avoid a physics which assumed that chaos lay in the foundations of nature. Quantum Theory seemed to throw everything into the air; but Einstein was still convinced that a new understanding of physics, possibly based on Field Theory, would reveal an intrinsic order in reality independent of our conceiving of it.

For Torrance, Einstein's conviction that such an order must exist, homologated the contention that, as scientific enquirers, we do not *invent* structures, but *discover* structures already there. In this way the empirical and the theoretical are interlocked. Torrance wanted theology to operate

---

"These dualist notions were re-introduced by folk like St. Augustine (the 'Two Cities' outlook). This brought back the Ptolemaic cosmology. The Reformation changed this. It introduced a world of motion, not a static state of affairs. Newtonianism is but another form of dualism: but nowadays we have a new, un-dualist, idea introduced by Einstein's Relativity in which form and being, substance and structures, are fused together. Pure sciences are working with this change, but Social Sciences are lagging behind."

4. Ritchie, Personal Lecture Notes, 2 (11th October, 1973): "God is deep. God is light, and in him is no darkness at all. Even though we encounter surds, nature is simple. Profundity, simplicity, and universality go together. We must allow nature to instruct us: but we overlay things with our own ideas. Nature must reveal itself in accordance with its own structure. So also in theology, it must reveal itself in its own structures."

5. See Torrance on Heisenberg in Torrance, *Theological Science*, 95–96.

with similar conviction: theology should be confident that it has to do with the true nature of God and with the true mode of God's interaction with the world; and not just with a human theorizing which may have no actual correspondence to reality.

## "God Does Not Wear His Heart on His Sleeve"

In making this statement, Einstein was pointing out that, although the natural sciences depend on careful observation, our manner of observing can be misleading. Consequently, an observer requires an understanding of the inner nature of what is being observed before he or she can in fact observe accurately. In connection with this, Torrance pointed to some of the flaws of the Newtonian view of the Universe. I had completed my mathematics degree only a few months before going to New College, and mention of Newton struck a chord. I was aware of a critical instance when Newton allowed his empirical observations to determine which aspects of his mathematical theories might be applicable to reality. Newton had allowed himself to be guided by what he thought he "saw" in nature, and by what he thought was "possible" in nature as he observed it. This made him disregard some aspects of his theoretical mathematics which, in Einstein's hands, would turn out to be of fundamental importance in understanding the nature of things.

∼

The next few lines are not from Torrance's lecture, and may be skipped without losing the overall argument. However, they illustrate how the observable, the theoretical, and the actual, can be mismatched. We start by considering one of the foundational equations of Newtonian mechanics: Force equals mass multiplied by acceleration:

$$F = ma$$

This is a truncated version of what Newton derived mathematically from the principle of the conservation of momentum ($mv = mv$). The full equation is:

$$F = ma + v.dm/dt$$

However, Newton dismissed the second part of the equation ($v.dm/dt$), which involves velocity being multiplied by the variation of the mass of an object in time. This was because Newton assumed any variation of mass to be meaningless since, in his day-to-day, common-sense, observation of nature, the mass of any given object was constant, independent of time, and independent of the velocity at which the object was moving. However, in contrast to Newton, and against common-sense instinct, Einstein did not exclude the possibility that mass may vary as velocity varies. This freed Einstein to develop his Theory of Relativity. What Newton had done was to trim the theoretical to the observable. He had allowed his common-sense observation of phenomena to dictate what must be possible. Newton assumed that the second part of the equation did not represent real life; therefore, because its irrelevance was "self-obvious," he dropped it. For all practical purposes, the extra part (v.dm/dt) can indeed be discounted quite legitimately when we limit ourselves to the low velocities which we experience day-to-day. However—and what Einstein discovered—when objects are moving close to the speed of light then realities are altogether different. Near the speed of light their mass does vary significantly depending on their velocity. Hence, although Newton had a profound understanding of the nature of things in his sights (through his full mathematical formula), he limited himself by allowing his common-sense observation of phenomena to trump what his mathematics was telling him. If Newton had believed his own mathematics, he may have anticipated Einstein's Theory of Relativity.

∼

Newton allowed himself to be dominated by the observable. Unfortunately, observations can mislead. Sometimes it is only when we grasp something of the logic of the inner rationality of the object—as presented in Newton's fuller equation—that we can then go back to nature, review our observing, and re-see what we think we saw. In this way an overall grasp of the true logic of an object compels us to look again and to reassess whether we actually saw what we thought we saw. In other words, although all science involves close observation of phenomena, our preconceptions may profoundly affect our observing. We may look: but we may not see. And we may not see: because we have not yet understood the inner rationale of what is before us. Hence, though we *observe* in order to *understand*, it is only after we *understand* that we are able truly to *observe* correctly.

Torrance transferred this to theology. He pointed out that if, in any field of knowledge, an enquirer concentrates solely on phenomena and interprets phenomena solely from within his or her existing mind-set, then he or she may well not appreciate what it is in the nature and logic of a thing which has made the phenomenon what it is. Thus, although observation is crucial, it is only when the enquirer grasps (even tentatively) the rationality which lies invisibly within phenomena, that the enquirer can begin to truly observe such phenomena aright. *Seeing* may give *understanding*: but only when we *understand* can we *see* properly what we are observing. Until we grasp something of the inner logic and true nature of an object, we may be unable to appreciate and grasp what is in plain sight.

Torrance argued that this was totally missed by much of modern biblical scholarship. What he meant by this was that, for example, the New Testament can only be read (observed) aright, if first the New Testament scholar appreciates the true nature of the central figure of the New Testament (Jesus) as both God and man, and works out from that center. In Torrance's view, liberal scholarship erred irreversibly by setting that theological rationale aside at the start, dooming itself from the outset to read the Gospels as myth!

In connection with this, Torrance referred to John 8:43, where Jesus responds to his opponents by saying (in Torrance's translation): "*You do not understand my speech (lalia) because you have not heard my word (logos).*"[6] Torrance argued that Jesus reverses what we might expect him to say. We might assume Jesus would say: "You do not understand my *word* (i.e., the fundamental message which I bring), because you have not heard my *speech* (i.e., the physical, audible, words which I speak)." But what Jesus actually says is that his opponents could not hear his speech (*lalia*) properly through their ears because they had not grasped—or had consciously rejected—the logic of his word (*logos*) which lay behind it. Torrance related this to the question of Christology, and especially to Liberal Protestantism's habit of reading the Gospels as myth.[7] Liberal Protestantism rejected the inner rationale of the Word of God *a priori*. It rejected the logic of the incarnation as being the vital key which unlocks the New Testament message. Liberal scholars insisted that we should only speak of how Jesus could be observed within a natural historical environment.

---

6. Ritchie, Personal Lecture Notes (Undated). Cf. Torrance, *Theological Science*, 197. NIV: "Why is my language not clear to you? Because you are unable to hear what I say." Revised Version: "Why do you not understand what I say? It is because you cannot bear to hear my word." Nestles' Interlinear: "Why do you not know my SPEECH? It is because you cannot hear my WORD."

7. Ritchie, Personal Lecture Notes (11th October, 1973): "We cannot always analyze from the side of the phenomena. We cannot analyze the historical Jesus because we are starting from the wrong structures. The Newtonian analytic method has collapsed."

But this automatically stripped away the supernatural from the Gospel witness. And so, at the very outset, it rejected an understanding of Jesus informed by the doctrine of the incarnation. Over against this, with Torrance, the doctrine of the incarnation was fundamental to understanding the Jesus of the Gospels and the rest of the New Testament. But, for Liberal Protestantism, the possibility of Jesus being more than simply an outstandingly spiritual man was dismissed from the start, and his being fully God and fully man was regarded as a doctrine foisted onto the historical Jesus by the Church Fathers. Liberal theology insisted that only natural historical phenomena can be considered as real events. Torrance viewed this as the enquirer *a priori* ruling out the possibility that the accounts we have of this man may in fact *only* make sense if we first grasp the true nature of his being, namely, that he is God become incarnate.

Torrance argued that the liberal approach was based on a so-called common-sense observation of phenomena; but that method destroys the very thing it seeks to know. In contrast, Torrance pointed out that in the natural sciences observation of phenomena always has to be reassessed after we perceive the logic of the reality behind the phenomena. He argued that, in similar fashion, Jesus of Nazareth can only be truly known, and can only be viewed aright, when first we understand who he is. And he can only be so understood after we grasp the logic lying behind who he is, namely that he is the incarnate Son of God, truly God and truly man. It is impossible to catch the historical Jesus simply in his humanity, because the limits placed on what that may mean will immediately exclude who he actually is. In liberal theology, the observable phenomenon of Jesus of Nazareth is everything. Or at least, whatever liberal theology reckons to have been the observable phenomena! But then he becomes Jesus, *sans* virgin birth, *sans* miracles, *sans* resurrection, *sans* ascension. None of this takes account of the reality lying behind Jesus of Nazareth: namely the incarnation. And the incarnation changes everything.

Just as our reading of the Universe is transformed when we allow the inner logic of reality to re-educate how we observe reality itself, so also our reading of the Gospels is transformed when we acknowledge Jesus to be God incarnate. Until we grasp the proper nature of what we are observing, we miss what is in plain sight. Thus, we cannot understand Jesus' "speech" (i.e., the physical, audible, observable phenomena) until we hear his "word" (i.e., the fundamental logic of the Gospel arising from who he is). All of this lay behind the divergent views expressed in the brains-trust discussion involving the Torrance and the two Professor Andersons.

### "God Is Deep"

Before consulting my student notes I remembered this quotation as: "God is deep but not devious." However, my notes indicate that we were given the shorter version as the heading to the section, though Torrance did cite the fuller statement in the course of the lecture. He linked Einstein's "God is deep" maxim to the New Testament verse: *"God is light; in him there is no darkness at all"* (1 John 1:5). What Torrance took from Einstein was that even if nature confronts us with entities such as irrational numbers, surd-like qualities, or the apparently paradoxical concepts which we meet in Relativity Theory or Quantum Theory, the scientist still believes that there is a logic to be discovered within nature itself, though this logic may lie so deep that it is difficult to access.

The sheer difficulty of the task may tempt us abandon the search for objective truth. Consequently, we may overlay reality with our own ideas. Or, we may be persuaded that any order detected in nature has been artificially created by our minds. We may be tempted to adopt a positivist stance, abandoning any hope of uncovering the true logic of reality. And, having become positivists, we may content ourselves with cataloguing and listing phenomena; or with predicting outcomes from statistical probability based on previous occurrences, rather than from a grasp of the intrinsic nature of a thing which enables us to unfold future behavior from that. The positivist observes habits of nature. He or she predicts from a basis of statistical probability. Not from an understanding of the actual nature of being.

Against all of this, Torrance was convinced that the best and most productive scientists worked from a conviction that in science we come to know nature as it is in itself. He was convinced that the same can, and must, be the case in theology. He argued that in the natural sciences the best theories are not mental constructs which happen to fit the data. Instead, they are theories which describe nature as it really is. But, precisely because nature is deep, the task demands dogged perseverance. And long-term perseverance is only possible if it is based in an unwavering belief in in the possibility of success. The laws of physics may be deep. But, because there is a Creator, there is a rational Universe able to be known by the human mind. The same convictions are required in theology.

At the same time, Torrance was aware that all scientific theories are incomplete approximations, and hence all theories are necessarily revisable *ad infinitum*. Hence we necessarily speak of an *apprehension* of truth rather than of a *comprehension,* since comprehension implies a complete and an exhaustive knowledge.[8] In class he illustrated this by contrasting an object cradled in an open hand, to the same object held in a clenched fist. The clenched fist represented the impossible claim of the human mind to completely encircle an object, thus gaining total comprehension of truth. The open hand represented apprehension, in which the mind cradles, rather than encloses, real truth within itself, always conscious that beyond its current understanding there is so much more. And yet, despite the necessarily tentative nature of all truth—including all scientific theories—the best theories do truly reveal something of the real nature of an object. Theories are not simply projections of human thought which happen to work, or which happen to fit the data. In the same way, theological knowledge involves *apprehension* rather than *comprehension.* In his paper on H. R. Mackintosh, Torrance acknowledged how his old teacher stressed that the human mind can only ever apprehend part of the reality under investigation, and can never comprehend the whole of it.[9] Nevertheless, and importantly, what can be known is *true* knowledge even if it has depths which have not yet been plumbed. This being the case, theological science is no different to the natural sciences.

---

8. Cf. Torrance, *Theological Science,* 296–97.

9. Torrance: "Hugh Ross Mackintosh: Theologian of the Cross" (Class Handout). Cf. Mackintosh, *Christian Apprehension of God.*

— *Chapter 6* —

# Theological Knowledge

TORRANCE'S VIEWS ON SCIENTIFIC method did not go unchallenged. He knew that within the scientific community itself there were alternative philosophies surrounding the scientific enterprise. And some of Torrance's own students, such as Bill Peat, Iain Paul, and Chris Kaiser, all of whom had been professional scientists in their own right, were well aware of this.[1] Each of them was sympathetic to Torrance's overall argument. But, from their professional knowledge, they were sharply mindful that not not all of their erstwhile colleagues believed that scientific theories describe reality as it truly is.

Torrance was mindful of this lobby. He knew that for some, theories simply happen to fit the data. And, in this school of thought, the truth and value of a theory lies in its consistency and pragmatic usefulness. Nevertheless, over against this, Torrance insisted that the scientists who historically have made the greatest strides in human knowledge were those gripped by the conviction that they were engaging with the true nature of being, and not simply creating mental models which happened to work. As with Einstein, Torrance viewed that latter position as a dead-end. This explains Torrance's dissatisfaction with methodologies which predicted outcomes only from probability and statistics, rather than from an unfolding of the inner rationale of the object in question. Torrance believed this was why Einstein was uneasy with Quantum Theory, and was why Einstein reckoned there must exist a unified Field Theory lying behind both Relativity Theory and Quantum Theory, which could yet

---

1. Iain Paul challenged Torrance's interpretation of Einstein, later writing a book for which Torrance provided the Foreword: Paul, *Science, Theology and Einstein*.

# Theological Knowledge

yield a coherent, unified, and objective, understanding of the universe. Though Einstein's personal search for a unifying theory was unproductive, Torrance regarded the quest as valid, and one which, someday, would find success.[2]

## Objective Knowledge

Do we know things as they are in themselves? Or do theories simply happen to fit the data? This philosophical problem has existed from the earliest days of modern scientific enquiry. The scientific revolution, involving the likes of Kepler, Galileo, and Newton, established empirical experimentation as the standard process through which we increase our knowledge of nature. Empiricism was given a philosophical basis by John Locke,[3] and its universal adoption brought about a change in the application of logic. Previously, *deductive logic* had been dominant. Deductive logic expands knowledge by syllogistic deduction from accepted propositions, with Descartes of the view that innate knowledge, implanted in the mind by the Creator, provides these propositions.[4] Over against this, the scientific revolution made *inductive logic* its primary tool. Inductive logic works on the assumption that, as the physical senses encounter reality through experimentation, the mind formulates statements from the gathered sense-data, and then constructs theories based on these statements. Thus, whereas deductive logic starts with an axiomatic premise, inductive logic starts with statements formed from discovered data. The huge success of the physical sciences from the sixteenth to the nineteenth

---

2. Since Einstein, Quantum Entanglement—the paradoxical phenomenon of an entity having two locations simultaneously—has become a major question. The search for a unified theory continues: though now such a search is perhaps based *within* Quantum Theory rather than *outside* of it as Einstein thought.

3. Locke saw the mind at birth as a blank slate or *tabula rasa*. Contrary to Descartes' pre-existing concepts, Locke taught we are born without innate ideas, and knowledge only comes from experience fueled by sense perception.

4. Descartes viewed humans as composite entities of mind and body, with priority to the mind. But, though he argued that mind and body are closely joined, he allowed a dualism between the two. Within this dualism the mind learns primarily from the power of innate ideas rather than from physical experience. It was over against this that Locke developed his theory of knowledge based on empiricism. Descartes' dualism (Cartesian dualism) is referenced frequently by Torrance, since Descartes' dualism between mind and body obstructed the ability of the mind to gain information in any encounter with the physical. This was inimical to Torrance, whose notion of intuitive knowledge required the mind to have direct encounter with physical reality.

centuries resulted in empiricism becoming the unchallenged scientific and philosophical tool.[5] Quite simply, it worked! It worked spectacularly. It produced concrete results. And it brought incontestable advances in understanding the world around us. And yet, at the same time, this apparently all-powerful empirical method, along with its concomitant assumption of the mind's ability to interpret sense-data correctly, did not go unchallenged.

Bishop George Berkeley questioned whether the mind can in fact know anything outside of itself or outside of the realm of ideas? He asked if it is even possible to prove that what we think we know through the senses is actually information from outside the mind at all?[6] Or was that an inherently unprovable proposition? It seems so. In his lectures on nineteenth-century theology, James Torrance put it to us this way: *"Thought cannot prove by thought alone that anything exists outside of thought!"*[7] David Hume's contribution was to argue that patterns which science "discovers" in the natural world—such as the sun rising every morning—are merely summaries of what an observer is *accustomed* to experience, but which the same observer can never *prove* to be part of the nature of things.[8] Instead, for Hume, "custom is the great guide of

---

5. The fundamental problem was that Enlightenment thinking assumed that any true knowledge comes through sense-experience. This evolved from the renaissance humanist approach which sought to root truth, not in an authority, but in nature. However, this rules out knowledge of God automatically. This was why Torrance was adamant that modern reflection on scientific methodology has shown empiricism and sense-experience to be an inadequate description of what actually happens in scientific discovery. Torrance argued that, alongside gathering empirical knowledge, there is an intuitive grasping of the nature of what is being explored. The mind grasps something of the wholeness of being, beyond the individual scraps of sense-data.

6. Bishop Berkeley only proved that we cannot *explain* how the mind learns from the senses. He did not prove that the mind does *not* learn from the senses. Samuel Johnson tried to destroy the theory by the expedient of kicking the person who was expounding Berkeley to him and asking the sufferer if pain was in his leg or just in his mind! But Berkeley's philosophy is more robust than that!

7. Torrance emphasized that all sciences depend on unprovable assumptions. This includes mathematics and logic as well as physics. He referred us to Kurt Gödel who, in the 1930s, proved that: in any non-trivial mathematical system, consistency and completeness cannot both be proven to be true of that system within the system itself; and that the issue can only be resolved through reference to a higher level of mathematical reality. On the basis of Gödel's Theorem, Torrance argued that all knowledge is only substantiated by reference upwards. Cf. Torrance, *Theological Science*, 255, and Torrance, *Space, Time and Incarnation*, 88.

8. Hume rejected Descartes' notion that knowledge may be based on innate ideas

human life."[9] What Hume meant was that we posit theories according to custom of experience; it is not because we understand the nature of things, and, on that basis, know why events are caused. However, in his example, Hume ignored Newton's gravitational-principle which does provide an underlying logic as to why the sun "rises" every day. As Stanley Jaki pointed out in his Gifford lectures, Hume was weak on actual scientific theory.[10]

Immanuel Kant took things further. Kant analyzed the predicament of the apparent impossibility of ever knowing anything outside of the mind. He tried to overcome the dilemma by creating the categories of *noumena* (what an object is in itself) and *phenomena* (our experience of that object). Thus Kant introduced a dualism between things-in-themselves and things-for-us; and he regarded things-as-they-are-in-themselves as quite unknowable.[11] Nineteenth-century theology, with its concentration on the *felt human experience of God,* and its abandonment of a search for what *God is in himself,* was one of the outcomes of Kantian dualism, brought to a peak by Schleiermacher with his focus on the feelings of the religious consciousness. Significantly, during his student days Karl Barth read and re-read Kant's *Critique of Pure Reason* and *Critique of Practical Reason.*[12] Barth admired Kant. He was impressed by his arguments. He

---

residing in the mind. Hume approved Berkeley's doubts concerning the ability of the mind to know anything external to it. Torrance, *Theological Science*, 118, noted approvingly that Hume did demonstrate that the notion of causality does not arise on logical grounds: but, precisely because of this, Torrance argued: "Because there is no logical road to these laws the scientist, in formulating them, must rely upon his *intuition,* that is upon the sheer weight or impress of external reality upon his apprehension, although once formulated he can test them indirectly through their success in bringing the widest range of experience under their illumination."

9. If for "custom" we read "probability," Hume's thought links with twentieth-century positivism.

10. Jaki, *Road of Science and the Ways to God.*

11. Cf. Torrance, *Theological Science*, 88–89. Also, Torrance, *Space, Time and Incarnation*, 43. For Kant, human knowledge applied only to the phenomenal realm, not to the noumenal. Since the "thing in itself" is by definition entirely independent of our experience of it, we are ignorant of the noumenal realm. This led Kant to suppose that the truly fundamental laws of nature, like the truths of mathematics, are knowable precisely because they make no effort to describe the world as it really is but rather *prescribe* the structure of the world as we experience it. For Kant, the reason imposes order: it does not discover order since the mind can never know the nature of the *noumena.*

12. Busch, *Karl Barth: His Life from Letters and Autobiographical Texts*, 40.

came to the conclusion that Kant's philosophy could never provide a solid basis for theology.

Thus, even empiricism—that apparently solid foundation upon which scientific knowledge could rest—was chipped away by philosophers skeptical of ever attaining true knowledge of anything outside of the mind. Nevertheless, until the closing decades of the nineteenth century, research scientists were largely untroubled by such philosophic doubts. As far as scientists were concerned, the empirical method worked. It brought results. And, in the real-world of scientists as opposed to the ideas-world inhabited by philosophers, solid progress was made almost every day. The claim of science to describe reality as it truly is in itself, seemed to be homologated by its triumphs. Philosophical discussions might enliven University staff-room conversation, but the sheer success of science meant that these philosophical issues could be marginalized, or simply categorized as interesting mental puzzles arising from the dilettante musings of dreamers.

Then came James Clerk Maxwell, Albert Einstein, and Neils Bohr. The theories which they produced demanded radically new conceptualizations and imagings of physical reality, of a type which went far beyond normal mental constructs. First, Clerk Maxwell suggested that imaging reality might involve fields of matter and energy rather than discrete objects and discrete forces. Then Einstein introduced Relativity Theory, which stretched the human conceptual framework to breaking-point.[13] Soon afterwards Neils Bohr and others formulated Quantum Theory. Suddenly the human perception of how things exist was not quite so straightforward. In this strange new universe what did our scientific theories mean? What did an equation mean? What status did they have in relation to reality? The theories worked. The mathematics worked. But did they work because they described what was out there? Or did they work only because they created models which fitted the data?

The new theories in physics which were developed in the late nineteenth and early twentieth centuries, demanded conceptual frameworks

13. Ritchie, Personal Lecture Notes, 5 (25th October, 1973): "In Quantum Theory we are up against something that we cannot *image*, because it is inherently unobservable." What Torrance meant was that although the conceptualities required by Relativity Theory and Quantum Theory can be expressed mathematically, and can be processed by mathematical techniques, the human imagination cannot visualize them. Hence, Quantum Theory in particular, as readily admitted by physicists, involves notions which would be reckoned self-contradictory if proposed anywhere else than in the "hard sciences."

so alien from what the human mind thought possible—both within nature and within the structures of thought itself—that it had to be asked whether scientific theories ever represented reality at all? Might David Hume have been correct all along? Is science simply a discipline which predicts outcomes based on custom molded by experience? Has science ever had an understanding of the objective structure and inherent logic of things? Has it been fooling itself that it had? The strangeness of the new theories which now had to be grappled with, and the difficulties in imaging and conceptualizing the physical reality which these theories necessitated, made metaphysical questions sharper than ever. On the one hand, realists, such as Einstein, maintained doggedly that in science we do uncover the true nature of things. On the other hand, positivists were firm in their conviction that science merely posits models which fit the data and which happen to work.

This meant that when Torrance looked across the University to the natural sciences, as disciplines whose methodology homologated his view of theology as a science, he entered troubled waters. In effect he was appealing to the *realist* tradition of modern scientific thought. But that was not the only player in the field. Nevertheless, Torrance held that it was the realist view of science which had been adopted by the best and by the most productive scientific thinkers. Building on this, he argued that the best theology has also been that written by men and women who have been convinced that God's self-revelation in Jesus Christ is a revelation of God as he truly is in himself. This lay behind Torrance's insistent declarations: "*In Jesus Christ we know God as he is in himself,*" and, "*There is no hidden God behind the back of Jesus Christ.*" For Torrance, this was the relevance of the *homoousios* for our knowledge of God. In classical Christology the *homoousios* means that the Son of God is the same being as the Father. Therefore, knowledge of Jesus Christ, the Son of God, is true knowledge of God as he is in himself.[14]

## Intuitive Knowledge

This leaves unanswered an important question. How can the mind know anything exterior to itself? Torrance was aware that epistemology (how we know things) lived with serious problems, which had been exposed by Berkeley and Hume among others. To overcome this impasse Torrance could have adopted the eighteenth-century Scottish Common

14. Ritchie, Personal Lecture Notes (November, 1973).

Sense Philosophy of Thomas Reid and Dugald Stewart. Reid and Stewart cut through the Gordian Knot of the epistemological "How?" by stating simply that it happens! We may never be able to prove how it happens. It just does. It is common-sense that it does! If Torrance adopted this stance he could eliminate immediately a host of problems, especially the question: how does knowledge of external reality enter the mind? But Torrance wanted something more substantial. In particular, he wanted to go beyond the traditional conservative-evangelical position that God provides statements in Scripture which the mind can then discourse upon. For Torrance, true knowledge comes through an encounter with *being*, not just through reflection on *statements about being*—whatever their source This led him to explore intuitive knowledge, a notion which became central to his theological method.

It is easy to misunderstand Torrance's concept of intuitive knowledge. It is not the same as Descartes' belief that God implants innate-ideas into the mind, which deductive logic may then exploit. Nor is it the same as instinctive-awareness. Nor is it the same as inspired-guesswork. Even less is it to be understood as gut-instinct. For Torrance, intuitive knowledge was a specific concept which he shared with the twentieth-century Hungarian-British philosopher of science Michael Polanyi—though Polanyi preferred the term "tacit knowledge" to "intuitive knowledge." As a working scientist, Polanyi made several important contributions. And yet, even as he did so, and as he reflected on the nature of scientific method, he came to the conclusion that positivism, which seemed to dominate contemporary science, was a vastly misleading theory as to how things are known, and in fact undermined humanity's achievement in understanding the universe as it truly is.

For Polanyi and for Torrance, intuitive knowledge was knowledge gathered when an open-minded enquirer repeatedly exposed himself or herself to an object, and when they repeatedly asked proper questions of that object, resulting in them gaining more than just the gathering of sense-data. In such an encounter between enquirer and object something of the nature of the object communicated itself to the enquirer beyond the collecting of data. In that situation, the logic of the nature of the object began to impose itself on the mind of the enquirer.[15]

---

15. Cf. Torrance, "The Place of Michael Polanyi in the Modern Philosophy of Science" (Class Handout), 1: "[Polanyi regarded discovery as] the free creation of thought which cannot inductively be gathered from sense-experiences but which arises in our minds under the impact of the inherent intelligibility (*Verständlichkeit*) of the universe,

This notion of intuitive knowledge attempted to describe—though never to explain—how the mind gains knowledge of reality exterior to the mind. Knowledge is gained in the encounter of mind and object, as the mind "leaps across" a logical gap in the attainment of a new conception.[16] For Polanyi, working in the *natural sciences*, this encounter took place through the iterative process of experimentation. For Torrance, working in *theological science* this encounter took place through God's voluntary self-revelation in Jesus Christ, mediated through Spirit, Scripture, and prayer. It is at this point that an earlier illustration becomes highly relevant. It is the image of Torrance preparing for his sermons on the *Book of Revelation* by reading, and re-reading, and re-reading, the biblical text in an attitude of prayer, and seeking to allow the Word of God to replace his presuppositions and to remodel his thinking.

Thus, in this notion of "intuitive knowledge," it is in the encounter of mind and object (taking place in a manner appropriate to the particular discipline), that an awareness of the true nature of the object is intuited, with the object itself "speaking" to the mind. Crucially, the "How?" of this is never fully made clear. Thus the notion of intuitive knowledge *describes* the process, without *explaining* how it happens. But, that this is actually how things happen was axiomatic for both

---

and with the kind of wordless thinking that goes on when the scientist is caught up in wonder and in the indefinable acts of intuitive apprehension upon which his creative structures rest." Also page 4: "Basic to everything is an intuitive apprehension of nature in its intrinsic relations—and by intuitive apprehension is meant rational but non-logical non-inferential knowledge. Scientific hypotheses are not logically derived from experience. Scientific knowledge advances through *freely invented concepts*, i.e., not fictions, not freely invented conventions, *but concepts that creatively arise in our minds under the compulsion of the objective structures of nature*."

16. Cf. Ritchie, Personal Lecture Notes (22nd January, 1976): "Intuitive apprehension: ideas as free creations of thought, under intimacy of experience: not logico-deductive or abstracted from observation. Intuitive apprehension of inner structures of reality. Process of knowing is unfathomable (Polanyi). Axioms are known only through discovery, not beforehand; not fixed premises or *principia* in the old sense . . . Polanyi talks of intuitive, anticipatory, tacit, apprehension of reality—yet ultimately we rely on unfathomable processes." Cf. Torrance: "The Place of Michael Polanyi in the Modern Philosophy of Science" (Class Handout), 7: "[Polanyi's 'tacit knowledge'] is essentially an *intuitive insight*, the insight of a mind informed by intuitive contact with reality, an inductive insight with a semantic or ontological reference which is objectively correlated to an aspect of nature seeking realization, as it were, in the mind of the inquirer . . . It is an authentically heuristic act in which the understanding *leaps across* a logical gap in the attainment of a new conception, and then, guided by an intuitive surmise evoked by that conception probes through deepening coherences to lay bare the structure of the reality being investigated."

Polanyi and Torrance. Torrance never attempted to solve the ultimate 'How?' of epistemology. He could not do so. No one can do so. As James Torrance pointed out, "*Thought cannot prove by thought alone that anything exists outside of thought!*" Hence, it is inherently impossible to demonstrate through pure thought how thought is related to something outside of thought, far less is it possible to show how anything outside the mind can be known by the mind.[17]

This brings us to the H. P. Owen seminars which Torrance set up in our final year, to familiarize us with the thinking of our new external examiner. Our group consisted of myself, Alistair Wynne, Tom Noble, Bill Peat, and Lance Stone, with Torrance himself leading the discussions. In my seminar notes for the 28th October, 1975, I noted Torrance's answer to a question posed by Bill Peat, in which Torrance said that Owen understood intuition inadequately, because Owen regarded intuition as no more than a general awareness of reality. Torrance pointed out that, for Owen, our knowledge of the inner rational structures of reality depends on the discursive reason creating theories around data which our senses have gathered. But, for Torrance, that was a Thomist approach. First, data is gathered. Second, statements are derived from that data. Third, the mind uses these statements to infer a general theory which the enquirer assumes is how things actually are.[18] Torrance saw things quite differently. Over against the Thomist/Owen position that theories are developed through the mind rationalizing *statements* derived from data, Torrance argued that *intuition* operates through, "an *intellective grasp* of rational structures themselves."[19] But what is this "intellective" grasp? What Torrance meant was that, beyond what Thomas and Owen describe, there is, in the encounter of enquirer and object, created a situation in which something of the rationality and logic of the object is intuitively grasped by the enquirer when—but only when—the object is questioned in a manner appropriate to it. This brings an "intellective" grasp of the *wholeness* of a rational structure.[20] Thus, the mind does not simply logicize *statements* which have been formed from gathered data.

---

17. Cf. Torrance, *Theological Science*, 184.
18. Cf. Torrance, *Theological Science*, 77, 142–43.
19. Ritchie, Personal Class Notes (28th October, 1975).
20. Cf. Ritchie, Personal Lecture Notes (18th October, 1973). Torrance held that all great intellectual advances involved synthetic thought, not just analytic thought. The mind grasps the big picture. The mind apprehends something of the wholeness of things.

Instead, the mind directly encounters the rationality of the *object*. Hence, true science involves much more than the discursive reason constructing models from statements about data. Instead, true science involves a direct encounter with the rationality of being itself, made possible because an appropriate scientific process has taken place.

Torrance explained that, for Aquinas, although what is in the mind has first been in the senses, the actual rational and intelligible structure of reality is only worked out in the mind by the mind. In contrast to that position, Torrance held that, as we allow an object to present itself to us, and as we interact with that object over and over again in an appropriate manner, then something of the intrinsic intelligibility of the wholeness of the object is apprehended by the mind. It is this interaction which brings about an intellective grasp in which we apprehend something of the wholeness of the object in question. Thus, it is not bare *statements* about data which our minds apprehend (size, temperature, color, chemical analysis, etc.); instead, something of the rational structure and logic of the *object* communicates itself directly to the mind as a whole. The mind gains an apprehension of the object, and this takes the mind deeper than the logicizing of statements could ever do—though statements can be part of the discipline of that encounter. In all of this, the crucial issue is that something of the wholeness of an object is communicated directly in the encounter between object and mind.

In the class-seminar, Torrance explained that Owen's Thomistic method was like old science which assumed that an enquirer gathered sense-data, information from which was put into the form of statements, and which statements then became the basis for the construction of theories. The theological equivalent of the Owen/Thomist position was seeing divine revelation as providing data in the form of propositional statements, which statements the reason then composed into theological doctrines. Over against this, in Torrance's view, revelation is not primarily statements, but is God communicating himself in Jesus Christ. And, it is the personal being of God in his revelation which communicates the inner logic and rational structure of God and of the ways of God which are witnessed to by Scripture. And so, for Torrance, neither the scientist nor the theologian apprehends the inner rationality of an object by working deductively from statements. Instead, for the theologian, something of the wholeness of God in his being and act is communicated and apprehended in our encounter with his self-revelation in Jesus Christ.[21] Hence, when we read Scripture, we do not just soak up statements (propositions) which the reason rearranges into doctrines. That would be a Thomist hermeneutic. Instead, the reading of Scripture, in prayer, in the Spirit, brings encounter with *God*, not just encounter with *statements about God*. That, Torrance would argue, is in fact a high doctrine of Scripture. This view of Scripture is discussed further in the next section.

For Torrance, in truly knowing something, we do not operate under the "*logical* compulsion" of a group of statements (statements may mislead through their limitations). Instead, we operate under an "*intellective* compulsion," which Torrance understood as being a compulsion forced on us by the inherent intelligibility of the object. In one of the handouts, "Scientific Dogmatics," I underlined the repeated strong and varied phrases which he used to try to get this across to us,[22]

- [Knowledge] is *forced upon us* when we are true to the facts we are up against.
- This is the way *we have to think* if we are to do justice to the object we are investigating.
- The rational person, free though he is, thinks as *he is compelled to think* by the external world.
- In science we ask questions and answer them *under the compulsion* of what is over against us.
- Our thoughts take shape in accordance with the nature of what we experience and under its *pressure upon us*.

In other words, in this intuitive apprehension—whether in the natural sciences or in theological science—the object communicates not simply data, but itself. And, as the enquirer goes back to the object again and again, then the mind intuits something of the actual nature of the object

---

21. Cf. Torrance, *Atonement*, 4: "Thus we cannot begin to understand the atonement by bringing to it principles of formal rational continuity or by adopting an abstract theoretical explanation. In seeking to unfold the meaning of the death of the Son of God, therefore, we must have recourse to putting together conjunctive statements based upon the *inherent synthesis* to be found in the person of the mediator and not in any logical or rational presuppositions which we bring to interpret what he has done for us . . . We must *follow* Christ and think only *a posteriori*, seeking throughout to be conformed to the mind of Christ himself as the truth."

22. Torrance, "Scientific Dogmatics," 1 (class handout).

in question. It is the rationality of the object which compels our minds to think a certain way. *How* this happens is not explained. Indeed, it *cannot* be explained. But, *that* it happens is assumed in all sciences. This was Torrance's starting-point. And, for Torrance, the use of intuitive knowledge in theology was legitimized by its use in the natural sciences.

Armed with this, Torrance cut a swathe through the philosophical issues surrounding the problem of the mind knowing anything external to itself, including knowing anything about God. A purely empirical approach deems all knowledge of God to be impossible. This is necessarily the case because, since God is spirit and not matter, he cannot be accessed empirically. On one level, Torrance accepted the power of that argument: hence his rejection of the so-called proofs of God from nature. But, and going beyond that position, Torrance held that, as the enquirer encounters God in his voluntary self-revelation in Jesus Christ—an encounter taking place through Scripture, prayer, and the immanence of the Holy Spirit—then the logic of revelation is intuited. Thus, what we are given to work with in theology is not simply the historical data of the Gospels, but the logic of the divine reality which alone makes sense of the Gospels. That logic is the incarnation. It is that rationality, apprehended in this manner, which is the ground for all Christian theology.

How do men and women access this self-revelation of God? We do not grasp *God* with our minds. Instead, God grasps *us* in his self-revelation in Jesus Christ. This then becomes knowledge accessible to us because of the action of Word and Spirit. In all of this, God is himself determining the manner in which he is to be known, which is in the Word of God, by the Spirit of God, through prayer and worship. Hence, through Word and Spirit, a truly scientific and objective (controlled by the object) knowledge is communicated to the enquirer.

As first-year students this was strange territory for us. Unknowingly, it lay behind our opening assignment. Over the years Torrance set various essays for his new students, with titles such as: "*Assess the significance of Matthew 11:27 and Luke 10:22 for the doctrine of the Person of Christ*," or, "*Consider the Epistemological Relevance of the Holy Spirit.*"[23] Ours was the former. And the axiom that no one knows the Son except the Father, and that no one knows the Father except the Son and those to whom

---

23. Torrance's interpretation of these critical verses differed significantly from Harnack's in his influential 1899/1900 Berlin lectures, later published in English as *What Is Christianity?* Harnack argued that these words merely point to Jesus' self-awareness of having a special divine mission.

the Son chooses to reveal him, was critical for Torrance's theology.[24] God is known in and through Jesus Christ. God is known as he chooses to be known. God is not under our scrutiny at our pleasure. Nevertheless, knowledge of God is *true* knowledge.

## Scriptural Knowledge

How did Torrance's concept of intuitive knowledge relate to knowing God through Scripture? We glanced at this earlier, but it now demands more extended consideration. At New College, Torrance's view of Scripture was criticized by liberal and conservative students alike. For liberals, Torrance was hopelessly Biblicist. They reckoned that, when all was said and done, he was an old-fashioned fundamentalist, and his erudite arguments involving scientific methodology were a bare covering for a primitive Biblicism. From the opposite perspective, conservative-evangelicals viewed his approach as too elaborate and potentially dangerous. They felt he was on a hazardous path, and that his concept of intuitive knowledge was an *open sesame* to a totally subjective interpretation of Christian faith.

Conservative-evangelical students, such as myself, held that everything in Christian theology could and should be deduced from statements given in Scripture. We accepted that Scripture has different literary genres—poetry, history, letters, wisdom literature, etc. However, notwithstanding the variety of genres, we believed that there are clear statements (propositions) in Scripture, and that it is these statements (propositions) which provide the objective data for Christian theology. The conservative-evangelical tradition argued that that was how the early Church constructed its theology, was how the Church Fathers prepared for the theologically definitive Councils of Nicaea (325), Constantinople (381) and Chalcedon (451), and was how the sixteenth-century Reformers understood the relationship between revelation, Scripture, and theology.

Torrance labelled this approach as Fundamentalism. He criticized it as an attempt to build theology from *statements* about revelation, rather than from revelation itself which is the *personal* self-communication of God in Jesus Christ. And, on this issue, he was prepared to challenge traditional interpretations of the biblical hermeneutics of major theologians. Over the years he published many papers which analyzed the approach to Scripture practiced by figures such as Athanasius, Hilary, Calvin, and

---

24. Torrance, *Preaching Christ Today*, 6.

other theological giants, arguing that their method dovetailed with his.[25] In connection with this, when I researched "Theology and Logic" as my final year special subject, he gave me a copy of his paper "Intuitive and Abstractive knowledge from John Duns Scotus to John Calvin," which touches on this area. In that paper he argued that a practice of intuitive knowledge was integral to how Scripture had actually been handled by Duns Scotus, Calvin, and others.[26]

1. *Scripture and Statements.* As conservative-evangelicals, we acknowledged that Torrance and Barth's emphasis on Jesus as the ultimate Word of God did have considerable biblical justification (John 1:1; Hebrews 1:1,2, etc.). However, our concern was that this emphasis on Jesus as the Word of God was applied by Barth and Torrance in a way which downgraded the written text of Scripture from being regarded as the true Word of God. We knew that Barth spoke of a threefold form of the Word of God: the proclaimed Word of God in the preaching of the Church; the written Word of God in Scripture; and the incarnate Word of God in Jesus Christ.[27] And, although Barth's presentation of the issue had a beguiling architectonic beauty, this threefold form seemed to suggest a hierarchy of importance, with increasing levels of inspiration and authority as the spotlight moved from the obviously fallible *proclaimed* Word, through the *written* Word, to the absolutely authoritative *incarnate* Word. The question was: within this gradation of truth was Barth taking Scripture as seriously as we wanted him to?

Before going to New College I had been advised that, for Torrance and Barth, Scripture was not the Word of God in itself, but only *became* the Word of God when the Holy Spirit made it so in a particular situation. This put theological defense mechanisms on high alert. Allied to this, elsewhere in the Faculty we had to cope with what we regarded as the liberal destruction of the integrity of Scripture. Understandably, we were wary of any view which seemed to undermine Scripture's veracity, or detract from Scripture's adequacy as the source of theological truth. This made it difficult for us to appreciate the nuances of Torrance's position. Only later did I come to see that Torrance's intention was to make

---

25. Cf. Torrance, *Divine Interpretation*.

26. Torrance wrote this paper for the 1966 Oxford and Edinburgh Congress celebrating the 700th anniversary of Duns Scotus' birth. Torrance, "Intuitive and Abstractive Knowledge from Duns Scotus to John Calvin," 291–305.

27. Barth, *CD* I/1, 98–140.

the doctrine of Scripture stronger, not weaker. And, only later, did I appreciate the context of Barth's teaching on Scripture within his *Church Dogmatics* I/1, namely, his debate with Liberal Protestantism. Correcting Liberal Protestantism's deviation from Christian orthodoxy was Barth's primary concern. We touch on this in our chapter on Harnack.

At the time, along with many of my conservative-evangelical fellow-students, I was uneasy with Barth and Torrance's approach. Broadly speaking, the conservative-evangelical position was that the whole of Scripture is the inspired Word of God, and that every word and sentence within it is God's Word objectively. As such, Scripture is the given locus of God's revelation, a revelation which has been expressed through narrative and propositions. Over against this was Barth and Torrance's insistence that the true focus of revelation is elsewhere: God is himself his revelation: he and no other. For Barth and for Torrance, Jesus Christ as the incarnate Word, *homoousios* with the Father, is the locus and the content of God's self-revelation in his own person, with the Word of God in Scripture witnessing to that one and only divine self-revelation. We interpreted this—incorrectly, as it happened—to mean that for Barth and Torrance, Scripture is not in itself the Word of God until God chooses to make it so. We saw this as responsible for phrases being used increasingly in church services such as, "Let us listen *for* God's Word in Scripture," rather than the authoritative, "Let us listen *to* God's Word in Scripture."

This raised worrying questions. Was Scripture no more than a collection of wise-sayings? Did it only occasionally give spiritual insight? Did Torrance's position imply that God's self-revelation in Jesus Christ could be something mediated directly by the Holy Spirit, with only a loose reference to Scripture? Did it result in subjectivism despite Torrance's avowed determination to root theology objectively? Might his method have the unintended consequence of sanctioning the notion that the Spirit gives new revelation to individuals, contradicting statements found in Scripture? Our suspicion and unease increased when Torrance insisted that God communicates primarily as personal being rather than through propositional statements. We saw this as undermining our conviction that Scripture has clear and timeless statements which are the axioms of theology and faith.

2. *Scripture and Incarnation*. These, and other questions, prompted me to read through Barth's *Church Dogmatics* I/1, in which Barth set out his doctrine of Scripture. This led to reading more of him. To my surprise, I

found that Barth did state that Scripture "is" the Word of God. So I had to think again. Perhaps Barth had been judged too hastily. However, in the 1970s, unlike more recent times, conservative-evangelical theologians were unanimous in finding Barth deficient in this vital area. Also, inevitably, there were other questions to be answered. For example, why was Torrance so reluctant to speak of Scripture as containing propositions? Surely a basic statement such as "God is love" (1 John 4:8) was a timeless proposition? Granted, the term "love" has to be fleshed out: but, after that is done (1 John 4:9–11), why cannot this Scripture verse—and, by implication, many other Scripture verses—be regarded as propositions which can be woven together to construct the great doctrines?

As conservative-evangelicals, we had our own understanding of the work of the Spirit in revelation. First, the Spirit inspires the words of Scripture: this is the objective work of the Spirit in revelation. Second, the Spirit opens up the human mind to understand the words of Scripture: this is the subjective work of the Spirit in revelation. But what we found was that Torrance's understanding of the objective and subjective aspects of revelation was radically different. He wanted to set his doctrine of Scripture within the logic of the incarnation; and so, for Torrance, the objective and subjective aspects of the work of the Spirit both took place in Jesus Christ, with the *reception* of revelation as important as the *giving* of it. As God, Jesus Christ is the *giver* of revelation through himself being the Word of God. But also, as man, Jesus Christ is the *receiver* of that revelation through being the one addressed by that Word. And the Holy Spirit is God in his capacity to open up the creature to hear and to know the Creator in and through Jesus Christ. In this way, Torrance rooted both the giving and the receiving of revelation in the incarnation. Hence, for Torrance, both the *divinity* and the *humanity* of Christ were central to theological epistemology.[28]

It is true that the conservative-evangelical view of Scripture also saw a link between the doctrine of Scripture and the doctrine of the incarnation. But of a somewhat different kind. Conservative evangelicals referred to the *analogy* of the incarnation vis-à-vis Scripture. By this we meant that, just as Jesus was truly human in every way yet remained sinless,

---

28. Torrance, *Theological Science*, 292n1. Cf. Torrance, *Atonement*, 8: "Jesus has come to fulfil the covenant will of God both from the side of God, fulfilling all the promises of God to his people, and from the side of man, walking in all the way that the people of God were commanded to, and as such to be the servant of the Lord in mediating a new covenant."

so Scripture is also truly human—insofar as it retains the linguistic and grammatical idiosyncrasies of its human authors—yet remains inerrant. This analogy aimed to rebuff the criticism that Scripture could only be divinely inspired if its authors had been turned into robotic ciphers who wrote down mechanically what the Holy Spirit "dictated" to them.

Torrance had a different understanding of the relationship of the incarnation to God's revelation in and through his Word. Torrance's emphasis was that the giving of revelation by God, and the reception of revelation by humanity, both occur in Christ, with revelation taking place in the unity of his person, the *homoousios*. Jesus is truly God and truly man. He is God speaking his Word to humanity. He is also humanity receiving that Word from God.[29] Moreover, as a man Jesus *grew* in his knowledge of God. Thus Jesus' human knowledge of God was not imported directly from his divinity, as if along a fiber-optic incarnational cable. Instead, "*Jesus grew in wisdom and stature, and in favor with God and man*" (Luke 2:52). This verse was quoted repeatedly by the Church Fathers as they sought to counter any suspicion that Jesus' humanity was in appearance only.[30]

3. *Scripture and Scholarship.* Slowly, bit by bit, I began to appreciate that Torrance had a tremendously high doctrine of Scripture. It became clear that, in practice, his doctrine of Scripture was as elevated as that held by any of his students, if not more so. Reverence for Scripture was central to Tom Torrance's Christian piety. From an early age he had read through the Bible twice every year.[31] Moreover, on various contested issues in academic biblical studies he held to a decidedly traditional position.[32] For example, he defended the precision of memory exercised by the authors of the Gospels and the Acts of the Apostles.[33] Similarly, he affirmed the

---

29. Walker, Firbush Lecture, 30th November, 2019.

30. Cf. Athanasius, *C. Ar.* 3.26; Gregory of Nyssa, *Against Eunomius* 4.4; Gregory of Nazianzus, *Or. Bas.* 43.38; etc.

31. Torrance, *Preaching Christ Today*, 10.

32. Cf. Torrance, *Theology in Reconstruction*, 22: "What we are to concern ourselves with then [supposedly] in reading St Mark's Gospel is not with what Mark claims to be talking about, but rather with what went on in Mark's soul and what his editorial creations tell us of his attitude to existence." Torrance tore apart the liberal assumption that written texts are all about the state of mind of the author and not about what they claimed to report. That was the easy, cheap, and superficial way to dismiss what has been a priori decided to be unacceptable.

33. Torrance, *Theological Science*, 322n1.

theological unity of Scripture, through the Old and the New Testaments, a position fundamental to his understanding of the relationship between God's dealings with Israel and the person and work of Jesus Christ. Consequently, he viewed the Old Testament as Christocentric as the New Testament. Likewise, in class Torrance let it be known that he favored an early date for John's Gospel, this being one of the few areas in which he agreed with the maverick Bishop John Robinson, whom he described as a fine scholar, but hopeless theologian![34] Torrance also held that the command of the risen Jesus to institute baptism in the name of the Father, Son and Holy Spirit (Matthew 28:19), came from the lips of Jesus himself and was not an intrusion by the early church.[35] He further insisted that the statement, "No one knows the Son but the Father and no one knows the Father except the Son and those to whom the Son reveals him" (Matthew 11:27/Luke 10:22), was spoken by Jesus himself, dismissing the view of liberal scholars such as Harnack who insisted that such complex theology could only have been inserted by the later church community.[36] In all of this, Torrance based his position on the conviction that if Jesus Christ is in fact who the Scriptures say he is, namely truly God and truly man, then these are exactly the statements we should expect Jesus to make. They perfectly illustrated Torrance's thesis, based on John 8:43, that it is only when we understand who Christ is, and only when allow our thinking to be controlled by that logic (*logos*) and what flows from it, that we can actually hear his speech (*lalia*) aright.

At the same time, as 1970s students, we noted that Torrance had what we regarded then as highly liberal views in some areas of biblical studies. For example, he accepted that Isaiah may not have been written by a single author.[37] In the 1970s, the single-authorship of Isaiah was a red-line in conservative-evangelical biblical scholarship. However, this red-line has blurred considerably. Modern conservative-evangelical scholarship now focuses on the canonical unity of the Isaiah text, and has less commitment to a single authorship. There are now many conservative-evangelical scholars—though not all—who are comfortable with referring to First, Second, and Third Isaiah in relation to blocks of text within the book (Isaiah 1–39; 40–55; 56–66). Few now hold to a single

---

34. Cf. Robinson, *Re-Dating the New Testament*.
35. Torrance, *Preaching Christ Today*, 7.
36. Torrance, *Preaching Christ Today*, 6.
37. Cf. Torrance, *Atonement*, 42, 46–47.

eighth-century BC author.[38] Today, Torrance's position on this, and on similar issues of biblical scholarship, would not be viewed as heterodox in conservative-evangelical circles.

4. *Scripture and Christology.* Torrance revered Scripture. We sensed it in class. We felt it in his use of the Bible. We experienced it in the exegesis which supported his theology. However, within this high-view of Scripture Torrance was determined to apply theological concepts precisely; and it was his commitment to theological precision which perhaps made us misunderstand him. We failed to realize he was trying to introduce us to a more theologically exact understanding of the core event of revelation, namely the self-revelation of God in Jesus Christ. At no point did he ever contemplate diluting Scripture as the Word of God. Contrary to our preconceptions, Torrance never down-graded Scripture. What he wanted us to grasp was how Scripture, as God's written Word, fits into the overall schema of God's self-revelation through Jesus Christ. Eventually we did understand that his approach raised Scripture to an even higher level.

The crux of the matter is this. In Torrance's schema, although we know everything about God *through* Scripture, Scripture can never itself be the primary *object* of our knowledge. The true object of theological knowledge is God himself. And, God's ultimate Word concerning himself is his personal communication in his Son, Jesus Christ (John 1:1; Hebrews 1:1, 2). That does not, in any way, demean, reduce, replace, or by-pass Scripture as the inspired Word of God. But, what it does do is to place Scripture within the overarching movement of God's self-revelation. God's Word is God himself: but we know that Word in and through Scripture. What this means is that when Torrance expressed his discomfort with a propositional approach to Scripture he never meant to deny that in Scripture there are clear statements—propositions if we like—which are foundational to theology and faith. His concern was that we should not view these statements as ends in themselves, as he believed was the conservative-evangelical approach. Instead, we look through these statements to the reality lying behind them, namely God's Word in person, Jesus Christ. However, "through" never meant, as we supposed it to mean, that such statements may be discarded and superseded when we embrace a supposedly higher knowledge beyond what Scripture gives.

38. I am indebted to Dr. Jamie Grant, Lecturer in Biblical Studies at Highland Theological College, for the current position of conservative-evangelical opinion on the issue.

Torrance rooted his doctrine of Scripture within a christological (hence a trinitarian and incarnational) framework. Within this christological setting, we are not to just think *statements*. Instead, we are to think *reality* through statements. And all of this takes place within the context of a living encounter with Christ as we read Scripture. God's Word creates within us the very possibility of us hearing that Word. In class, I noted Torrance saying,

> God's Word can create (*ex nihilo*) in us the ability to hear the voice of God. We must have a constant giving to it. This is beyond any natural powers that we have of our own. This Word must become imprinted on us. To apprehend God, we need an auditive, intuitive, knowledge. We can only hear God if our hearing is sanctified. This is the empirical relationship and approach that we must have in any scientific structure, because God in his own nature is creative Word.[39]

My early mistake was to assume that the notion of looking *through* biblical statements somehow implied going *beyond* biblical statements. That was never what Torrance meant. His point was that statements *qua* statements can never be the object of enquiry (even in the natural sciences.) Rather, it is always the reality to which statements point which is the object of enquiry. To focus on *statements* is to be Thomistic. To focus on the *reality* to which these statements refer is to be Christian. Hence, Torrance was passionate about the fact that God does not just reveal *statements about himself*. Instead, God reveals *himself*. Therefore, in receiving revelation we encounter God himself, and not simply statements about him which the mind may then rearrange to form doctrines. Instead, as we read and meditate upon Scripture, and as we surrender our minds to the guidance of the Spirit, God communicates himself.

⁖

It is this intellective, intuitive, apprehension of God's being and his ways—always disciplined by prayerful reading of Scripture—which enables us to re-read Scripture in a way which is molded ever more deeply by the logic of God's mighty acts of creation and redemption. And, only when we grasp the divine rationale lying behind Scripture, a rationale which is rooted in the Trinity and the incarnation, does Scripture come together in our minds and make sense. Without that overall grasp of the

39. Ritchie, Personal Lecture Notes, 6 (Autumn, 1973).

theological whole, scholars cannot get beyond narrow and limited interpretations of the biblical text.

This was well expressed in Alasdair Heron's article "*Homoousios* with the Father," in a volume edited by Torrance to commemorate the sixteen-hundredth anniversary of the Nicene-Constantinopolitan Creed. Heron pointed out that one of the essential differences between Arius and Athanasius in the fourth century was that Athanasius grasped the overall logic of the christology of the New Testament. It was that grasp of the inner rationale of Scripture which enabled him to read the Scriptures quite differently from Arius who, quite simply, couldn't see the wood for the trees. Arius just didn't "get it." In contrast, concerning Athanasius, Heron wrote that he, "stresses the identity of being between the Father and the Son, and the assumption by the Son of our human nature, . . . together they constitute the 'scope' (*skopos*) of the overall message of Scripture, *and thus the horizon within which Scripture itself must be interpreted.*"[40]

How do we read Scripture? We read it as the living Word of God. We do not read it in a way which kills its life by a barren application of the historico-critical method which from the outset excludes the living triune and incarnate God. Instead, a christologically-based hermeneutic creates a virtuous circle: Scripture points us to who Jesus Christ is; we encounter Jesus Christ in and through Scripture; and, in that encounter, we apprehend—ever more deeply—the God who reveals himself.

---

40. Heron, "*Homoousios* with the Father," 71 (italics added).

— *Chapter 7* —

# Theological Concepts

UNDERSTANDING TORRANCE WAS CHALLENGING. Nonetheless, the veil of incomprehensibility started to lift when it dawned on us that, at the heart of Torrance's whole argument, there was an absurdly simple truth. The key lay in Torrance's conviction that theology is an objective scientific discipline when, and only when, it allows its object (God) to determine the appropriate mode of enquiry. It was a eureka moment when that penny dropped.

That discovery in the Dogmatics lecture room paralleled closely what had happened in the school mathematics class in Jedburgh. Our teacher was a Mr. Darrow, who had come to Scotland from Poland as a refugee after World War Two. There was nothing lacking in Mr. Darrow's teaching; but there was in my understanding. For a couple of terms, I was in the dark. Then suddenly—and it was *suddenly*—one afternoon it became as clear as day. I grasped what the principle of algebraic substitution meant, and that it could apply to anything: a number, a concept, an object, or even an equation. Having "got it" everything else followed. A similar epiphany took place at New College. Once I understood Torrance's fundamental principle, so much else fell into place. To think scientifically is to think in accordance with the nature of the object. To think otherwise is to introduce a fatal disjunction between knowing and the object known, and between mind and reality.

Just as many of C. S. Lewis' writings in defense of Christianity exposed contradictions lying within some anti-theistic and anti-Christian arguments, so Torrance's work exposed contradictions in thinkers, ranging from the eighteenth-century David Hume to the twentieth-century positivists. Concerning Hume, Torrance argued that if Hume's approach were taken to its logical conclusion, then it would not only invalidate the possibility of religious thought (Hume's aim) but would also disqualify the methodology of the natural sciences (probably not Hume's aim!)

Torrance encouraged us to attend the 1974/75 and 1975/76 Gifford Lectures in Edinburgh given by Professor Stanley L. Jaki on "The Road of Science and the Ways to God."[1] Jaki was a fascinating figure. He was Hungarian-born. He was a Benedictine priest. He held PhD doctorates in both theology and physics. He had professorial appointments at Oxford and Yale. Moreover, he had also been one of the first to see the wider implications of Gödel's incompleteness theorem.[2] The lectures took place in the William Robertson Building of the University in Edinburgh's George Square, and I recall Jaki starting one of the sessions by telling the audience how moved he had been earlier that day when visiting David Hume's grave in Edinburgh's Calton Hill cemetery. However, notwithstanding his genuine admiration of Hume, Jaki argued that although Hume appeared to have much to say about science his actual scientific knowledge was weak. Jaki's verdict was that Hume's philosophical skepticism was a dead-end, not just for religion but for any science which sought to know what reality is actually like. That was also Torrance's verdict.

Nonetheless, for Torrance, theological science had a much higher task than invalidating hostile critiques of Christian faith. At New College the task of Christian Dogmatics was the positive elucidation of Christian theology, not apologetics as such. Its primary task was not confounding critics of faith, but developing a positive knowledge of God and his ways. Torrance saw that as the best of all apologetics. *Deus dixit.* God speaks. And, in that speaking he creates the very possibility of a knowledge of himself.

## Images and Imaging

After my eureka moment I began to understand what Torrance really had in mind when he made his frequent references to science, and to its great figures such as Isaac Newton and Albert Einstein. Or did I? It was all to do with their methodology. Or was it? Was Torrance only focused on methodology? Perhaps. And yet we sensed there was more. And the reason why we suspected there might be more was because Torrance

---

1. Jaki, *Road of Science and the Ways to God.*
2. Jaki, *Relevance of Physics*, 129.

seemed to discuss modern science not simply in terms of its methodology but in terms of its concepts. He made frequent reference to the new *conceptualities* necessitated by modern physics, and not just to the *methodologies* which led to their discovery. Significantly, Chris Kaiser, who at the time was completing his theology PhD (1974) under Torrance, and who already held a PhD in astrophysics, had taken as his thesis topic, "The Logic of Complementarity in Science and Theology," which touched on the challenges facing the human mind when trying to conceptualize or to image fundamental realities.

Clearly then, there was more in the interconnection of science and theology than merely a common approach to methodology, important though that was. When Torrance himself reflected on the huge steps taken in modern physics he had come to realize that these advances had been possible only because physicists had allowed their minds to entertain radically new structures of thought and imaging. And, one of the fundamental scientific changes which Torrance made us aware of was the shift from the Euclidian-Newtonian view of space and time as a *container-box* mentality, to the radically *relational* and *integrated* view of space-time necessitated by the discoveries of Clerk Maxwell, Einstein, and Bohr.[3] Might it be, in some similar fashion, that theology required not only a new methodology but also a new way of conceptualizing and new structures of thought in order to cope with the transcendent nature of its subject-matter? In class Torrance stated, "We cannot be good theologians unless we give up thinking in images." And, underscoring this, he added,

> The Greeks thought with their eyes; [but] the Hebrews thought with their ears [because they took the second of the Ten Commandments seriously]. We are dominated by the Greek way. Hence, when we think about what we hear, we immediately put it into a visual pattern. Hence we miss God so much because his mode is Word. We must learn to think auditively.[4]

He illustrated this by referring to upside-down spectacles, "The problem is the *conceptual* image, not the *visual* image." He lamented that three hundred years of phenomic science had left us with a real need to alter our conceptual framework; and, though it is natural for us to want to

---

3. Cf. Torrance, *Space, Time and Incarnation*, 22–51.
4. Ritchie, Personal Lecture Notes, 6 (26th October, 1973).

picture and image what we think, there is a pressing need in both science and theology to operate with imageless relations.[5]

Building on this, Torrance strove to separate theological conceptualization from old ways of seeing things; and, instead, to move towards notions which involved a more integrated theological continuum in line with modern scientific thinking and in line with the relational, imageless, concepts demanded by Field Theory, Relativity Theory, and Quantum Theory. As mentioned above, Torrance knew that modern investigation into the nature of physical reality had resulted in physicists discarding the notion of space as a container-box which was independent of time, and which was independent of the events occurring "within" it.[6] The old view, so closely allied to Newtonian mechanics, had been replaced by the concept of a space-time-continuum which is itself formed and affected by the events which occur "within" it. Under this radically new way of imaging reality, the hitherto helpful Newtonian notion of discrete objects being acted upon by discrete forces at a distance was transformed. Now there was the idea of a continuum of integrated fields in which the focus was on the *inter-relationship* of matter and energy, and on the *inter-relationship* of space and time. As an aside during one lecture, Torrance told us that when he explained this to Karl Barth, especially the transformation of thinking necessitated by Einstein's theories, Barth put his hands to his head, exclaiming, "I must have been blind not to see that!"[7]

Torrance was aware that, in theology, concepts were frequently treated as isolated entities. Over against this, he argued that any truly foundational concept can only be understood aright within its inter-relationships. Here he built on the notion of the Trinity as the ground and

5. How is God both three and one? How is the oneness of God consistent with the Christian belief in three persons? How can Jesus Christ be fully God and fully man? Torrance never discussed these as problems of logic. If he had, he would have asserted that the logic problem is not on God's side but on ours. This is because it is the nature of being which determines the logic and conceptuality appropriate to it. Thus, the real issue in logic is how *created being* is rational, not how God's *trinitarian being* is. A simple analogy may help. If we lived in a totally two-dimensional universe we could never visualize what a three-dimensional universe would be like, even though we could conceptualize it mathematically (and not only for three dimensions, but for four, five, six, etc.). The ability to employ mathematics in a skillful and accurate manner is not the same as being able to visually imagine an entity.

6. Torrance, *Space, Time and Incarnation*, 22.

7. This wording is as recalled from the class lecture. Torrance, *Space, Time and Resurrection*, x, quoted Barth as exclaiming: "I must have been a blind hen not to have seen that analogy before!"

grammar of all theology. It is the inter-relationship of Father, Son and Holy Spirit which provides the conceptual foundation for understanding all of the acts of God. At the same time, what must be avoided is writing a pseudo-trinitarian theology in which, for example, God the Father is neatly associated with creation, God the Son with salvation, and God the Spirit with whatever remains! That would be using the Trinity as a three-drawer theological filing system. Instead, God as Father, Son, and Spirit, in their inter-relationship with one another is involved in every act of God, with the logic of triunity driving itself into every corner of theological thought, and affecting the way in which we describe everything that God is, everything that God says, and everything that God does. In a true trinitarian theology, both form and content are controlled and informed by the triune nature of God.

But the form of inter-relationship (*perichoresis*) found in the Trinity is not necessarily replicated in the physical structures of the cosmos. To insist that must be so, and to impose "trinitarian" structure on the created order, would be to posit an analogy of being or form (*analogia entis*) between the Creator and the creation. This would not be taking seriously the fact that the cosmos is created out of nothing (*ex nihilo*), and that God in his freedom has given the cosmos its own logic of being. Similarly, neither is it the case that the form of inter-relationship between the divine and human natures of Christ is exactly the same as that found in the Trinity—though Torrance moved close to stating that it is.

## Models and Modelling

Modern science has opened itself up to radically new conceptualities, and to entirely new ways of understanding what the structures of created being are actually like. What has been required, increasingly, is imageless thinking; and, if this is the case within the natural sciences, a similar fundamental rethinking of conceptualities must surely be required in theological science. If the human mind has had to turn itself inside-out when faced with what the created and material universe is actually like, how much more must it need to adapt when confronted by the logic of the transcendent being of God and the logic of God's interaction with that universe? These considerations will influence the final section of this book, in which we discuss the concepts of incarnation and atonement; not as individual events separated in time and space, but as integrated reality cohering in the person of Jesus Christ as God and man.

At New College, we understood little of this to begin with. And yet, enough was communicated to make me read, for the first time, works on the philosophy of science. Long evenings were spent in the stackrooms, deep below the New College Library, in which I found a small, but relevant, collection of books and pamphlets. An early discovery was a volume on Sir David Brewster, the nineteenth-century physicist from my home town of Jedburgh. There were articles by Einstein in which he discussed his view of science. Even more helpfully, I came across a copy of Werner Heisenberg's, *Physics and Philosophy*. Studying these did not bring immediate illumination. Nevertheless, bit by bit, reading these alongside Torrance's own work, *Theological Science,* I began to piece together what I thought he meant.

I knew about Relativity Theory. In my mathematics degree I had worked with some of its equations. And Jacob Bronowski's recently broadcast BBC TV series, "The Ascent of Man," had touched, in popular fashion, on some of the apparently paradoxical aspects which Relativity Theory engenders. I knew a bit about Quantum Theory, though again the conceptualities which it demanded were difficult to make sense of, as professional physicists admit to this day.[8] Initially, I thought that Torrance was importing some of these new scientific conceptualities into his theology directly. Later I understood that they were more a spur for parallel thinking, rather than being used in a one-to-one application.

However, what did become clear to me, again gradually, was that thinking scientifically not only involves adopting a scientific way of knowing things (epistemology), but, as a result of that methodology—in which the nature of the object determines and reforms our thinking—also involves forcing our minds to develop new structures of thought, and new forms of imaging and non-imaging, which better express the logic of the reality under examination. The structures of rational thought, and the type of mental conceptualization which we are familiar with, have been immensely influenced by the container-box view of the universe in which time and space are thought of as a box within which objects exist and

---

8. See Dawkins, *Unweaving the Rainbow: Science, Delusion and the Appetite for Wonder.* Dawkins suggested that nobody truly understands quantum theory, possibly because natural selection shaped our brains to survive in a world of large things where quantum effects are smothered. Though his explanation is questionable, what is clear is that Dawkins recognized the staggering nature of the concepts involved.

events happen. And this container-box conceptuality has influenced the very possibilities of our thinking, even molding the basis of our logic.[9]

What Torrance argued was that Clerk Maxwell, Einstein, and Bohr, discovered that the universe, on both the macro-level of the cosmos and the micro-level of atomic particles, does not conform to the container-box paradigm, but demands a new way of seeing how things exist. Of course, at this point, our use of the word "seeing" is itself indicative of the problem which our highly visual form of thinking is faced with in these areas. Helpfully, modern science has enabled us to understand that nature demands new conceptualities which allow our minds to be aware that events mold and affect the time-space continuum itself. The container-box concept is how we think space and time exist. As a concept, the container-box model is perfectly adequate for ordinary, "low-velocity," experience. However, when we attempt to understand nature's inner workings more deeply, and when we look to boundary-condition-events which help constitute the foundations of reality, we are forced to reassess what we think we have seen and what we think we have experienced. We are compelled to reassess how we viewed the phenomena before our eyes. That forces our minds to grapple with whole new structures of being, which hitherto we thought to be impossible or self-contradictory.

Torrance never argued that the specific conceptualities and mental gymnastics involved in, let us say, Quantum Theory, in which an object can apparently be in two places at the one time, should be applied directly in theology to explain, for example, how the Trinity can exist, or how the incarnation can take place. That would be a crass, inane, and erroneous application of sophisticated concepts. Moreover, it would confuse God's unique mode of being with a mode of created being, in a modern variant of the *analogia entis*, which would be as fatally destructive as previous versions have been. Instead, any new and proper conceptuality in a particular science has to be found within the nature of the particular object itself, with no expectation that analogies of structure will exist across disciplines. However, precisely because scientists have made us aware that the nature of the created universe demands new structures of thought if we are to make sense of it, then it comes as no surprise that understanding the nature of the Creator makes far greater demands. Moreover, when the Creator interacts with the created order, in and through the incarnation, then that event introduces us to something extra, well beyond the structure of being with which we are familiar.

9. Ritchie, "Theology and Logic."

## Thought and Theo-Logic

Field Theory, Relativity Theory, and Quantum Theory take us beyond the serviceable, but limited, push-pull physics of Newton's universe. They take us out of the simple container-box model of Euclidean Geometry. And they turn our way of imaging and modelling space and time inside out. Similarly, but in vastly profounder measure, the Trinity and incarnation make us rethink our theological concepts entirely. In all of this, it is precisely because the object itself, in any field of true scientific enquiry, refashions the way we see things, that we can never rule out, *a priori*, having to understand reality in a way which demands new models derived from new forms of conceptual imaging, even new ways of logical thinking. Torrance wrote,

> The theologian who thinks theo-logically, from a center in God and in accordance with the logic of God, must never forget that his thought will inevitably have a novelty of form baffling the natural thinker, and that the new content which he seeks to express in grammatical and logical language may impose too heavy a strain upon it. As Jesus taught us, the new wine will burst the old wine-skins.[10]

Torrance was aware that not only human concepts but human language is stretched to breaking point when we attempt to express such things. In my seminar notes I recorded him referring to Athanasius, "All our language has to be stretched to speak of God"; and referring to Hilary, "Great strain is put on our language in speaking of God."[11] At Firbush in 2019, Bob Walker further argued that it is not only theology which challenges the capabilities of language: all human language, even speech about ordinary things, is inescapably anthropomorphic. And yet, God provides us with ideas within this inevitable anthropomorphic context. God uses the molded creaturely word.

The exploration of such themes occupies much of the rest of this book. Aware of the principles lying behind Torrance's way of thinking theologically, we shall delve specifically into his core principle that the work of Christ in the atonement is rooted in the person of Christ in the incarnation, with no radical disjunction between the two. And yet, it does

---

10. Torrance, *Theological Science*, 280.

11. Ritchie, Personal Seminar Notes (18th November, 1975). Torrance, *Theological Science*, 209, referred to Hilary's point that images are to be regarded as helpful to man rather than as fitted to God (*De Trinitate* 1.19).

so without flattening out the distinction between Bethlehem and Calvary, and without diluting the centrality of the event on Calvary in any way. It is to these issues that we now turn.

— *Part Three* —

# Christology

— *Chapter 8* —

# "Man of Israel, Lord God"

IN ALL OF HIS theological work, Torrance stressed the importance of Israel in relation to Christian faith. Not political Israel, but Israel as God's covenant people. He opened the 1955 Church of Scotland report on baptism by placing the sacrament within the context of Israel's covenant relationship with God.[1] In his 1983 book *The Mediation of Christ*, he included a moving passage on the same theme, occasioned by his visit to Israel in 1976 as Moderator of the General Assembly.[2] And, in his published lectures on incarnation and atonement, the mission of Christ in relation to God's covenant with Israel is emphasized consistently, with the very opening paragraph of *Atonement* stating that the Son of God, "comes into the situation prepared for him in Israel" and that he "acts both critically and creatively in fulfilment of the Old Testament patterns of understanding and worship provided within the covenant."[3] There exist many more examples in Torrance's published works.

At New College, the centrality of Israel in Torrance's thinking was highlighted in examination questions. One question posed in our final year paper on Pneumatology and Ecclesiology was: "Discuss the relation of the Christian Church to Israel in the light of St Paul's principle that the branches do not bear the trunk, but the trunk the branches."

1. Church of Scotland, *Biblical Doctrine of Baptism*, 11–12.
2. Torrance, *Mediation of Christ*, 52–56.
3. Torrance, *Atonement*, 1. "It was his universal covenant of grace which he began to set out in Israel, in the midst of humanity, in order to work a way to the blessing of all nations in its complete fulfilment. In this covenant God gives himself to humanity and assumes humanity into covenant communion with himself" (7). Also, "He has come to fulfil the will of God manifested in covenant relation with Israel" (25).

Another question asked: "What is meant by the Incarnation? How would you relate it to the interaction of God with the creaturely world, and the interaction of the Word with historical Israel?" As his students, it was clear to us that the importance of Israel—within the covenant purposes of God—was woven into Torrance's entire theology.

For Torrance, the Hebrew vocabulary used by the Old Testament to describe atonement (*goel, kipper, padah*) was a vocabulary necessitated by the person and work of Jesus Christ.[4] In other words, when the New Testament authors took Old Testament vocabulary into their writings, they were not cherry-picking Old Testament words and concepts as useful metaphors which might happen to describe the atoning work of Christ. Instead, in the providence of God it was the once-for-all atoning work of Christ which had in fact driven these concepts, and their vocabulary, back into Israel's understanding of God's redemptive purposes. Thus, the Old Testament atonement liturgy was what it was because of Christ, not *vice-versa*. Given this, and given Torrance's consistent emphasis on Israel, it is unsurprising that, in designating the incarnation as foundational to all Christian theology, Torrance described Jesus not simply as man and God, but as, "Man of Israel, and the Lord God."[5] Jesus is not any man. Nor is Jesus only a representational man. He is Man of Israel. And, in being Man of Israel, he is the one in whom God's covenant is fulfilled.

A holiday which my wife and I made to Prague in the Czech Republic reinforced this profound relationship between Israel's faith and the Christian Gospel. A visit to the Jewish Quarter of any Central-European city brings the tourist face-to-face with the impact of the holocaust, and so it was in Prague. Nonetheless, something else also stood out for us. Next to the entrance to the old Jewish Cemetery of the city is the Ceremonial Hall. This was where the traditional Jewish burial ritual started. The corpse was cleansed. The body was bathed. The hair was washed. The nails were cut. And this cleansing symbolized the spiritual cleansing which is necessary before any man or woman meets a holy God. One of the displays in the Ceremonial Hall gave the words which the officiating Rabbi recited during this ritual; and, in one of the set prayers, the Rabbi addressed the issue of a true cleansing. He asked, "*Who is it who cleanses you?*" Then answered, "*The God of Israel cleanses you.*" In essence, that question and answer is the whole Christian Gospel. This is because,

---

4. Torrance, *Atonement*, 25–96, esp. 67.
5. Torrance, *Preaching Christ Today*, 9.

when the logic of that question and answer is pushed to its extremity, the Gospel message becomes its inevitable consequence. God himself, and only God himself, does the cleansing. God himself, and only God himself, does the atoning action.[6] And what it points to is that God is not just the ultimate cause lying behind the work of atonement; he is in fact the immediate means and the direct personal agency of what is done. That Jewish bereavement liturgy pointed unerringly to a presupposition implanted deep within the foundations of Israel's faith: namely, that God himself is our salvation.

As God's covenant people, Israel had that premise embedded within their experience of God as savior and redeemer. God alone can redeem. God alone can save. God alone can cleanse. And it is arguable that this understanding was part of God's preparation of his people Israel for the incarnation, for the cross, and for the resurrection. Tragically, Israel failed to make the connection between this core principle of their faith with the actual presence of God among them in Jesus of Nazareth. But, from the vantage-point of a Gospel perspective, the connection is clear: God cleanses us in Christ, not just by *providing* what is necessary for our salvation, but by himself directly and personally *doing* and *being* what is necessary. When God came to Israel in Jesus Christ, Israel was challenged to recognize the full implications of truths long rooted in their faith, and to take the resultant Gospel joyfully to the world. "*Who is it who cleanses you?*" "*The God of Israel (himself in person) cleanses you.*"

What this means is that the consistent theme of the Bible, through both the Old and the New Testaments, is: "*God is himself the Gospel.*" That was why Tom Torrance affirmed so strongly the theological unity of the whole of the Bible. It is the God of Israel *in person* who saves and redeems. And what Christian faith affirms is that what God *provides*, *becomes*, and *does*, in being the Gospel, he *provides*, *becomes*, and *does* in the person of Jesus Christ. As such, Jesus is the Gospel. This was the theme explored at the Firbush Conference of November, 2018.

And yet, this pithy, powerful, and attractive phrase, "Jesus is the Gospel," is capable of being understood from different perspectives, not

---

6. Cf. Torrance, *Atonement*, 23, where he interpreted Mark 10:45 ("The Son of Man came not to be served but to serve, and to give his life as a ransom for many") from the context of Psalm 49:7–8: "No man can ransom himself, or give God the price of his life." Also, "God is primarily the subject, for it is ultimately God himself who atones, who blots out sin, pardons it, casts it behind his back, invalidates it or annuls it" (*Atonement*, 34).

all of which embrace what Torrance would regard as a full or properly balanced theology. "Jesus is the Gospel" can become a slogan rather than a statement imbued with the full richness of the Christian message. Hence, in order to clarify what the phrase can mean within Christian theology, the next group of chapters consider it under three headings: "Jesus as Teacher," "Jesus as Agent," and "Jesus as Savior." Our argument is that, although the first two are true as far as they go, they simply do not go far enough. That they embody important and correct aspects of the Gospel is not in doubt. But, in themselves, each is an insufficient depiction of the Christian message. It is the third which portrays the Gospel in fullest measure, and which gives the most satisfactory expression to what was implicit in Israel's faith.

*Jesus as Teacher.* Consideration of this epithet will acquaint us with Torrance's reaction to Liberal Protestantism. Though his response to Liberal Protestantism is rarely mentioned in Torrance studies, that response molded his thinking significantly, especially his methodology. This was because Liberal Protestantism was, in many respects, the epitome of a theological system adopting the wrong type of "objectivity," limiting itself to insights gleaned through the historico-critical method, and setting aside at the outset what Torrance saw as the fundamental logic of the Gospel, namely the incarnation. In analyzing Torrance's reaction to Liberal Protestantism, we engage particularly with Adolf von Harnack, whose approach crystallized an interpretation of the Christian Gospel, and an approach to theology, which was widely popular at the start of the twentieth century. Barth had come to reject the whole basis of Liberal Protestantism, and Torrance had a comparable response, and one which was critical in his theological development. The Ritschlian and Harnackian approach to Christology, as filtered through H. R. Mackintosh's critique in *Types of Modern Theology*, loomed large over Torrance's studies at New College in the 1930s. And, when James Torrance gave us his lectures on nineteenth-century theology, Harnack was *the* pivotal figure. Importantly, Harnack's ideas are not limited to the nineteenth century. His insistence on identifying the Christian Gospel with the ethical teaching of Jesus, and on discarding traditional doctrinal orthodoxy vis-à-vis the person and work of Christ, is an emphasis reappearing frequently in contemporary liberal theology. As such, Harnack represents a way of understanding Christianity which retains widespread currency. For Harnack, "Jesus as Teacher" was everything. Over against this position, Torrance (and Barth) saw revelation taking place not just through the teaching of Jesus, but in the very person of Jesus Christ as God and man. God reveals himself to man in Jesus Christ because the Son of God is *homoousios* with the Father. For Torrance (and Barth) Jesus as the God-Man was everything. For Harnack it was the first doctrine to be ditched.

*Jesus as Agent.* Here our discussion will touch on Torrance's relationship to Westminster Calvinism, which was a formative dynamic in his approach to Christology and soteriology. We have already noted Torrance's long-running disagreement with facets of traditional Reformed theology. One of the most important of these disagreements centers on Torrance's conviction that Protestantism focuses on Jesus as an *instrument* or *agent* through whom God accomplishes his purposes, but that this brings with it a loss of appreciation that God's purposes are achieved in the *person* of Christ himself as the God-Man. For Torrance, the purposes of God in Christ are achieved through Christ *being who he is*, not just through Christ *doing what he does*. Consequently, for Torrance, as for Barth, reconciliation and revelation take place not simply *through the agency* of Jesus, but *in the being* of Jesus Christ as God and man. God reconciles and reveals himself to men and women in Jesus Christ because the Son of God is *homoousios* with the Father. But, was Torrance's understanding of traditional Reformed Protestantism correct or fair? Was it true that traditional Reformed Protestantism regarded Christ simply as an agent or as instrument? How do we read Torrance in the light of this debate?

*Jesus as Savior.* If, from Torrance's perspective, "Jesus as Teacher" and "Jesus as Agent" are true but inadequate explications of what is involved in making the statement "Jesus is the Gospel," then the phrase 'Jesus as Savior' may be a helpful corrective. Expounding this option will involve us discussing how Torrance wove together the person and work of Christ, the incarnation and the atonement. It will also involve us in discussing further the form and the content of theological statements. This will bring to light some major conceptual issues which arise from Torrance's theology.

— *Chapter 9* —

# Jesus as Teacher

DURING THE WINTER OF 1899–1900, and on the threshold of a new century, Adolf von Harnack delivered a series of sixteen lectures in Berlin. He spoke largely extempore to a class of some six hundred students who were drawn from all the Faculties of the University. Harnack was a dominating figure in European theology. He was a protégé of Albrecht Ritschl. And he was a teacher to whom theological students flocked from all over Europe. An audience member recorded the lectures in shorthand, and, at the close of the series, presented Harnack with a complete script of what he had said. After some editing this was published in German as *Das Wesen des Christentums* (*The Essence of Christianity*). In 1901 the work was translated into English by Thomas Bailey Saunders under the title *What Is Christianity?*

The result was a sensation. Harnack struck a chord. There was a hunger for a modern Christian faith which was sensible rather than superstitious, practical rather than dogmatic, educated rather than fantastical, but still capable of emphasizing the nearness of God to the human soul. Harnack supplied such a religion. In his lectures, he contracted theology to what he saw as the essence of Christianity. For Harnack, this consisted in the original ethical teaching of Jesus, plus an awareness of the continued presence of God to the soul. He rejected miracles.[1] He

---

1. Harnack dismissed most New Testament miracles, though he allowed there may be arcane, undiscovered, laws of nature which enable some of the unusual phenomena to occur: "Although the order of Nature be inviolable, we are not yet by any means acquainted with all the forces working in it and acting reciprocally with other forces" (cf. *What Is Christianity?*, 26–28).

rejected the apocalyptic elements associated with Jesus' teaching.² And he rejected absolutely the notion of Jesus as the God-Man.³ Harnack's system had huge appeal. It seemed to be a level-headed and intelligent presentation of Christianity in a day of doubt and skepticism.

The book was as eagerly sought after in Scottish households as it was anywhere. In May, 1901, the *Scotsman* newspaper carried an extensive review which noted that in Germany the published lectures had enjoyed an extraordinary vogue, "almost rivalling the latest problem novel in popularity."⁴ The reviewer commented that Harnack was perhaps the most widely read and influential of all living German theologians, and remarked that Harnack's appeal was aided by his literary elegance. This elegance was in stark contrast to "the cumbrous and barely intelligible chaos of sentences which passes for style in the works of the typical Teutonic theologian." Harnack had simplicity. He had directness. He had "a fine religious tone." But, above all else, it was the content of the lectures which made *What Is Christianity?* the religious blockbuster of the age. The reviewer was aware of a spiritual hunger "among the educated classes," which Harnack's distillation of the essence of Christianity seemed to meet. Having shorn the Gospel from superfluous myth and supernaturalism, Harnack offered an attractive religious and ethical Christianity.⁵ Even today, a read through Harnack's lectures is an enriching spiritual experience. Enriching, that is, so long as we set aside considerable

---

2. Johannes Weiss and Albert Schweitzer later argued that Harnack's naïve appeal to Jesus' "simple sayings" had to be modified: there were no "simple sayings" since Jesus' teaching was inextricably bound up with an apocalyptic eschatology. Torrance argued that Harnack interpreted Jesus' teaching in an entirely non-eschatological sense "largely because of the Kantian and Ritschlian presuppositions that the Kingdom of God is the realm of moral ends or values" (Torrance, *Atonement*, 270–71). Torrance also pointed out that recent scholarship has: "brought scholars back to grapple with the enormous place occupied in [biblical documents] by *eschatology*, that is, the setting of the historical Jesus in the context of the divine intervention in history." Torrance had a wider understanding of "eschatology" than it simply referring to future events. It referred to the Word and Act of God breaking into the whole of history in Jesus Christ.

3. Cf. Torrance, *Karl Barth: An Introduction to His Early Theology, 1910–1931*, 73. Cf. James Torrance's comments on Harnack, "Vicarious Humanity of Christ," 127–47, esp. 131–32.

4. *The Scotsman* (13th May 1901).

5. In contrast, Torrance stated: "There can be no radical dichotomy between a moral and spiritual conception of redemption on the one hand, and on the other hand a cultic and dramatic conception of redemption, which *from the human point of view could be regarded as primitive and mythological*" (Torrance, *Atonement*, 36; italics added).

reservations. We deal with some of these reservations later, as they highlight profound issues which Torrance reacted to.

## 1. THE HARNACK GOSPEL

The *Scotsman* reviewer identified three main elements in Harnack's exposition of the essence of Christianity. (a) The Kingdom of God and its coming. (b) God the Father and the infinite value of the human soul. (c) The higher righteousness and the commandment of love.[6] When pressed, Harnack simplified Jesus' whole doctrine to two headings: God as the Father; and the human soul so ennobled that it can and does unite with him.[7] For Harnack, these principles demonstrated that the true Gospel is not dependent on a particular time in history or on a particular geographical location, but is religion in its purest form. Thus, true Christianity is the essence of all religion. And it is so because Christianity focuses on the Fatherhood of God and the union of the soul with the divine.

If Torrance's starting principle was that Jesus as the God-Man provides the theological logic which alone makes sense of the New Testament, then Harnack's was the opposite. In Harnack's view, early and original Christianity can only be discovered if, at the outset, we eliminate the doctrines of the Trinity and the incarnation. These mask the true Gospel, which can only be found in the sayings of Jesus or in the primitive faith of the first Christians. And the task of "scientific" scholarship—as scientific was understood by Harnack—was to use historico-critical tools to identify these original components. However, in adopting that approach, Harnack was guilty of disregarding the freedom of God to act in ways which the historico-critical method could never accommodate. As Torrance put it, "Harnack had failed to see that, while scientific activity is concerned with the pure knowledge of its object, for that very reason the nature of the object must be allowed to prescribe the specific mode

---

6. Harnack, *What Is Christianity?*, 51.

7. Harnack, *What Is Christianity?*, 63. Elsewhere Harnack expanded his two points to four: God the Father; Providence; the Position of Men and Women as God's Children; and the Infinite Value of the Human Soul. In these, "the whole Gospel is expressed" (68). Later, he stated: "The inner and essential features of the Gospel are: Unconditional Trust in God as the Father of Jesus Christ; Confidence in the Lord; Forgiveness of Sins; Certainty of Eternal Life; Purity; and Brotherly Fellowship" (180). Each day Harnack's expression of the kernel of religion and Christianity evolved. But, though the number of critical points varied, the thrust of his argument did not.

of rational activity to be adopted in knowing it."[8] Harnack's method—and that of the Liberal Protestant tradition from which he came—was a prime example of the employment of a false idea of scientific objectivity in which being "scientific" and being "objective" was confused with putting aside the truly supernatural elements of Jesus' life and ministry. Much of Torrance's future work on theological science took place against this background.

For his Berlin audience, Harnack portrayed Jesus as a midwife bringing true religion to birth. As such, for Harnack, a phrase such as "Jesus is the Gospel" would express the belief that Jesus' ethical principles were so perfectly embodied in Jesus' life as to be identified with Jesus' person. Moreover, because Jesus was inhabited by God (Absolute Spirit) in a unique manner, he was not just *a* teacher of high principles, but was *the* teacher without parallel in human history, leading humanity to an awareness of the highest religion possible. For Harnack, biblical texts such as, "God was in Christ" (2 Cor 5:19) pointed to a inimitable confluence of the Absolute Spirit with Jesus' spirit, resulting in him having this unique role as *the* teacher for humanity.

In his vast *History of Dogma,* published between 1886 and 1889, Harnack had explored the development of Christian doctrine through the centuries. One of his main arguments was that much orthodox Christian theology was a deplorable import from Greek philosophy. He insisted that early Christian thinking, including some of the New Testament itself, had to be understood from a Hellenistic context, since Hellenistic thought-patterns had distorted the whole course of Christianity. Harnack took that as a given, as did others whose education in classical culture and the classical languages reinforced this hypothesis. In the century since Harnack, scholarship has back-pedaled on this reading of early Christian theology, aware that it largely ignored Hebraic/Jewish drivers of thought as opposed to Hellenistic/Classical ones. Certainly, at New College, Torrance emphasized that New Testament documents, and the theology which the Church Fathers developed in the light of the New Testament, must be interpreted from a Hebraic mind-set as much as from a Hellenistic one.[9] However, at the time, Harnack read Christian theology through Greek philosophical spectacles. He saw a disconnect between the simple teaching of Jesus of Nazareth, and the complex theological

---

8. Cf. Torrance, *Karl Barth: An Introduction to his Early Theology, 1910–1931,* 148.
9. Cf. Torrance, *Preaching Christ Today,* 7.

statements made at Nicaea and Chalcedon. Consequently, what Harnack sought to present to his audience was a practical Christianity, unrelated to the "speculative" theology of the Church Fathers who, in his opinion, fatally compromised genuine Christianity.

## Harnack: Truth and Timelessness

Torrance disagreed with Liberal Protestant assumptions. One major area of divergence concerned Harnack's principle that ultimate spiritual realities must be based in timeless truths, and not in accidental historical events. By the late nineteenth century, Gotthold Lessing's maxim had become widely-accepted: *"The accidental truths of history can never become the proof of necessary truths of reason."*[10] In other words, absolute truth, in any area of human experience, must be independent of any accidental historical circumstance through which that truth has been discovered. No historical event can, in itself, be the basis for ultimate truth. At New College, it was James Torrance, in his lectures on nineteenth-century theology, who discussed with us the implications of Lessing's phrase. As students, we found that series of lectures immensely helpful because, by that stage, most of us had read some nineteenth-century Liberal Protestant theology. Instinctively, we felt it to be lacking. But we struggled to get a handle on why that was so. We saw it at fault on various individual doctrines. But, in terms of grasping why its overall schema gave rise to its lack of orthodoxy, that was another thing. James Torrance's lectures gave the insight we needed. And, on Lessing's maxim, the brothers James and Tom were of one mind.[11]

James argued that what Lessing expressed, and what Liberal Protestantism had taken on board, was the Enlightenment desire to base knowledge in general truths of reason rather than in particular truths of revelation given at specific points in history which, by their transient nature, are intrinsically unrepeatable and not amenable to verification. When Lessing's principle was applied to theology it was interpreted to mean that truth can only be based in what is universally available to all humanity, at all times, and in all places. Truth must lie in the general (the

---

10. This was in a longer statement: "Since no historical truth can be demonstrated, then nothing can be demonstrated by means of historical truths: therefore, the accidental truths of history can never become the proof of necessary truths of reason." See Lessing, "On the Proof of the Spirit and of Power," 51–55.

11. Cf. Torrance, *God and Rationality*, 108.

## Jesus as Teacher

universal and timeless), and not in the particular (the accidental and historical). Hence, the only valid, objective, and scientific theology or ethics is one which is accessible by all, in every place, in every era.

Religious and moral issues, as well as philosophical ones, lay behind Lessing's thinking. If God is fair and just (essential attributes of divinity), then he must give all people, in all places, at all times, the same equal opportunity to know him. Hence, true and pure religion must consist in truths universally accessible in all places, at all times, and not in a particular historical event of revelation. Significantly, in Barth's early *Göttingen Dogmatics*, as Barth strove to free himself from the influence of Harnack, Barth referred to Lessing's maxim repeatedly, realizing he had to take another path. Similar to Barth, what the Torrances emphasized was that Christianity is not built on timeless truths—which Jesus merely clarified and made relevant to his hearers—but is built on a particular historical self-revelation of God in Jesus Christ. Specifically, the particular *event* of incarnation, cross, and resurrection, is what gives the Christian Gospel its rationale. This "Scandal of Particularity" was anathema to Liberal Protestantism.

But for Harnack, following Lessing, it could only be the general and the universal (God as Spirit) which was of primary and permanent importance. The particular and the local (the historical Jesus) merely assisted in introducing men and women to transcendent reality. Indeed, the ideals of Christ could remain true and valid even if the disciples had invented the entire story of Jesus as a vehicle for their thoughts. Jesus' vital contribution was to liberate men and women to know this transcendent reality as God their Father, by cutting across the dogmas of his day.[12] Jesus released deep-seated religious instincts which God had implanted in men and women. Once more they could have direct communion with God. This direct communion brought new birth into a holy life, in which, "purity and brotherly affection" were of first importance.[13]

Tom Torrance was aware of where this led, pointing out that Ritschl interpreted Christ solely in terms of what he means for us in our moral need and understanding.[14] In similar fashion, in his Berlin lectures Harnack taught that Lessing's dictum meant that true religion consisted of eternal divine ideals, especially practical moral and ethical ideals.

---

12. Harnack, *What Is Christianity?*, 166.
13. Harnack, *What Is Christianity?*, 167–68.
14. Torrance, *Space, Time and Incarnation*, 44.

Eternal, transcendent, truth had been mediated in and through Jesus Christ. In order to retrieve this truth, the modern Church had to follow Jesus' example and liberate the pure Gospel from spurious metaphysical doctrines such as those of the God-Man and the atonement. Only then could the Church attend to its main task of applying spiritual and ethical truths in the social and political domain.

In all of this, Harnack assumed that the essence of true religion is a *universal timeless* truth, not a *particular historical* truth. As such, specific and peculiar Christian doctrines such as the atonement, the incarnation, and the Trinity, had nothing to do with the Gospel which Jesus taught. Such doctrines are inherently unknowable to the general mass of humanity, since they require a particular revelation, given at a particular point of history, to particular people. For James Torrance, the "Scandal of Particularity" has been a stumbling-block for theological liberals, not only of Harnack's era but ever since. Harnack was convinced that Jesus taught general religious truths, available to all humanity in all places at all times, albeit with unique insight and authority.

## Harnack: Text and Interpretation

In the course of his argument, Harnack appealed to a Protestant principle concerning Scripture. If, as early Protestantism argued, any man or woman could open their Bibles and find the Gospel clearly stated within its pages, then the Gospel must be, "something so simple, so divine, and therefore so truly human, as to be most certain of being understood [by] individual souls."[15] Harnack was asking: What would truly unaided, unguided, uninfluenced, and truly untutored, men and women, if left alone with the Scriptures, actually be able to discover? What simple spiritual experiences and convictions would they be able to identify in its pages? In Harnack's opinion, they most definitely would not find, *by themselves*, the sophisticated doctrines of a later era. Therefore, given that the true essence of faith must be findable and discoverable by any Christian left alone with his or her Bible, then surely true faith can only lie in the simple saying of Jesus.[16] An untutored reader *could* discover these in the New Testament. But, an untutored reader *could not* discover, by himself or herself, the metaphysical notions of the incarnation or Trinity! Thus the sayings of Jesus are what must be important. Not the later doctrines.

15. Harnack, *What Is Christianity?*, 275.
16. Harnack, *What Is Christianity?*, 278, 292.

## Jesus as Teacher

As a historian, Harnack's bread-and-butter was handling and assessing sources, and he argued that the relevant material pertaining to the original teaching of Jesus was to be found in two places. First, in Jesus' own sayings. Second, in the effects or impression which Jesus, or the spirit of Jesus, made in his very first disciples. And the task of historico-critical scholarship was to identify such material in the earliest stratum of sources.[17] The concept of "impression" was important for Harnack.[18] Not just the "impress" Jesus made on the disciples; but the "impress" which in turn they made on the early church, plus the faith which that "impress" has evoked and stimulated through history to the present-time.

Crucially, vital to Harnack's entire argument was a late-dating of the Gospels. This was because a late-dating more easily accommodated one of Harnack's key assumptions: namely, that blocks of church teaching from several generations *after* the time of Jesus had been imported into the Gospel narrative. The role of scholarship was to disentangle the original sayings of Jesus from this later soup, enabling the kernel to be identified. Curiously and conveniently, that kernel coincided with Harnack's theology! However, the validity of Harnack's separation of so-called "later ideas" from original Christianity depended heavily on his confident assumption of late-dating for the Synoptic Gospels—a fashionable view at the time, but no longer a given.[19] But this assumption enabled Harnack to separate what he regarded as *early* (Jesus) material, from what he categorized as *later* (church tradition) material. And, in Harnack's schema, early material could be identified *a priori* by it being simple and practical, whereas late material could be identified *a priori* by it being sophisticated and intellectual. But this was a circular argument. Harnack used his desired conclusion—that the essence of the Gospel was simple ethical teaching—to decide what was original to Jesus. And Harnack knew he had to move any semi-sophisticated theological christological statements in the New Testament as far as possible in time from Jesus and the primitive church. The later the date he could attach to the

---

17. For Harnack, the authoritative sources for the Jesus' message were overwhelmingly the first three Gospels. He saw John's Gospel as hopelessly compromised. Harnack reassured his audience that the historico-critical work of two generations had succeeded in restoring in the main outlines of that original message and with it the overall credibility of the synoptic gospels, which D. F. Strauss thought he had destroyed. Cf. *The Scotsman* review (13th May 1901).

18. Harnack, *What Is Christianity?*, 31.

19. Harnack, *What Is Christianity?*, 22. Remarkably, Harnack claimed that Luke's Gospel was written during the reign of the Emperor Domitian (AD 81–96).

more complex christological statements of the New Testament, the easier it was for him to maintain his position of distinguishing between what he regarded as the essence of Christianity from later "imported" thinking.

Predictably, Harnack's treatment of John's Gospel was even more extreme than his handling of the Synoptic Gospels. He was well aware of several phrases in John's Gospel which do anticipate, in some measure, the God-Man Christology of the Church Fathers. And, as James Torrance pointed out to us, this was precisely why Harnack disliked the Fourth Gospel. He rejected *a priori* any possibility of Jesus having ever taught the "I am" sayings. They did not fit with Harnack's preconception of what Jesus could have said.[20] Harnack took it as axiomatic that Jesus never preached about himself. Therefore, Jesus' true teaching had to be disjoined from Johannine statements about his person. As James Torrance stated, "It was an *a priori* assumption for Harnack that the Gospel, as Jesus understood it, deals with the Father only, not God the Son."

In contrast to Harnack, and with far-reaching theological implications, Tom Torrance dated John's Gospel early. For Torrance, it was not only perfectly possible for Jesus to have said what John claimed he had said, but it was to be fully expected of Jesus, precisely because he was truly God and truly man. Thus, the theological presuppositions of Harnack and Torrance with respect to the person of Jesus Christ dictated the way they read the biblical text, and what they could allow to be true within it. This was where Harnack and Torrance diverged concerning Matthew 11:27/Luke 10:22: "*All things have been committed to me by my Father. No one knows the Son except the Father, and no one knows the Father except the Son and those to whom the Son chooses to reveal him.*" For Torrance, this came from the lips of Jesus. For Harnack, it could not possibly have done so. It is too intellectual. It is too abstract. It strays from the simple ethic which Harnack predetermined must have been Jesus' message. It introduces the possibility of Jesus being more than simply the man from Nazareth. Harnack could not, under any circumstances, allow that to be the case. In this, Harnack followed Ritschl. And, in James Torrance's words, "For Ritschl, Jesus was not one with God in being (*homoousios*) but was one in will and purpose. Beyond this, Ritschl would not go, for it would be metaphysical speculation."[21] Over against this, and in deliberate and conscious contrast to the Liberal Protestant position, placing

---

20. Ritchie, Personal Lecture Notes (9th December, 1975).
21. Ritchie, Personal Lecture Notes (5th December, 1975).

the *homoousios* at the centre of Christian theology was Tom Torrance's life-long principle.

## Harnack: Uniqueness and Incarnation

How Harnack, and Liberal Protestantism with him, understood any notion of the uniqueness of Jesus Christ, was a factor in shaping Tom Torrance's theology. Harnack refused to accept that the uniqueness of Jesus Christ consisted in him being truly God and truly man. Jesus is Teacher. Jesus is *not* God and man. And yet, as a churchman, Harnack still wanted to say that Jesus and Christianity were unique. But how? In Berlin, Harnack quoted Goethe on Christianity being the highest ideal in intellectual and spiritual culture: "Let intellectual and spiritual culture progress, and the human mind expand, as much as it will; [but] beyond the grandeur and the moral elevation of Christianity, as it sparkles and shines in the Gospels, the human mind will not advance."[22] Harnack mirrored this when he said, "The Christian religion would not be the highest and the ultimate religion unless it brought every individual into an immediate and living connection with God."[23] For Harnack, Jesus did exactly that. It was that which made Christianity the highest possible religion.[24] It had a unique ability to fashion humanity into one people, enabling "the last and highest stage in the history of humanity" to be reached.[25] But it was not because Jesus was the God-Man.

Instead, for Harnack, Jesus was unique because he taught and embodied the fundamental truths of religion in a way which no one else ever had, and with an unsurpassable purity and strength.[26] Jesus freed true religion from Pharisaical rules. Jesus radically transformed values,

---

22. Quoted by Harnack, *What Is Christianity?*, 4. Harnack compared the worldwidede spread of Christianity with the limited orbit of Islam and Hinduism. He regarded these religions as localized, imprisoned within their ethnic origins, and lacking the universality which must be a characteristic of true religion which puts men and women in contact with the eternal and the absolute. Because, in his view, true Christianity was not tied to a specific nation or ethnic group, it touched the eternal, and was unconstrained by the particular. Harnack lived within a Christianized culture, and never envisaged the appeal of other religions which the twentieth century would bring.

23. Harnack, *What Is Christianity?*, 165.

24. Harnack, *What Is Christianity?*, 179.

25. Harnack, *What Is Christianity?*, 189.

26. Harnack, *What Is Christianity?*, 48.

"of which many before him had a dim idea."[27] Jesus' genius lay in his ability to give simple expression to profound and important truths, "as though he were only reminding men of what they know already, because it lives in the innermost part of their souls."[28] Above all else, Jesus taught a "higher righteousness and the commandment of love." "The whole of the Gospel is embraced" under this heading, and, "to represent the Gospel as an ethical message is no depreciation of its value."[29] At the root of this is love. Love must completely fill the soul. Love is what remains when the soul dies to itself. Love is the new life already begun. We experience this when we, "steep ourselves in the Beatitudes of the Sermon on the Mount" which are Jesus' ethics and Jesus' religion, "united at the root."[30] Jesus' teaching has unique power because of the authority of the personality which stands behind it. But not because he was the God-Man.

Many of Harnack's presuppositions lay behind Hugh Anderson's line of argument when he, Tom Torrance, and George W. Anderson debated "Who is Jesus?" in the New College student common-room. These assumptions meant that Harnack rejected the incarnation as an historical event. In sharp contrast, the incarnation was central for Torrance. And, for Torrance, the incarnation was not just a dogma to be ticked-off in a check-list of orthodoxy. Instead, for Torrance, the incarnation was, and is, the driver of the whole logic of revelation and reconciliation. Revelation and reconciliation took place in and through the being of God in Jesus Christ. precisely because he was, and is, truly God and truly man. Not so for Harnack.

To maintain his argument Harnack had to over-simplify the New Testament witness to the person of Christ. In particular, he had to play down the inconvenient truth that there are multiple passages, even within the earliest strata of New Testament documents, which indicate that the first Christians gave to Jesus the same honor, glory, majesty, and worship, as ascribed by Israel to Yahweh. Harnack's selectivity meant he

---

27. Harnack, *What Is Christianity?*, 68. The uniqueness of Jesus' teaching was not in its originality: Pharisaical teachers had already proclaimed that, "everything was contained in the injunction to love God and one's neighbor." But in one respect Jesus' teaching did have an original feature. This was the notion that the kingdom of God "is already here" (54). Overall, it is only in Jesus that we: "find any message about God and the good that was ever so pure and so full of strength (for purity and strength go together) as we hear and read of in the Gospels" (47–48).

28. Harnack, *What Is Christianity?*, 68.

29. Harnack, *What Is Christianity?*, 70.

30. Harnack, *What Is Christianity?*, 72, 74.

did not analyze passages such as Philippians 2:1–11 (cf. Isaiah 45:23b), which make sense only if the earliest believers gave to Jesus the same honor, glory, and worship, as given to the Lord God of Israel. Harnack knew such statements exist in Scripture. And he was aware that they do require, "assent to a series of propositions about Christ's person," and that they do give a basis for the sophisticated christological formulae of later centuries.[31] Harnack could only dismiss these and their implications by declaring, *a priori*, that they were never part of the very earliest primitive Christianity. He conceded that Paul made statements which led later generations to speculate on the person of Jesus (two natures), and on how redemption was accomplished (substitutionary atonement). That could not be denied. But Harnack regretted that Paul had become, "author of the *speculative* idea" that Christ was possessed of a peculiar nature of a heavenly kind.[32] Harnack steadfastly refused to see such statements as part of the original Gospel, even though these statements lie within the earliest extant Christian writings, namely the Pauline epistles.

Even at the height of his powers and influence, Harnack's view on the uniqueness of Christ was not unchallenged. The *Scotsman* reviewer of 1901 commented: "Few theologians in this country, we suspect, will accept [Harnack's] interpretation of the 'divine Sonship' to which Jesus undeniably laid claim." But, reviewers aside, Harnack was hugely influential. And his teaching fed into a late nineteenth, and early twentieth century, liberal theological culture. It was over against that powerful movement that Barth and Torrance developed a theology which was consciously predicated on the uniqueness of Jesus Christ as truly God and truly man. But it would be insufficient simply to contradict the Liberal Protestant school on individual doctrines. They had to strike at the root. They had to identify what was wrong with it systemically. Consequently, in order to change the direction of modern theology, they needed to develop a methodology which took seriously God's freedom to be the living God, God's freedom to become flesh and dwell among us, and God's freedom to be in himself revelation and reconciliation in Jesus Christ.

Consequently, Torrance developed a methodology contrary to that of Harnack and his school. Harnack's core axiom was: In order to read the New Testament scientifically, a scholar must *eliminate* from his or her mind notions of incarnation and Trinity, and only work with whatever

---

31. Harnack, *What Is Christianity?*, 185, 192.
32. Harnack, *What Is Christianity?*, 185 (italics added).

the "scientific" historico-critical method will allow. Torrance's core axiom was: In order to read the New Testament scientifically, a scholar must *start* with who Jesus is as the incarnate Lord, because only *within* that understanding does the biblical witness make sense. For Torrance, the historico-critical method was a useful tool, but utterly incapable of coping with the reality of God's freedom to become the incarnate Lord, which is the reality undergirding the entire logic of the New Testament.

## Harnack: Cross and Resurrection

Similar issues surround Harnack's theology of Easter. For Harnack, Calvary and the Empty Tomb were *revelatory* events, intended to teach general truths, and not *achievement* events which, through a specific action of God in history, brought a core spiritual reality into being which would not exist otherwise. Here, Harnack distinguished between *Geschichte* and *Historie*. *Geschichte* referred to the "meaning" or "interpretation" of events, whether or not the events were factually true. *Historie* referred to the "told story" or "claimed narrative" surrounding events. Using this distinction, Harnack distinguished between the Easter *faith* (*Osterglauben*) which was *Geschichte*, and the Easter *message* (*Osterbotschaft*) which was *Historie*.[33] And in Berlin Harnack sought to persuade his audience that the story of doubting Thomas (John 20:24–31) was told for the express "purpose of impressing on us that we must hold the Easter *faith* even without the Easter *message*."[34] The Easter *faith* could remain valid even if the Easter narrative were not historically true. The Easter *message,* or narrative, was simply a vehicle used by the Gospel writers to communicate the Easter *faith*.[35]

Torrance saw things differently. Torrance pointed out that the secular presuppositions behind the historic-critical method—which automatically reject the possibility of God acting in history through incarnation, miracles, resurrection—meant that liberal scholars such as Harnack had already dismissed screeds of factual data (*Historie*) even before they started to consider what the meaning of the remaining New

---

33. Harnack, *Das Wesen des Christentums*, 95.
34. Harnack, *What Is Christianity?*, 160–61.
35. Ritchie, Personal Lecture Notes, 11th October, 1974: Alasdair Heron explained to us that, "*Geschichte* involves the interpretation of history; *Historie* involves the 'objective facts' of history, such as primary data, annals, etc."

Testament text might be (*Geschichte*).³⁶ The Christmas story was not allowed to be a fact. The miracle stories were not allowed to be facts. Jesus' deeper sayings were not allowed to be authentic. The story of Jesus' physical resurrection was not allowed to be a fact. All these were rejected at the outset as impossibility. What this meant was that the meaning of the Easter *faith*, which Harnack saw as the entity with permanent value, was developed apart from any consideration of, for example, the significance of the empty tomb as historical reality!

In conscious opposition to this approach Torrance developed his own theories of what constitutes a properly objective theological science, insisting upon a reintegration of historical events (incarnation, miracles, resurrection, etc.) with divine revelation. Without such a reintegration, the New Testament witness is left barren and fraudulent. For example, if we eliminate the "fact" (*Historie*) of the miracle of the incarnation *prior* to asking what the Gospel narratives "mean" (*Geschichte*), then we make it impossible *a priori* to ever see any theological importance for the incarnation! Hence, for Torrance, the historical event (*Historie*) was absolutely critical and indispensable. As event, it was integral in *bringing a new state of affairs into being*. This was why Torrance criticized Harnack for detaching, "the historical Jesus from the actual presentation of the mystery of Christ in the biblical documents and in the tradition of the church."³⁷

With his Liberal Protestant assumptions, Harnack's view was that the meaning of a story may be true even if the told story were no more than myth, declaring to his audience that though many legends about historical figures are not factual history (*Historie*), "we may spread them with a good conscience, because they embody correct historical judgments (*Geschichte*)."³⁸ Hence, for Harnack, the Easter *story* was but

36. Torrance, *Incarnation*, 270; *God and Rationality*, 109.

37. Torrance, *Preaching Christ Today*, 7.

38. In a letter to the *Scotsman* (27th August, 1906) a a correspondent commented on some of the historical illustrations in the first volume of Harnack's *Reden und Aufsatze*, writing: "History [according to Harnack] is two-fold—the history of what happened and the history of what was thought about what happened. The legendary story about an 'eminent' person, the saying ascribed to him which he never uttered, does not belong to history of the former kind, though told as such, but it may have its value as a contribution to history of the latter kind, if it aptly characterizes a person or correctly depicts a situation. The legend is a criticism of history told as history. When told about an eminent person it is an attempt, to characterize him, to sum up in one phrase or anecdote his whole significance. Actual history is seldom so accommodating as to let us see the great man at the climax of his development in a dramatic situation in which his most distinctive qualities are brought to light. Legend, therefore, comes to our

a vehicle for communicating an eternal truth, which is the Easter *faith*. Once that "truth" has been grasped, the "story" can be left behind. And the Easter *faith*, for Harnack, was "the conviction that the crucified one gained a victory over death; that God is just and powerful; that he who is the firstborn among many brethren lives."[39] But, concerning the historical appearances associated with the first Easter, "There is no tradition of single events which is quite trustworthy": consequently, "how can the Easter faith be based on them?"[40] As always with Harnack, it was the *teaching* (an eternal truth) which was important, not the *event* (an accidental contingency of history). The Easter *faith* was true even without the empty tomb stories of the Easter *message*. The young Barth was aware of this approach, though he never adopted this de-historicized version of Christianity.[41]

For the Torrances, the distinction between *Historie* and *Geschichte* was a prime example of dualist thinking, separating phenomena from understanding, and separating event from revelation. James Torrance's verdict was, "Ritschl relativizes the significance of Jesus and paves the way for Ernst Troeltsch, i.e., that Jesus is the *historical occasion* for God introducing the ideal into the world; and Harnack was going to draw the conclusion that after the principle has come in, then the person does not matter."[42] For Harnack, the important thing was that the grave of Jesus became, "the *birthplace* of the indestructible *belief* that death is vanquished, that there is a life eternal."[43] At the same time, Harnack felt able to speak of his own faith: "On the conviction that *Jesus lives* we still base these hopes of citizenship in an Eternal City which make our earthly life worth living and tolerable." Jesus 'lives.' But Jesus' tomb may not be empty.

~

assistance. By some striking anecdote about him, or some pregnant saying ascribed to him, it sets him off, as it were, and sums up the impression he produced. For instance, ... Constantine the Great is said to have asked for baptism on his death-bed with the remark: 'Let all ambiguity vanish now.' It is quite incredible that he really said that. But this legend brings to expression, in a way 'that could not be surpassed, the fact that up to the last his mind was not quite made up between Christianity on the one side and Paganism on the other.'"

39. Harnack, *What Is Christianity?*, 161.
40. Harnack, *What Is Christianity?*, 162.
41. Busch, *Karl Barth: His Life from Letters and Autobiographical Texts*, 56.
42. Ritchie, Personal Lecture Notes (5th December, 1975).
43. Harnack, *What Is Christianity?*, 162 (italics added).

## Jesus as Teacher

Concerning Calvary, Harnack asked his audience to imagine what being a Christian meant for the first converts. He suggested three things.[44] First: recognition of Jesus as the Living Lord. Second: a spiritual experience, involving consciousness of a living union with God. Third: leading a holy life, in purity and brotherly fellowship. Significantly, as James Torrance pointed out, Harnack's list of essentials did not include expiatory atonement through Christ's death on the cross. Harnack was not unaware that Paul wrote, "Christ died for our sins according to the Scriptures" (1 Cor 15:3,4); but he rejected the idea that Christ's death and resurrection dealt with the problem of sin. Instead, Harnack categorized the notion that "Christ died for our sins" as Paul's, *"particular speculative idea."*[45] Having neatly side-stepped Paul, Harnack insisted that the majority of the first Christians simply saw Jesus' death and resurrection in terms of announcing Jesus as Lord, and not as something with expiatory significance.

At the same time, Harnack knew that some early Christians believed that Jesus' death dealt with their sins and that Jesus rose again physically, but he saw no need to adopt that position.[46] He argued that, although for them Jesus' death had the value of an expiatory sacrifice, it was not actually so. Harnack claimed that Calvary exposed the whole notion of vicarious blood-sacrifice as having always been invalid. In his opinion, that was what the *Letter to the Hebrews* really meant.[47] Harnack told his audience that blood-sacrifices did not cease because they had been *fulfilled* in Jesus. Instead, they ceased because Jesus showed that the whole notion of a blood-sacrifice to make expiation had always been wrong, *even if the sacrifice were Jesus himself.* Jesus' death was in no sense a vicarious sacrifice.

To support his case, Harnack interpreted Isaiah 53 as simply meaning: "Greater love has no man than this, but that he lays down his life for his friends."[48] What does the cross mean? What is its lasting significance? For Harnack, it was by the cross of Jesus Christ that "mankind gained such an experience of the power and purity of a love *true to death* that

---

44. Harnack, *What Is Christianity?*, 152.

45. Harnack, *What Is Christianity?*, 154 (italics added).

46. Harnack, *What Is Christianity?*, 156–58.

47. Harnack, *What Is Christianity?*, 158. In Harnack's view, the *Letter to the Hebrews* taught that Jesus' death on the cross was an expression of love, demonstrating that, for once and for all, *no blood*—not just the blood of bulls and calves—washes away sin.

48. Harnack, *What Is Christianity?*, 158.

they can never forget it, and that it signifies a new epoch in their history."[49] This was a Moral Example theory of salvation, with Harnack also dallying with the idea that righteous suffering is salvific: "Everywhere that the just man suffers, an atonement is made which puts us to shame and purifies us."[50] Significantly, Harnack changed the translation of Matthew 20:28/ Mark 10:45 from Jesus giving his life, "*as a ransom [Lösegeld] for many*," to Jesus giving his life, "*as a service [Dienst] which he was rendering to many*" as an example to be followed.[51] Though this translation is unsupported by the Greek text, it is what Harnack wanted the text to say.

Torrance reacted strongly against Harnack's position.[52] For Torrance, the whole life of Jesus was an act of increasing solidarity with sinners. Jesus took into himself the wretched, fallen, brokenness of humanity, from the moment of his conception in the womb of Mary until the bearing of human sin reached its climax at Calvary. And so, for Torrance, reconciliation was an *event* cut into the very flesh of Christ, not just an *announcement* of an eternal spiritual truth.

Although Harnack dismissed Paul's emphasis on expiation as a speculative idea, he did praise Paul's achievement in freeing true religion from ceremonies and rules,[53] and for teaching that authentic religious experience was *in the Spirit* and not in law or in dogma. As such, Paul transformed the Gospel into the "universal religion."[54] When commenting on the Reformation principle of "justification by faith," he treated it only as the general *realization* that "God is *for me*."[55] Harnack was insistent that justification does not bring a change of *status* in relation to God. It simply brings a change in our *understanding* of that relationship. That,

---

49. Harnack, *What Is Christianity?*, 159 (italics added).

50. Harnack, *What Is Christianity?*, 159. Cf. 158: "Anyone who will look into history will find that the sufferings of the pure and the just are its saving element."

51. Harnack, *What Is Christianity?*, 160. In German, *ransom* is *lösegeld*, the term normally employed in Matthew 20:28 and Mark 10:45 in German Bibles. In our view, Harnack has three instances of "sleight of hand": (1) His reinterpretation of the concept Son of God; (2) His way of reading the *Letter to the Hebrews*; (3) His skewed translation of Matthew 20:28 and Mark 10:45. Over against Harnack's reading of Mark 10:45 (Matt 20:28) see Torrance, *Atonement*, 22.

52. Cf. Torrance, *Atonement*, 68.

53. Harnack, *What Is Christianity?*, 176.

54. Harnack, *What Is Christianity?*, 180.

55. Harnack, *What Is Christianity?*, 284–86.

## Jesus as Teacher

in Harnack's view, was the Gospel rediscovered by Luther, though Luther, after starting well, relapsed into the metaphysics of orthodoxy.[56]

For Harnack, the cross had nothing to do with substitutionary atonement. Instead, it was a paradigm of justice giving way to mercy, and was the supreme example of the paramountcy of brotherhood and self-sacrifice in the service of one's neighbor.[57] At the cross, pure religion was actualized in an act of self-sacrifice. Jesus allowed himself to be condemned because, having *taught* his disciples to renounce all their lawful demands and all their just rights, he also put aside his rights when faced with injustice. He crucified his self-interest. He went the way of Calvary.[58] The cross established the principle that, when love is shown in the face of enmity, evil will be overcome by gentleness. In dying to self, Jesus revealed and embodied the eternal life of God within the soul. True religion is love. The definitive sign of love is dying on behalf of others. That was the meaning of the cross. This Liberal Protestant version of Christian faith was part of the theological background to Torrance's student days. But, for Torrance, something objective happened at the cross. Something happened in history which changed things in the relationship between God and humanity. The cross did not simply *reveal* a truth. The cross *effected* a salvation.

Harnack lamented that metaphysical speculations, such as the doctrines of the incarnation and the Trinity, had become test-statements of Christian faith. He bewailed the fact that the Greek church, "still entertains the conviction today that in these doctrines it possesses the essence of Christianity, regarded at once as a mystery, and as a mystery that has been revealed."[59] He asked his Berlin audience: "Does intellectual assent to complex doctrines, such as is required in some churches, have any connection with the faith of New Testament figures such as the Syrophoenician woman or the centurion at Capernaum?"[60] "Is that not a poor

---

56. Harnack, *What Is Christianity?*, 291.

57. Harnack, *What Is Christianity?*, 77.

58. Harnack, *What Is Christianity?*, 110–11, argued that though Jesus' primary command is to "Love your enemies," it is right to fight for house and home when violently attacked since Jesus, "was not thinking of such cases."

59. Harnack, *What Is Christianity?*, 235.

60. Harnack, *What Is Christianity?*, 237. Harnack (238) deplored the way in which true religion had been superseded by tiresome ritual, especially in the Greek Church: "There is no sadder spectacle than this transformation of the Christian religion from

exchange for a living religious experience?" Surely, "It is *religion* (the love of God and neighbor) which gives life a meaning: *knowledge* cannot do it."[61] Throughout his lectures, Harnack stuck to his main theme: that the importance of Jesus lies in his ethical teaching, and in placing experience of God at the heart of religion. Harnack bewailed the dominance of christological theories. They perverted the majesty and simplicity of the Gospel. They introduced dangers "of a kind such as cannot arise with Jesus' sayings."[62] Put aside God-Man theories! Put aside atonement theories! Return to the sayings of Jesus! Return to the awareness of God which Jesus taught! Only Jesus' sayings are to be relied on![63]

Harnack predetermined how he would read the New Testament. He shelved everything which deviated from what, *a priori*, he believed primitive Christianity to have taught. And he wielded the historic-critical method in a manner which, *a priori*, removed any deep theological statements from the primitive witness. Having done so, he then claimed that the earliest documents had none! This made it impossible for Harnack to read the New Testament in the light of some of its own remarkable texts which—as he reluctantly acknowledged—did whisper that Jesus was God and man, and did speak of an atonement through the cross. As Torrance might put it: Harnack read the Word of God *after* having eliminated the essential theological grammar which alone gives it sense and coherence, namely that Jesus is God incarnate, "Man of Israel and Lord God."

## 2. THE ORTHODOX REACTION

James Torrance summarized Harnack's position as: "Jesus raised moral energy," "Jesus did not ask for confession of sin," "Jesus did not say that all

---

a worship of God in spirit and in truth into a worship of God in signs, formulas, and idols . . . It was to destroy this sort of religion that Jesus Christ suffered himself to be nailed to the cross, and now we find it re-established under his name and authority!" The only saving feature of much of formal religion is that it provides a place where Jesus' sayings are read" (242). Yet, there is some hope: "By not having suppressed the Gospel, but by having kept it accessible, even though in a meagre fashion, the church still possesses the corrective power in its midst" (244).

61. Harnack, *What Is Christianity?*, 300 (italics added).
62. Harnack, *What Is Christianity?*, 184 (italics added).
63. Harnack, *What Is Christianity?*, 184: "The way in which [Paul] ordered his religious conceptions, as the outcome of his speculative ideas, unmistakably exercised an influence in the wrong direction." Inconveniently for Harnack, the Pauline corpus is indisputably early.

were sinners," and, "Jesus said "Yes" to the best in modern culture."[64] This last point was key. Harnack's thinking developed within a German philosophic culture which regarded God as Absolute Spirit, and that within such a culture the human spirit had opened itself up to Absolute Spirit to such a degree that culture itself manifested the qualities of Absolute Spirit. Therefore, true religion could be retro-read from the impact of Absolute Spirit on the human spirit as expressed in its culture—its art, science, philosophy, and ethics—as much as from the pages of ancient Scriptures. Indeed, insights and religious feelings gleaned from the effects of the impress of Absolute Spirit upon the human spirit, and from the answering response of human culture after long exposure to that divine Spirit, may be more reliable indicators of divine realities than words from old documents. That was why, in Harnack's tetchy 1923 correspondence with Barth, Harnack argued that humanity advances in its religious understanding through reflecting on its advance in culture, as much as through its meditation on Scripture.[65]

## World War I

At the start of the twentieth century, and within the milieu of a self-confident European Christendom, Harnack's star was at its zenith. But, in 1914, Harnack took the fateful step of publically supporting the Kaiser's war policy. Many admirers were now confused. How could that square with what he had written about true Christianity, especially its emphasis on love, self-resignation, and putting aside the rights of the self? When Barth discovered that Harnack was one of ninety-three German intellectuals who signed a manifesto identifying themselves with the Kaiser's war policy, Barth began to question what Harnack stood for: "It was like the twilight of the gods when I saw the reaction of Harnack, Herrmann, Rade, Euken, and company to the 'new situation,' and discovered how religion and scholarship could be changed completely, into 42cm cannons."[66]

64. Ritchie, Personal Lecture Notes (J.B.T) (13th January, 1976).

65. Cf. Rumscheidt, *Revelation and Theology*, 30, 33. This lay behind Barth's "No!" to Natural Theology, and his concern that German culture was dangerously close to being deified.

66. Quoted in Busch, *Karl Barth: His Life from Letters and Autobiographical Texts*, 81. Cf. Torrance: "There was no word about corporate guilt or salvation in Harnack which could help man in the First World War. This lack led to a false fusion of Christianity and culture in Germany" (Ritchie, Personal Lecture Notes, 13th January, 1976).

So began Barth's theological journey, convinced that theology should henceforth never be based, to any degree, in the achievements, insights, or ideals, of human culture, even if that culture claimed it grew from a meeting of the human spirit with the Absolute and the Eternal. Instead, theology must only be rooted in God through his Word.

Harnack's war stance also perplexed his devotees in Great Britain, including those in Scotland.[67] For generations, scores of students had travelled to Germany to sit at his feet. The initial reaction was disbelief. Surely there was no connection between high German culture, including its theology, and German militarism? But, as the war proceeded, the two were bracketed together increasingly, though not always justifiably.[68] Then the personal attacks on Harnack began. In August, 1916, the British press reported Harnack speaking in support of Germany's war aim of winning back her colonies and re-establishing her Empire.[69] Then the press reported Harnack addressing a meeting in the Great Philharmonic Hall in Berlin at which he said, "Every one of us approves the use of aerial weapons against England, and rejects the idea of showing any consideration for them."[70] According to the *Scotsman*, Kaiser Wilhelm personally approved this speech, telegraphing his congratulations to Harnack. Two months later, the *Scotsman* reported that, "the eminent German theologian" supported unrestricted submarine warfare and aerial bombing of England.[71] By now, the sobriquet "eminent theologian" was sarcasm, not respect; though the term did indicate how Harnack had once been regarded. Other reports of Harnack's jingoism were published in British newspapers throughout the conflict.

---

67. Cf. *Scotsman* (Letter, 3rd September, 1914): "If Harnack deserved any reverence or gratitude for services to Christendom, he has destroyed all claim to either, and has well earned British contempt by his fire-eating and slanderous utterances. Harnack is one of the willing and obsequious tools of the partnership, constituted by, "*Meinself und Gott*."

68. The minister of South Morningside United Free Church in Edinburgh, Charles A Salmond, in a long letter to the *Scotsman* (7th March, 1916) averred that the new German theology produces no heroes such as "a Luther, a Knox, a Bunyan, a Chalmers, a Duff, a Livingstone, as in earlier times it inspired the glorious company of the Apostles and martyrs. What world uplifters of that ilk has the new theology produced, either in Germany or among ourselves?"

69. *The Scotsman* (4th August, 1916).

70. *The Scotsman* (14th August, 1916).

71. *The Scotsman* (16th October, 1916).

Churchmen on both sides supported their nation's war effort. That was understood. But Harnack had been seen as *the* mouthpiece for European—not just German—Christianity. How could Harnack support the Kaiser's warmongering? His Berlin Lectures of 1899/1900 had made an immense impact. As had his teaching of so many British clergymen. How could he, of all people, support unrestricted submarine warfare and the bombing of British civilians, given the Christianity he so eloquently presented in his lectures? Was something rotten at the core of a once revered German culture and German Christianity? The Duke of Argyll certainly thought so. In a withering letter to the *Scotsman* the Duke declared that young men who studied in Germany before the war had, "put off their faith at the feet of Harnack."[72] Others tried to defend their old teacher.[73] Despite these loyal and faithful apologists, Harnack's reputation was severely compromised.

## The Aftermath

In 1918 the War finished. Passions cooled. Academic theological work resumed. And, with it, came a reassessment of Harnack's fundamental position. In the 1933 Croall Lectures, H. R. Mackintosh dissected the Ritschlian theology which lay behind Harnack's position on several issues, including: the person of Christ, the meaning of the cross, and the understanding of justification and reconciliation.[74] And, in the 1937 series

---

72. The *Scotsman* (19th October, 1917): "They were educated at one of those very German Universities (spiritual homes?) which for generations have been teaching the worst forms of materialism and varying degrees of unbelief. Just as young ladies were sent to Paris to learn to put on their clothes, so young men were sent to the Universities of Kültur to put off their faith at the feet of Harnack . . . [and] these German Universities whose pernicious influence has borne no small a part in bringing about the present cataclysm."

73. Oliver Shaw Rankin from Sorbie, made a spirited defence of Harnack in reply to the Duke's condemnations. *The Scotsman* (23rd October, 1917): "In the letter from Inverary Castle . . . there is a statement about young men sent 'to put off their faith at the feet of Harnack.' I shall make the Duke a fair offer, namely, let him give examples of any persons who have put off their faith at the feet of Harnack, and I shall gladly produce at least two examples of Scotsmen who studied at the feet of Harnack and died in the faith fighting for their country, and who would certainly not have been of the Duke's calumnious opinion. There are numerous people, as against the hypothetical ones supposed to have lost their faith, who have had their faith strengthened through the excellent spirit of Professor Harnack."

74. Croall Lectures 1933: Mackintosh, *Types of Modern Theology: From Schleiermacher to Barth*.

G. S. Duncan of St Andrews pointedly entitled his opening discourse: "Jesus: No Mere Teacher."[75] The title "No Mere Teacher" was provocative. It took direct aim at Liberal Protestantism, at Harnack, and at everything which that theology represented. A reporter from the *Scotsman* recorded Duncan stressing,

> We cannot separate facts from faith as Harnack did. Nor can we eliminate the eschatological character of Jesus' message as Harnack did. Nor can we dismiss the fourth Gospel as Harnack tended to do. Nor can we deny that the Jesus presented to us in the Gospels is far more than "mere teacher."[76]

For Duncan, the New Testament claim that Jesus is "Son of God" pointed to something far deeper than what Harnack could ever allow. Duncan insisted that there is no good evidence that a Jesus essentially different from the New Testament witness ever existed. And Duncan identified Harnack as having a specific problem with the New Testament portrayal of Jesus as "Son of Man." Importantly, both titles (Son of God, and Son of Man) come from the earliest strata of the New Testament, and Harnack's treatment of both had been outrageously inadequate.

Mackintosh and Duncan's appraisals were typical of the inter-war reaction to German Liberal Protestantism. This meant that when Torrance went to New College in October, 1934, he arrived at a Faculty well versed in German theology and appreciative of its contributions, but also keenly aware of its dangers. H. R. Mackintosh influenced Torrance beyond measure, with Torrance enthralled by his teacher, and reading Mackintosh's *Types of Modern Theology* several times.[77]

Also influencing Scotland in the 1930s, and emerging as an alternative to Harnack and the Liberal Protestantism which he represented, was Karl Barth. Barth's impact, already considerable, had even greater sway after his visits to Scotland in 1937 and 1938 to deliver his Gifford Lectures. Now settled in Basel after expulsion from Bonn by the Nazis, Barth was somewhat surprised that he, of all people, should be invited to be a Gifford lecturer, given that Lord Gifford established the lectures as an exploration of Natural Theology. In his first address Barth made clear his position on Natural Theology over against what he saw as the weaknesses

---

75. Croall Lectures 1937: Duncan, *Jesus, Son of Man: Studies Contributory to a Modern Portrait.*

76. *The Scotsman* (14th April, 1937).

77. Torrance, "Hugh Ross Mackintosh: Theologian of the Cross."

of both Roman Catholicism and Protestant Modernism. This gave him the opportunity to stress unequivocally that, "The revival of the gospel by Luther and Calvin consisted in their desire to see both the church and human salvation founded on the Word of God *alone*, on God's *revelation in Jesus Christ*, as it is attested in the Scripture, and on faith in that Word."[78] It was this type of thinking, in which Barth developed a modern theology based on the Word of God alone—and not in a culture or religious awareness supposedly produced by the effect of Absolute Spirit on the human spirit—which had earlier gripped and excited Tom Torrance.

As a student, the young Barth had eagerly, though never uncritically, absorbed Harnack's ideas. He had been enthused by a theology which put the "Political Question" and the "Social Question" at the heart of a practical and socially relevant Christianity. Barth had viewed that as the future, leaving behind his own father's dry orthodoxy. Then 1914 brought a crisis of thinking. If it were true that European "Christian" culture was the product of the imprint of the Absolute Spirit upon the human spirit, how could 1914 occur? From that point onwards, as far as Barth was concerned, the way in which theology tried to link culture and Christianity was inadequate, misleading, even idolatrous. Consequently, Barth found himself drawn back towards his father's traditional Protestantism and its realism. He re-appreciated its emphasis on the darkness of human sin, and the need for atonement. That now spoke with more relevance than did Liberal Protestantism with its roots in romanticism. And so, for Barth, in contrast to Harnack, the coming of God's kingdom was not to be understood as the coming of a set of ethical ideas. Far less was it about human culture becoming coterminous with the ideals of Absolute Spirit. Rather, the coming of God's kingdom was the breaking in of the rule of God as a crisis event over against the kingdoms and cultures of this present world. God's Word was God's "No!" to human wisdom. And God's Word was God's "No!" to all culture built on that wisdom.

Barth made a discovery. Christianity is not an idea; however noble such an idea may be. And Christianity is not about encounter with Absolute Spirit. Instead, Christianity is a name. The name is Jesus Christ. That was Barth's initial way of expressing what would become for him a fundamental principle: namely, that *Christianity IS the Person of Jesus Christ* in his being and his act. It was working out the implications of that principle which started Barth on his extended theological adventure, first

---

78. Barth, *Knowledge of God and the Service of God*, 8–9 (Barth's emphases).

in his *Göttingen Dogmatics* and then in his *Church Dogmatics.* Christian faith is not an idea or a concept. Christianity *is* Jesus Christ. Everything centers on his person. It is utterly inadequate to understand Jesus as just a teacher, or as an example, or as a guru of religious experience. Instead, Jesus is himself revelation and reconciliation in his very being. He is the Gospel by being so in his person. It was this theology which fed into Torrance's own thinking, enriching every aspect of Torrance's faith.

In his Berlin lectures of 1899/1900 Harnack attempted to present a Christian faith which would satisfy modern men and women. He was convinced that the essence of Christianity is Jesus' teaching, which teaching corresponded in the most profound way possible to the religion which God had originally implanted in the souls of men and women everywhere. In Harnack's view the Church took a wrong early turning. Dogma sucked the life from true faith, Theological theories destroyed dynamic Christianity. The Church became preoccupied with creedal formulae and apocalyptic myths. Fixation on Jesus as the God-Man, and on the cross as a place of atonement, "threatened the very existence of the Gospel, by drawing away men's thoughts and interests in another direction."[79] Devotion to Christ mutated into formal Christology.[80] Living faith transformed into propositions. True religion became identified with doctrine, rather than with living in the Spirit.[81] And yet, the simple Gospel was there to be rediscovered. But, to do this, the Church must throw aside the God-Man theory, and must strip itself of atonement ideas. For Tom Torrance such a project would be unbiblical and misguided. For Torrance, Harnack failed to grasp a fundamental principle of Christian faith: namely, that God has come, in his divine freedom, to be both revelation and reconciliation in the person of Jesus Christ. Jesus is no mere Teacher.

---

79. Harnack, *What Is Christianity?*, 185.
80. Harnack, *What Is Christianity?*, 193.
81. Harnack, *What Is Christianity?*, 211.

— Chapter 10 —

# Jesus as Agent

WE NEED TO GO beyond Harnack. Jesus not only *taught*. He also *did*. He *did* something in his incarnation. He *did* something on the cross. He *did* something in his resurrection. And, for the earliest Christians, it was what he did as an *act* of redeeming mercy at Calvary which made salvation a reality. What they realized was that salvation is non-existent without these events *qua* events. Jesus was, and is, the agent or instrument of salvation, not just a teacher. And yet, might even the terms *agent* and *instrument*, like that of *teacher*, fall short of expressing the fullness of what God accomplished in and through Jesus Christ?

In 1966, James Philip, the minister of Holyrood Abbey Church in Edinburgh, expounded the *Westminster Confession of Faith* chapter by chapter at the congregation's mid-week service. That took place some years before I came to Edinburgh as a student, but the addresses had been published in-house as four booklets, and were available from the church bookstall.[1] From 1970 onwards, during my undergraduate years, I was a regular attender at Holyrood Abbey Church, and James Philip became a key influence on my thinking. I read his work with enthusiasm. His booklets, plus Louis Berkoff's *Systematic Theology*, were my first instructors in Reformed theology.

Torrance, however, felt that traditional Reformed theology, as represented by Philip, Berkhoff, and the Westminster tradition, fell short. For Torrance, Jesus was not just an agent who did something to accomplish salvation for us. Instead, Jesus was, and is, salvation in his own person. In his reading of Scottish Reformed theology, Torrance lamented that, with

1. Philip, *Westminster Confession of Faith: An Exposition*.

a few exceptions, it tended to view Jesus' work of atonement in mainly functional terms, with Jesus presented chiefly as an instrument to achieve an end. He regretted that much Scottish Reformed theology failed to incorporate the incarnation into the work of atonement, failed to fuse the *being* of Christ with the *act* of Christ, and failed to integrate the *person* of Christ with the *work* of Christ. At least in any adequate fashion. In Torrance's view, this Scottish tradition, so heavily influenced by the Federal Calvinism of the *Westminster Confession of Faith*, had departed from the very best theology of the original Reformers in which God was spoken of—as Barth would put it—in "a correlation of his being and act, and in a togetherness of his being-in-the-act and his act-in-the-being."[2] Consequently, Torrance judged that much of Scottish theology had given the incarnation and life of Jesus only a superficial redemptive significance, interpreting Jesus' incarnation and earthly life almost solely in terms of Jesus preserving his sinlessness on the way to Calvary where the real act of salvation took place.

Torrance's assessment of Scottish theology was only partly true. Rabbi Duncan, for one, was well aware that Bethlehem and Calvary should be kept together. And Rabbi Duncan was not alone. Mainstream Reformed theology had always stressed the importance of Christ's *active obedience*—obedience offered throughout the whole of Jesus' life—as essential to the salvation which he accomplished. Jesus, as the Last Adam, lived the life we should have lived. Throughout his life, and not only on the cross, Jesus substituted his humanity which had been made perfect through obedience, in place of our broken humanity which had been ruined by sin.[3] I certainly heard echoes of this from James Philip.

Nevertheless, within traditional Reformed theology there was always the danger of a reduced interpretation of the obedience of Jesus, and of viewing it only in terms of Jesus preserving purity and sinlessness until the day he was nailed to the cross as the unspotted, unblemished, lamb of God. Torrance insisted that much more was involved. Jesus did not mark time until Calvary. Jesus was not simply protecting his moral and spiritual perfection until he became an atoning sacrifice. Instead, Jesus acted vicariously throughout his life, actively creating a new humanity, which,

---

2. Cf. Rumscheidt, *Revelation and Theology*, 194.

3. Philip, *Westminster Confession of Faith*, Part Two, 34. Cf. Crowe, *Last Adam: A Theology of the Obedient Life of Jesus in the Gospel*. Crowe, of Westminster Theological Seminary, argues that all four Gospels present Jesus's obedient life as having saving significance.

through his resurrection, would become our humanity, and would become our salvation, through our union with him.

## 1. THE FORENSIC/LEGAL MODEL

The *Westminster Confession of Faith* molded Scottish Reformed theology and piety from the seventeenth century onwards. Torrance viewed that tradition as one which divorced the *being* from the *act* of Christ, with unwelcome consequences. Despite spending his earliest years in China, Torrance saw himself a Scottish theologian, and was sharply aware of the Westminster system. This influenced the development of his theology of the person and work of Christ. In the following paragraphs we critique some aspects of Westminster theology from Torrance's perspective.

### Salvation through Legal Declaration

At the heart of Westminster theology is the forensic/legal model of the atonement, a model which emerged from the Reformation. This describes salvation in terms of a judicial process in which our sin is *legally* charged to Jesus' account, and Jesus' righteousness is *legally* charged to ours. Sinners are *declared* (reckoned/counted) to be righteous (legally) because of what Jesus has done, even though they are not *made* righteous (ontologically). This was what James Philip taught, and which I found helpful as I began to think through the faith more theologically. Philip wrote,

> The word [justification] itself belongs to what the theologians call 'forensic terminology,' i.e., terminology that properly belongs to the sphere of law, the law court, and the legal system. The meaning of the word, as used in the New Testament, *never means 'to make righteous,'* but rather 'to declare righteous' or 'to accept as righteous.' When Paul says that God justifies the sinner, he does not mean that *he makes* the sinner righteous, but that *he declares* the sinner righteous, accepting him as righteous in his sight.[4]

As Philip made clear, central to the Westminster understanding is the notion that justification never means to *make* righteous. Instead, in the forensic/legal model of the atonement, Jesus is agent in a legal process in which he gives appropriate recompense (propitiation) for another's sins, in order that God may *declare* (but not *make*) the sinner righteous, and in order that God might be both just and the justifier of those who believe

---

4. Philip, *Westminster Confession of Faith*, Part Two, 30 (italics added).

in Jesus (Ephesians 3:26).⁵ As our substitute, Jesus took upon himself all of the infinite *legal* liability due to us because of our sin.⁶

There is no doubt that the forensic/legal model is present in the Scriptures.⁷ It is used by Paul to explain the meaning of the atonement, especially to clarify the central Gospel truth that what God accomplished for sinners through Jesus Christ was a full, complete, and sufficient atonement. Sin, and the guilt of sin, are no longer reckoned (accounted) to those who are in Christ. Their penalty has been charged fully to him. He has paid the price in full. As such, God declares sinners to be righteous, and free from guilt, in and through his Son. They are now justified (in the right) before God. And they are so irrevocably, because on the cross the penalty for all their sin—past, present, and future—was made in full. Therefore, legally, no longer can sin and its penalties have any claim on the redeemed children of God. The forensic/legal model is especially effective at clarifying these key truths. And yet, at the same time, in his exposition of the *Westminster Confession,* James Philip conceded that the metaphor of the law court, the forensic/legal model, sometimes struggles to express the full meaning of justification.⁸

Like James Philip, Tom Torrance strove to root his theology in Scripture. As such, he accepted that there is a profound, and a necessary, forensic/legal aspect to the atonement. Scripture says it. Theology demands it. As Torrance himself wrote, there has to be an "essential unity between dramatic and forensic redemption: that is, redemption by sheer act of grace and by justification."⁹ And Torrance was well aware that, without a forensic aspect to the atonement, a purely ontological emphasis would "degenerate into a doctrine of deification through union with deity."¹⁰ He also agreed that a vital consequence of the work of Christ is that sinners are indeed *declared* to be legally free of guilt, and are indeed *declared* to

---

5. Philip, *Westminster Confession of Faith*, Part Two, 30.

6. Philip, *Westminster Confession of Faith*, Part Two, 33.

7. Numerous biblical texts employ forensic/legal concepts. E.g. Ps 32:2; Rom 2:13; 3:20; 4:5; 5:13–14.

8. Philip, *Westminster Confession of Faith*, Part Two, 35.

9. Torrance, *Atonement*, 33 (37–38, 61, 90, 99–101). See also, Torrance, *Atonement*, 53, where he affirms the cultic-forensic dimension of the atonement within a three-way emphasis involving: the dramatic aspect of atonement; the cultic-forensic aspect of atonement; and the ontological aspect of the atonement. All three are aspects of both the OT atonement liturgy *and* the work of Christ.

10. Torrance, *Atonement*, 55.

be legally righteous before God. He never disputed that.[11] In Christian faith, it is of paramount importance that, on the Day of Judgment, the divine verdict on the redeemed is that they are declared to be "Not guilty." If that Divine verdict and declaration cannot be made, then all that Christ has done is of no effect.

At the same time, Torrance argued strenuously that understanding the atonement solely in forensic/legal terms is inadequate, and leads to a reduced understanding of who Christ is and of what Christ has done. What Torrance wanted to do was to undergird the biblically valid forensic/legal dimension of the atonement with an incarnational model. This was because he was convinced that it is the incarnational model which provides the definitive logic of atonement. And he believed that an appreciation of that ultimate rationale would transform our understanding of the atonement into something much more than seeing it only in terms of a legal transaction between God, Jesus, and sinners. For Torrance, the incarnational reality of the person of Jesus Christ alone provides the proper framework for understanding the Christian teaching of salvation. Because of this, Torrance argued that, for all its strengths, the forensic/legal model gives us a Jesus who is but an agent or divine instrument in a process, rather than a Jesus who is salvation himself in his person. And he maintained that only this latter understanding could express the fullness of the biblical witness, and the depth of the faith of early Christians.

---

11. Cf. Torrance, "Atoning Justification" (class handout): "Imputation describes the perfected work of grace. It indicates that justification is forensic in the sense that it is grounded on the once and for all judgment of Jesus Christ on the cross, but it indicates that what happened there, while complete in its reality, is yet to be fully disclosed at the Advent of Christ." Torrance touched on this in his paper "Hugh Ross Mackintosh: Theologian of the Cross," when he refers approvingly to Mackintosh's view: "Mackintosh agreed with [MacLeod-Campbell] in refusing to separate the Incarnation from the Atonement, and thus in declining to offer a doctrine of atonement in terms of a merely *external* or *judicial* transaction between God and sinners, as though Christ's righteousness and our guilt were both externally transferable. Far from rejecting the forensic element in the atoning and propitiatory work of Christ, however, he interpreted it as falling within the inner being of Jesus in terms of his active as well as his passive obedience under the judgment of divine Holiness and Love." Torrance contrasted Mackintosh with James Denney who: "Interpreted St Paul's doctrine of union with Christ only in moral or judicial terms." In *Theological Science*, 27, Torrance argued that MacLeod-Campbell sought to understand the atonement "in its own light" by keeping "within the limits of its own evidence" so that he would not be misled by untested preconceptions. Torrance read MacLeod-Campbell as trying to put aside the preconceptions of Scottish Calvinism and thinking through the atonement in its own light.

## Luther and Melanchthon

The forensic/legal model is a powerful theological tool. It has helped clarify the meaning of the cross for many Christians, myself included. And, in the sixteenth century, it was the model which enabled the Reformers to move away from notions of salvation based on the disastrous penitential theology of the pre-Reformation period, which had undermined Christian faith and piety throughout Europe. In the all-encompassing penitential system, men and women attempted to make themselves righteous before God by expunging their sins through good works, pilgrimages, pious acts, prayers, receiving the sacraments, doing penance, or buying indulgences. Over against that entire system, Protestant theologians emphasized that the problem of sin and guilt is dealt with by God alone. It is God who does it, not us. It is God's action, not our action. It is God's gift, not our achievement. But, in order to underpin and validate their theology, Protestant theologians had to develop an adequate alternative description of how this can be.

Medieval theology offered a simple explanation. It taught that God infuses grace into the sinner (primarily through the sacraments), and that this infused grace justifies sinners (albeit temporarily), by putting them in a state of grace (also temporarily). The crucial mechanism in this process is an *infusion* of grace, a concept which made perfect sense to the medieval mind. Hence, when Martin Luther emphasized the Reformation doctrine of sinners being justified by *faith* and not by *works*, he knew that simply stating that sinners were justified by faith was not the end of the matter. He still had the problem of explaining *how* it can be that sinners are cleansed and made righteous.

At the start, Luther continued to think along medieval lines. He still believed that God somehow infuses grace into sinners by his Spirit, though not through the sacraments but through true faith in Christ. This meant that Luther still understood the "How?" of the process in terms of an infusion of grace.[12] Then Philip Melanchthon came along, empha-

---

12. The notion of an infusion of grace introduces the related concept of a person being "in a state of grace" (at least for a period of time until needing another infusion). Within such a model, "becoming righteous" is temporary since it is self-evident that any man or woman sins again. Melanchthon's emphasis on justification as "being declared righteous" rather than "becoming made righteous" was intended to avoid that scenario. In Melanchthon's model, because justification concerned a divine declaration rather than a human becoming, then it could be permanent and irrevocable. Thus, Reformed theology moved away from the notion of sinners being 'made righteous' as

sizing the forensic/legal nature of justification.[13] In 1521, whilst Luther was still struggling with the concept of grace as an infused entity, Melanchthon wrote in his *Loci Communes* that grace is not in fact a *"thing"* which is *"in us,"* but is the *"attitude"* of God *"towards us."* Hence, sinners are put right with God, and are justified, not by an *infusion* of grace, but by God's *attitude* of grace in which God declares legally that we are now *reckoned* to be righteous before him because of faith in Christ. It is the legal relationship between God and the sinner which changes. It is that legal relationship which is decisive.

What Melanchthon did was to introduce Luther to the concept of a legal imputation. There is no *infusion* of grace. Instead, God *reckons* Christ's righteousness to be ours. And so, in answer to questions such as: "How does Christ's righteousness become ours?" and "What mechanism enables it to happen?," Melanchthon had a model which solved many problems, and not only for Luther. This way of expressing the Gospel was adopted by nearly all the Reformation Fathers, including Calvin.[14] Because of God's attitude of grace, God establishes a legal imputation which has been underwritten by his irrevocable word. Grace is imputed legally. Grace is not infused. In this way Protestant theology freed itself from the medieval notion of infused grace with its attendant dangers and errors. Grace is relational. Grace is the attitude of a reconciling God towards sinners. And grace, thus understood, is at the heart of the whole Reformation theological revolution. Reflecting this emphasis, one of the questions in the Dogmatics II, 1974 Autumn Term examination, was: *"'In both Luther and Calvin, the grace of God in Christ is re-established at the center of theology.' Explain and discuss."*

---

the basis of their justification, since it was seen as self-evident that no man or woman remains in that state of holiness.

13. Green, *How Melanchthon Helped Luther Discover the Gospel*. Cf. McGrath, *Reformation Thought: An Introduction*, 108–10.

14. Cf. Calvin, *Geneva Catechism*, Q. 118: "Merely through his goodness, without any regard to our works, he is pleased to accept us freely in Jesus Christ, imputing his righteousness to us, and does not impute our sin." Calvin formulated this in response to the question whether, through our merits, we are able to induce God to be kind to us. Calvin used the model of a legal imputation from God to eliminate the idea of self-generated merit. Calvin's Scripture reference behind Q&A 118 was Titus 3:5–7.

Part Three: Christology

## 2. THE WESTMINSTER TRADITION

There is no doubt that Melanchthon's powerful forensic/legal model helped to liberate the theology of the Reformation from Medievalism. A century later, the same model was adopted by the 1646 *Westminster Confession of Faith*, which, in 1690, became the confessional standard of the Church of Scotland. In chapter 11, the *Confession* states,

> [God freely justifies the elect] *not by infusing righteousness* into them, but *by pardoning* their sins, and *by accounting and accepting* their persons *as righteous;* not for anything wrought in them, or done by them, but for Christ's sake alone; nor by imputing faith itself, the act of believing, or any other evangelical obedience to them, as their righteousness; but by *imputing* the obedience and satisfaction of Christ unto them, they receiving and resting on him and his righteousness by faith; which faith they have not of themselves, it is the gift of God.[15]

The key statements here are that God freely justifies: (1) "*not by infusing righteousness,*" but (2) "*by pardoning sins,*" and (3) "*by accounting and accepting our persons as righteous.*" The wording is all important, with a considerable theological history lying behind it. In stating that God justifies, "*not by infusing righteousness,*" the *Westminster Confession* employs terminology which deliberately rejects the medieval infusion-model which Luther struggled with, and which Melanchthon freed him from. Over against that medieval infusion-model, the *Westminster Confession* stresses that God *accounts* and *accepts* persons as righteous because of the legal imputation of the obedience and satisfaction of Christ. Elsewhere, when the *Westminster Confession* refers to the obedience and satisfaction of Christ, it includes the life of Jesus as well as the death of Jesus. In this context, the obedience of Christ is the righteousness of his whole life; and, the satisfaction of Christ is the merit of his atoning death.

---

15. WCF, 11: "On Justification." The *Confession* continues: "Faith, thus receiving and resting on Christ and his righteousness, is the alone instrument of justification: yet is it not alone in the person justified, but is ever accompanied with all other saving graces, and is no dead faith, but works by love. Christ, by his obedience and death, did fully discharge the debt of all those that are thus justified, and did make a proper, real and full satisfaction to his Father's justice in their behalf. Yet, in as much as he was given by the Father for them; and his obedience and satisfaction accepted in their stead; and both, freely, not for anything in them; their justification is only of free grace; that both the exact justice, and rich grace of God might be glorified in the justification of sinners."

Critically, in the *Westminster Confession*, the imputation of Christ's righteousness is a forensic/legal imputation. It is not the infusion of an entity; not even an entity called grace. Moreover, the *Westminster Confession* does not teach that sinners are *made* righteous, since that would steer too close to the medieval infusion-model. Instead, it emphasizes that sinners are legally accounted to be righteous because of faith in Christ who, as the Last Adam, lived a life of full obedience before paying the debt of sin upon the cross.[16] In all of this, the crux of the matter is that righteousness is not *infused* into sinners. Instead, righteousness is *imputed* or *credited* on a legal basis. The price of sin is charged to Christ's account—legally. He pays the price—legally. His righteousness is accounted to sinners—legally. No ontological issue is involved.

In contrast to this, but without relapsing into medieval notions of an infusion of grace, Torrance wanted to state that in Christ sinners are not just *declared* righteous, but are *made* righteous. Torrance was convinced that justification involves more than simply a legal declaration that God now regards reconciled sinners as righteous in Christ, though such a legal declaration is always part of justification, but as its outcome not its mechanism. Torrance was adamant that we are *made* righteous in Christ. Something *ontological* occurs. Not just something *legal*. In *Space, Time and Incarnation*, he wrote, "Justification is not only a *declaratory* act, but an *actualization* of what is declared."[17] He continued, "Justification becomes not only the non-imputation of sins but the clothing of the sinner with the righteousness of Christ."[18]

There is no doubt that the intention of the *Westminster Confession*, from start to finish, is evangelical. It sets out to preserve the core Reformation emphasis on grace. And it is determined to present salvation as a pure act of divine grace. Most of all, it seeks to protect Reformed thinking from the risk of that divine grace being compromised in any way. This explains its heavy emphasis on predestination, with the double-decree stated early, and molding all that follows.[19] James Torrance, in his lectures on Scottish Theology, lamented that the double-decree was introduced in the *Westminster Confession's* opening chapters, viewing that as fatally compromising everything which followed. Yet, it was not placing the

---

16. The *WCF* proof text is Rom 4:5.
17. Torrance, *Space, Time and Resurrection*, 62 (italics added).
18. Torrance, *Space, Time and Resurrection*, 63.
19. *WCF*, 3.

divine decree early which was wrong. After all, Karl Barth also embedded the doctrine of predestination at a similar juncture in the overall schema of his *Church Dogmatics*. However, for James Torrance, it was the *Westminster Confession's* presentation of predestination as a double-decree which was a problem, since that particular interpretation critically fed into all its subsequent theology.

Within the Westminster tradition itself, the doctrine of predestination, especially in the form of the double-decree, is seen as undergirding and protecting the doctrines of grace. Grace can only be grace if God does it all. No human contingency, however minor, can influence or affect any of God's saving acts. If it did, then that divine grace becomes conditional on human action, however slight the human element may be. The writers of the *Westminster Confession* were concerned to avoid any scintilla of the heresy that sinners may be made righteous by their own efforts, no matter how limited their contribution.[20] All is of God. All has been done in Christ. All is of grace. And the salvation which Christ procures, is accomplished through God declaring sinners to be righteous because of the obedience and satisfaction of Christ. The ultimate concern of the *Westminster Confession* is grace. And the mercy which flows from grace must be rooted fully, totally, and completely in God himself in Jesus Christ. It is because of grace, and grace alone, that sinners are accorded a change of legal status before God.

We cannot discuss every point of difference between the Torrances and Westminster theology. That would be a long and involved process. However, from a Torrancian perspective, we do ask whether the *Westminster Confession's* adoption of an exclusively forensic/legal model allows it to say all that needs to be said about the atonement? Does the dominance of the forensic/legal model create problems as well as solving some? Does it provide an adequate expression of the 'How?' of the atonement?

### The Westminster Legacy: I

One of the prominent contemporary advocates of Westminster theology in the United States is Westminster Theological Seminary, Pennsylvania, whose position was well-expressed on the Seminary's official website in 2018.[21] Written by Brandon Crowe, the statement articulated the

---

20. Cf. *Larger Catechism*, Q&A. 71. This guarded against the semi-Pelagianism of the medieval penitential system.

21. https://faculty.wts.edu/.

traditional Westminster understanding of how Christ's righteousness is imputed to sinners:

> Imputation most often refers to the legal (or *forensic*) crediting of Jesus's perfect righteousness to believers by faith for justification. Imputation communicates that believers are made right with God (or *justified*) on the basis of the obedience of Christ (both active and passive . . . ). By Jesus's active obedience he meets the demands[22] of perfect righteousness God has always required of humanity. By Jesus's passive obedience, he pays the penalty due to humanity on account of sin. Additionally, beyond the imputation of Christ's full obedience to believers, imputation may also refer to the counting of believers' sins to Christ as the sin-bearing substitute . . . Imputation describes the *legal* means by which our perfect representative's actions can benefit us by faith. Apart from the perfect obedience of Christ imputed to us, we are not able to meet the demands of a holy, just, and perfect God. Imputation is therefore at the heart of the gospel message: the requirements for acceptance with God cannot be met by sinful humanity . . . Adam's first sin is imputed to all humanity descending from him naturally, and therefore Adam's sin has *legally* binding consequences for all who are born 'in him.' Likewise—but better—Christ's entire righteousness has *legal* consequences for all those who are 'in him,' and this is explained by means of imputation (cf. Rom. 5:12–21).

This statement expressed the classic Westminster position in which the Glorious Exchange is interpreted as a legal declaration. Our sin is *reckoned legally* to Christ. His righteousness is *reckoned legally* to us. On that basis Christ is deemed to bear our sin, and we are deemed to be clothed with his righteousness. Crucially, within this forensic/legal interpretation, sinners are not *made* righteous, but are *declared* righteous. As already stated, Torrance could never regard that as adequate.

At this point we recall the words of the Jewish bereavement liturgy: "*Who is it who cleanses you?*" Being cleansed is vital. However, are sinners truly cleansed if the imputation of Christ's righteousness is only a legal imputation and not an actual one? Is it sufficient to state that Jesus was made legally responsible for our sin? Is a purely legal pronouncement

---

22. "Meets the demands": i.e., stays qualified to become the sinless lamb on the cross. Torrance wanted more. Torrance held that Jesus' active obedience not only kept Jesus in the right before God, but acted *vicariously* in our place. He lived his life positively in our place for us.

enough to satisfy the scorching holiness of God? Can God be satisfied with what might, unkindly but perceptively, be described as a legal fiction? Are sinners reconciled to God if the truth of the matter is that in themselves (ontologically) they are the same as before? In other words, is it sufficient to say that "Jesus is the Gospel" simply because his righteousness has been reckoned legally to be ours? Or is something more required? And, if something more is necessary, might it be that "Jesus is the Gospel" because he has *truly* undone our history of rebellion, has *truly* made us righteous, and has *truly* restored what was broken by sin? In this vein Torrance wrote,

> The theology that deals only in forensic terms and speaks only of a purely objective atonement in that sense, brings upon itself the suspicion of make-belief, and yet the biblical revelation speaks in the most astonishing terms of this substitutionary act of Christ: 'He who knew no sin became sin for us, so that we might be made the righteousness of God in him.'[23]

When James Philip expounded the *Westminster Confession,* he was aware that the law-court metaphor had inadequacies.[24] And he also knew that the forensic/legal mode of imputation was criticized by some as a legal fiction. In order to counter that criticism, Philip focused on the realism of the suffering of Christ on Calvary, and on the infinite cost of salvation through the death of Jesus: "The imputation of our sin to him was no fiction, but a grim and terrible experience in which he went into the outer darkness for our sakes."[25] In other words, the experience of Christ on the cross was no make-believe. It was reality. However, Philip's response did not really address the specific concern felt by Torrance and others. Torrance never accused Westminster theology of underplaying the realism of the agony of the cross, or of the cost of salvation. That was never disputed.

By critiquing Reformed theology's almost exclusive reliance on the forensic/legal model, Torrance wanted to strengthen—not weaken—the concept of substitutionary atonement in which Christ bore the penalty of the wrath of God against sin. Torrance's aim was to reinforce the notion of substitutionary atonement, not dilute it.[26] On the cross Jesus bore the

---

23. Torrance, *Atonement*, 125–26; see also 54.
24. Philip, *Westminster Confession of Faith*, Part Two, 35.
25. Philip, *Westminster Confession of Faith*, Part Two, 36.
26. Torrance, *Atonement*, 153–54.

wrath of God on the sin of men and women; and Torrance accepted that what Christ did was an act of penal, substitutionary, atonement—though he was uneasy with the term "penal" because of its inappropriate usage in some Satisfaction Theories with their apparent emphasis on a divine vindictiveness.[27] As Walker makes clear in his glossary of theological terms as used by Torrance, there was no doubt in Torrance's mind that, in our place, Christ took to himself the consequence and penalty of our sin.[28] Christ took the *penalty*. Christ took it *in our place*. And these two statements supply the core definition of penal substitution: a *penalty* taken *in our place*. Torrance's position on this surprised many conservative-evangelical students who thought him to be suspect on penal substitution. And James Torrance, who, like his brothers, also studied under Barth in Basel, told us that many of Barth's students had been likewise astonished when, contrary to their expectations, Barth expounded penal substitutionary theory as his own.

In point of fact, Torrance interpreted the cross as the event where Christ, in our place, suffered the penalty of sin and the wrath of God *in its most terrible form*.[29] And Torrance was determined to plumb the meaning of the darkness of Calvary even more deeply than a purely forensic/legal conception of justification allowed, and to move beyond that particular model to the ontology which lay behind it. At no point, did Torrance displace the forensic/legal by the ontological. Rather, his concern was to show that when we grasp the core ontology of the situation, all models of the atonement—including the forensic/legal one—gain even greater strength and profounder depth.

## The Westminster Legacy: II

In 2019, WTS updated its website, with a more extended account of its theological stance.[30] What it now put forward was excerpted largely from a chapter written by Brandon Crowe, entitled, "The Passive and Active Obedience of Christ," which appeared in a collection of essays edited by Matthew Barret.[31] In greater detail than before, the WTS statement emphasized that the two aspects of, "Jesus's unified obedience (his passive

27. Torrance, *Atonement*, 57, 72.
28. Cf. Walker's notes in Torrance, *Atonement*, 454, 460.
29. Torrance, *Atonement*, 125–26, 153–54.
30. Crowe, "Two Benefits of Justification."
31. Crowe, "Passive and Active Obedience of Christ," 443–46.

obedience and his active obedience) are both necessary for justification." First, Jesus' obedience in his death on the cross deals with the forgiveness of sins:

> The law requires punishment for sin. Sin cannot simply be swept aside and forgotten without recompense. Sin brings a penalty, leading to death, for every person born naturally since Adam. That penalty must be paid. This aspect of Jesus's obedience is not that controversial for the many today, who recognize the need for forgiveness of sins through the death of Christ.

Second, Jesus' obedience throughout his life deals with the right to eternal life:

> A right understanding of passive obedience also tells us that Jesus bore the wrath of God throughout the whole course of his lifelong obedience. This means that, as Geerhardus Vos has argued, the blood Jesus shed in his circumcision is no less atoning than the blood he shed at Calvary. This lifelong suffering is memorably captured in the *Heidelberg Catechism*, question and answer 37: "Only *perfect* obedience can meet the demands of eternal life; imperfect obedience simply cannot suffice."[32]

The 2019 WTS statement clarified that Jesus's obedience concerns a penalty which he paid, not only on the cross but throughout his life. And it is this entire action which corresponds to the forgiveness of sins in justification. The statement continued,

> Yet justification consists in more than the forgiveness of sins. For if we are 'only' forgiven for our sins, we still have not realized the requirements for eternal life, as laid out in God's law. Attaining eternal life requires perfect obedience. Here we must consider Adam, who was promised eternal life on condition of personal, entire, exact, and perpetual obedience. Adam, as we know, failed to exhibit the obedience necessary to realize this prospect of glorious, everlasting life. However, we should not think that with Adam's failure, the requirement of perfect obedience for eternal life is somehow swept away, as if with a wave of the hand. Instead, perfect obedience continued to be the

---

32. The *Heidelberg Catechism* is further quoted: "Question: What do you understand by the word: 'suffered'? Answer: That all the time [Christ] lived on earth, but especially at the end of his life, He bore, in body and soul, the wrath of God against the sin of the whole human race; in order that by his passion, as the only atoning sacrifice, He might redeem our body and soul from everlasting damnation, and obtain for us the grace of God, righteousness and eternal life."

requirement for the inheritance of eternal life. To be clear, this obedience must be *perfect obedience* and not the obedience of believers in sanctification. As Herman Bavinck cogently argues: 'Just as we must not artificially divide the passive and active obedience of Christ, so we must not divide the benefits of Christ's unified obedience, as if one could possess one without the other.'

Jesus, living our life in our place, and in our place rendering the obedience we should have given to God but did not give, fulfills all that Adam (as our Covenant Head) should have given but did not give. The statement added: "only with Adam in his sinless, created estate that the possibility of eternal life on condition of perfect obedience is possible." But, "Once sin enters the world, original sin affects all those born naturally after Adam." And, because all are tainted in Adam, who was the covenant (or representative) head of humanity, none can render that obedience to God. "Only *perfect* obedience can meet the demands of eternal life; imperfect obedience simply cannot suffice." This, according to the 2019 WTS statement, is where Jesus' entire obedience (passive and active) becomes critical:

> Jesus's obedience can therefore be understood to have passive and active dimensions, which correspond to the two benefits of justification. Forgiveness of sins corresponds to Christ's passive obedience; and the securing of eternal life corresponds to Christ's active obedience. And [following Bavinck] just as we must not artificially divide the passive and active obedience of Christ, so we must not divide the benefits of Christ's unified obedience, as if one could possess one without the other. It is not just 'this' or 'that' part of Jesus's obedience that provides the ground for justification; it is the *entire* obedience of Jesus that saves. As Calvin succinctly states: 'How has Christ abolished sin, banished the separation between us and God, and acquired righteousness to render God favorable and kindly toward us? ... He has achieved this by the whole course of his obedience.'

Torrance could have agreed with much of the above, though he might have expressed it differently. Yet, despite areas of potential agreement, there were two major points of difference between himself and classical Westminster theology.

First, the *vicarious* humanity of Christ. Torrance insisted that the obedience of Christ throughout his life on earth (commonly known as Christ's *active obedience*) was truly and fully vicarious on our behalf.

It was not simply part of Christ's own righteousness as a man: a righteousness which he took to the cross as the sinless lamb of God; and a righteousness which became part of him as the Last Adam, our new representative head. For Torrance, more was involved. For Torrance, Christ obeyed in our place, fulfilled the law in our place, worshipped and prayed in our place, and even believed in our place; and, crucially, he did this in a manner in which he was not simply forging a righteousness for *himself*—even on our behalf as the Last Adam—but was forging our righteousness *as if we were the ones doing so ourselves*. And so, he himself, "became *our* prayer, *our* oblation, *our* worship, *our* faith, *our* perfect answer to God the Father."[33]

Second, the *imputation* of righteousness. Torrance questioned how the Westminster tradition understood the notion of imputation. Torrance insisted that the righteousness of God is imputed to us on an ontological basis, not just on a legal/forensic basis. In Christ, we are not simply *reckoned* to be righteous by legal imputation, but are *made* righteous. Both of these issues are of substantial importance.

There is no doubt that, from his pulpit, James Philip expounded to the congregation a rich understanding of the passive and active obedience of Christ. I recall him, one Sunday evening, using the vivid illustration of a vandal breaking into an art gallery. The vandal defaces a portrait by an Old Master, first slashing it with a knife and then smearing it with dirt. On the crime (sin) being discovered, the question becomes: what must be done to put things rights? Clearly, the vandal needs to be caught and punished. But punishment alone does not put things right. The curator wants his picture back. Therefore, to put things truly right, the picture itself needs to be painstakingly restored to its original condition as if the crime had never even taken place. Only after that restoration are things how they had been originally. The theological parallels are obvious. Arresting the vandal and punishing him, corresponds to Jesus' *passive* obedience, in which, supremely on the cross, he takes the penalty for our having defaced God's image. But, God also wants his picture back! And so, it is the whole of Jesus' life in his *active* obedience, in which, on our behalf and in our place, he restores that marred and spoiled image of God. And that work of *restoration* through Jesus' active obedience is as essential as his bearing the *penalty* of sin upon the cross in his passive obedience. James Philip's art gallery illustration originated from as early as Athanasius; and

---

33. Torrance, *Atonement*, 70 (italics added).

it conveyed superbly the multi-dimensional nature of the obedience of Christ. Again, Torrance would disagree with little of this. But he would insist that the truly vicarious aspect of that active obedience should be absolutely central.[34]

At Firbush in November, 2010, the concept of the vicarious humanity of Christ, in so far as Christ's obedience truly becomes *our* obedience in him, was elaborated upon by Tom Torrance's younger brother David. During his presentation, David Torrance commented that, while nearly all liberal theologians reject out of hand the whole notion of Christ' vicarious humanity, some evangelicals are little better. He stated,

> Sadly, many evangelical theologians restrict the vicariousness of Christ to his atoning death, and become concerned if we speak of the vicarious life, vicarious resurrection, and vicarious ascension of Christ. They believe that in doing so, we detract from our understanding of Christ's substitutionary, atoning death. But this is a misunderstanding of Scripture. Christ's substitutionary atonement embraces his incarnation, life, death, resurrection, ascension, and Pentecost. And those who restrict the vicariousness of Christ to his atoning death, interpret the atonement purely forensically.[35]

Even if a theologian adopts the term "vicarious" he or she might not be using the word exactly as Torrance did. Though the term can be taken as a general synonym for "in our place," in what manner do we understand "in our place"? For many evangelical theologians Christ is "in our place" as our legal stand-in. That was David Torrance's point when he stated that some interpret the atonement only forensically. That is vicarious substitution of a type, but it is so only in a legal or forensic manner. For Tom Torrance, as for his brothers, Christ "in our place" involves a far more radical vicarious substitution, in which Christ truly becomes what we are, and, in him, we truly become what he is, as he lives on our behalf the life we have failed to live before God. Crucially, that perfect obedience which he offers to the Father in our place, truly becomes *our* obedience. And so, for Torrance, Christ acted in our place, not just as our

---

34. Cf. Torrance, *Atonement*, 8: "Jesus has come to fulfil the covenant will of God both from the side of God, fulfilling all the promises of God to his people, and from the side of man, walking in all the way that the people of God were commanded to, and as such to be the servant of the Lord in mediating a new covenant."

35. D. W. Torrance, "The Vicarious Humanity of Christ, Incarnate, Crucified, Risen and Ascended," Firbush, November, 2010.

legal substitute, but in a manner which affects us ontologically. We *truly become* obedient sons and daughters of God in him.

## The Puritan Legacy

We have underlined the importance of not misrepresenting the place of both the active and passive obedience of Christ in the theology of the Westminster tradition. At Firbush in April, 2011, this was underscored by Douglas Kelly, who picked upon some of the concerns expressed by David Torrance the previous autumn. Kelly is a scholar who understands both Torrance and the Westminster tradition. He gained his PhD at New College under Torrance in the 1970s, and he is also firmly rooted within Westminster Calvinism. In his presentation, Kelly argued that the very best Reformed theologians, including many of the Puritans, had always placed a high value on Christ's active obedience throughout his life, as well as on his passive obedience in his death.[36]

To illustrate his argument, Kelly referred to Calvin's *Institutes*, in which Calvin taught that the whole course of Christ's obedience is important to salvation.[37] He cited Volume Two of John Owen's works, with its emphasis that Christ's passive obedience is itself an *active* obedience since *obeying* is *doing*. He also pointed out that Owen stressed the importance of the whole filial relationship between God the Father and God the Son, which relationship the Son lived out in our humanity, *giving us to share in it*, and from which we may all receive. Kelly moved on to quote Thomas Goodwin, who taught that Christ's passive obedience will not suffice unless joined to his active obedience and vice versa. Kelly also

---

36. Douglas Kelly, "The Active Obedience of Christ," Firbush, April, 2011.

37. Calvin, *Institutes* 2.16.5: "When it is asked then how Christ, by abolishing sin, removed the enmity between God and us, and purchased a righteousness which made him favorable and kind to us, it may be answered generally, that he accomplished this by the whole course of his obedience. This is proved by the testimony of Paul: 'As by one man's disobedience many were made sinners, so by the obedience of one shall many be made righteous' (Rom. 5:19). And indeed he elsewhere extends the ground of pardon which exempts from the curse of the law to the whole life of Christ: 'When the fullness of the time was come, God sent forth his Son, made of a woman, made under the law, to redeem them that were under the law' (Gal. 4:4, 5). Thus even at his baptism he declared that a part of righteousness was fulfilled by his yielding obedience to the command of the Father. In short, from the moment when he assumed the form of a servant, he began, in order to redeem us, to pay the price of deliverance. Scripture, however, the more certainly to define the mode of salvation, ascribes it peculiarly and specially to the death of Christ."

mentioned Bavinck's *Systematic Theology*, Volume Three, which emphasized the dangers of restricting the atoning work of Christ to his suffering. Kelly could also have dipped into the nineteenth-century *Diaries* of Andrew Bonar who, as his theology developed, became increasingly aware of the importance of the obedience of the whole life of Jesus from Bethlehem to Calvary, in relation to salvation.[38]

The crucial issue in Kelly's paper, as he expounded the richness of the Puritan tradition, was that so much of its theology centered on Jesus, as the Last Adam, fulfilling everything which God ever wanted in the First Adam, his son. Reflecting on this, Kelly discussed the notion of the two Adams as crucial in Paul's theology of redemption; within this context, Kelly highlighted Torrance's insistence that, in the perfection of his human life, Christ was indeed the Last Adam undoing the work of the First Adam. Going further, Kelly asked: Why did Christ not go directly to the cross from either the manger or his baptism? His answer, reflecting what he saw as the Puritan understanding, was that, as the Last Adam, Christ's life had to be lived in order that a life of active obedience could be carried out, because that life of active obedience was itself a necessary and vital part of our salvation. Hence, within the Westminster and Puritan tradition, as properly understood, Jesus' obedient life was not lived simply in order to keep himself pure for the cross. Instead, it was lived in order to live a life of obedience *for us* as the Last Adam. In terms of effective application, the fruit of that obedience then becomes *ours* by legal imputation.

In his paper, Kelly touched on the question of whether the Westminster Assembly in the 1640s ever considered stating explicitly that Christ's active obedience was vicarious. He pointed out that the doctrine was indeed debated, and that the Assembly voted "Yes." However, three

---

38. In his *Diary* Andrew Bonar reflected frequently on the nature of Christ's imputed righteousness. (a) 2nd March, 1834: "Since last communion I have seen more than before of Christ's substitution in our room; his righteousness the only ground of our acceptance." (b) 29th May, 1863: "My leanness; but my soul is more than ever fixed upon Christ, and my conscience satisfied with *his obedience from Bethlehem to Calvary, and his drinking the cup of trembling from the manger till he drank out its dregs at the Cross*." (c) 20th July, 1890: "Reading Brainerd's Life: it seemed to me that he did not hold fellowship with the living Savior as he might have done, did not see himself covered with Christ's merits whereby God's eye was turned away from his imperfections, corruptions, ignorance, failures, because the *obedience of Christ was imputed to him*. I would be like Brainerd every day, mourning and sad, if I did not see myself so covered with the obedience of Christ that the Father saw me in him to be beautiful and attractive, because of the garment of righteousness" (italics added).

of its members argued that this emphasis might result in anti-nomianism if people believed that Christ obeyed vicariously in our place. Hence, the text of the *Westminster Confession* never highlighted this vicarious aspect of the active obedience of Christ.

Commenting specifically on Torrance, Kelly agreed that Torrance did not concentrate on Christ's legal accomplishments, but on his living out the life which pleases and honors the Father. And he recalled Torrance interpreting biblical verses, such as Ephesians 2:6, as pointing to Christ's life not only as a *sanctification* of our human nature, but also as a *reconciliation*. Thus Christ's active obedience is the life of true Sonship. And, in Gethsemane, Jesus acting vicariously in our place and from within our humanity, bent our human will back into God's will. All from the inside-out. Thus, though we are indeed reconciled to God by Christ's saving death, we are also reconciled by his saving life (cf. Barth, *CD* I/2, 301). Thus, Christ provides a vicarious response in his active obedience. Christ lives out a life of filial Sonship which neither Adam nor Israel ever did. As such, *representation* must be added to *substitution* as vital to atonement, something which Torrance found in Romans, chapters 5 and 6. Christ really took our place in terms of obeying, knowing, and worshipping God. But, significantly, Christ's vicarious response *upholds* ours, it does not *replace* ours. It truly becomes ours. And yet, unless it is fully *Christ's* it has no existence as *ours*.[39] Here Kelly, in his presentation of Torrance's position, applied the concepts of *anhypostasia* and *enhypostasia* which recur in Torrance's thinking.[40] For Torrance we are saved both by the death of Christ and by his life.

---

39. D. W. Torrance read several papers at Firbush Conferences in which he argued that Galatians 2:20 should be translated as "having the faith *of* the Son of God" rather than "having faith *in* the Son of God." He opined that the Authorized Version perhaps gives the best translation, consistent with classical Greek grammar, because the subject (Christ) is in the genitive case hence the translation should be "the faith *of* Christ." Theologically this would mean that *our* faith is grounded in *his* faith; i.e., he has faith, vicariously, for me. And yet, in union with Christ, that vicarious faith truly becomes my faith.

40. The concepts of *anhypostasia* and *enhypostasia* originally applied to the relationship between the humanity and the divinity of Christ. The Church Fathers taught that in becoming incarnate the Son of God did not assume to himself an already existing human person, but that the humanity of Christ only came into existence in the incarnation itself. Therefore, the humanity of Christ has no existence apart from in union with the divinity of Christ (anhypostasia); but, because of that union it has a true, complete, and full human existence in and of itself (enhypostasia) and is not a mere cipher of his divinity. As Torrance put it, in the incarnation the Son of God does

## The Righteousness of Jesus Christ

Kelly's paper prompted reflection on the nature of the righteousness of Jesus Christ. Was that righteousness *forged* through the obedience of Christ's life, lived out day by day? Or did Christ simply *preserve* a divine righteousness which he brought with him from the perfection of heaven to the incarnation? In other words, was it a righteousness which the man Jesus *created* in his humanity? Or was it a righteousness which Jesus *preserved* in his humanity? The New Testament allows both aspects, and the reason it does so is because the righteousness of Jesus Christ is the righteousness of one who is both truly God and truly man. This means that, on the one hand, what the redeemed sinner receives from Christ is the righteousness *of God* (2 Cor 5:21). On the other hand, it is also the righteousness of a man. Christ's righteousness was *generated* in his humanity through his life of obedience: as Torrance emphasized, "He *learned obedience* from what he suffered" (Heb 5:8).[41] Because the imputation of righteousness is central to justification, this deepens the atoning significance of Christ's life. That life, as it was lived, was what forged the very righteousness which becomes ours in union with him.

Central in all of this is the question of how righteousness, as the fruit of Christ's active obedience and passive obedience, becomes ours. In line with the Westminster tradition, the WTS statement focuses on a forensic imputation: "When we ask how the obedience of Christ can be reckoned to us, the best answer is by means of *imputation*. In brief, imputation means that in justification the obedience (or righteousness) of Christ—including both passive and active dimensions—is *forensically*, or *legally*, credited to believers by faith alone" (italics added). The statement

---

not assume or enter into an existing human person, but makes "room for himself in our physical existence, yet without being contained, confined, or circumscribed in place as in a vessel" (*Space, Time and Incarnation*, 13). The twin concepts of *anhypostasia* and *enhypostasia* have since been abstracted from their original context and applied as a general christological principle. For a clear exposition of what Torrance meant (and did not mean) by *anhypostasia* and *enhypostasia*, see Walker's article: "The Innovative fruitfulness of An-En-hypostasis in the thinking of T. F. Torrance," on the *Participatio* website, where Walker offers the following definitions: (a) *Anhypostasis*: the humanity of Christ has *no* existence in itself, independent of the incarnation. It is *an*-hypostatic (*non*—personally-subsistent); (b) *Enhypostasis*: the humanity of Christ has full human reality *in* the person of the incarnate Son. It is *en*-hypostatic (*in*-subsisting, i.e., fully human, personal reality *in* the *person* of the Son). Cf. Walker's glossary in Torrance, *Atonement*, 452.

41. Cf. Torrance, *Atonement*, 79.

goes on to emphasize that, "the righteousness that is imputed is the entire obedience of Jesus." Adam's sin was imputed to all humanity; however, as the Last Adam, born of a virgin, Jesus similarly stands at the head of a new humanity, but unaffected by the guilt and corruption of sin. Hence, "the remedy to the imputation of Adam's sin comes by means of the righteousness of the Last Adam, whose obedience is imputed to all who believe in him." Moreover, "The work of the Last Adam involves not only forgiving sin *but also realizing the perfect obedience* that the First Adam never achieved in order to secure eternal life" (italics added).

What we see is that the 2018 and the 2019 WTS statements both focus on a *legal* imputation of the righteousness of Christ. This is where Torrance would require Crowe and WTS to go further. Much of the WTS statement is excellent. It is rich in biblical insights. It protects the biblical understanding of grace. However, it operates with what Torrance would regard as an agency model. Jesus is the agent who, in his life, death, and resurrection, does what is necessary through being our legal *alter ego*, and his achievements are transferred to us by legal imputation. Torrance wanted more. For Torrance, what Christ did for our salvation was accomplished not simply *legally by means of his agency*, but *in his person as part of his ontological identity*. And, in terms of the application of that salvation to sinners, what Christ did in his life, death, and resurrection, affected not just their *legal status* before God, but affected the *very nature of their being*. His obedience was not simply *in place* of theirs; but his obedience truly *became* theirs.

⸺

Harnack saw Jesus as Teacher who taught salvation. Reformed theology has tended to present Jesus as Agent who achieved salvation. Both are correct in their own way. But what Torrance sought was a theology in which Jesus is more than teacher or agent. He wanted a theology in which Jesus is salvation in his person, and in which incarnation and atonement become as one in the person of Jesus Christ. Jesus is not merely an agent fulfilling a task, however holy that task may be. He is in himself the task accomplished.

To advance the argument we turn to 2 Corinthians 5:21: *"God made him who had no sin, to be sin for us, so that in him we might become the righteousness of God."* In the following chapters it will be important to bear in mind that Paul's phrase: "[*We*] *become the righteousness of God"* is in direct counterpoint to the connected phrase, "[*Christ was made*] *to be sin for us.*"[42] What this means is that if one is understood simply as a legal imputation, so may be the other. But, if one points to an ontological imputation, so must be the other. Our argument will be that the text expresses a theology which demands more than a forensic/legal understanding. Instead, the text, and the core theology lying behind it, presupposes that on the cross Christ was truly *made* sin, and that Christ was more than just the legally accountable bearer of the guilt of sin. Similarly, in Christ, sinners are truly *made* righteous, and are not merely reckoned as such legally. These arguments take us to the heart of Torrance's incarnationally centered understanding of atonement.

---

42. Among other references, Torrance, *Atonement*, 151, 367, bring out the importance of 2 Corinthians 5:21.

— *Chapter 11* —

# Jesus as Savior
## *Calvary*

DURING THE SECOND HALF of the twentieth century, William (Willie) Still was one of the Church of Scotland's most prominent advocates of Westminster and Puritan theology, applying it to great effect at Gilcomston South Church, Aberdeen.[1] It was through his influence that James Philip came to a deep-rooted Christian faith; and, during Still's ministry, Gilcomston became the church of choice for many students, with scores of men and women from the congregation called into full-time Christian service both at home and abroad. Coming from a Salvation Army background, Willie Still hesitated before settling on Westminster Calvinism as the theological school which, for him, best represented biblical Reformed theology. He was a bible expositor *par excellence.* He had a creative ability to think outside the box. And, in his prime, he was in high demand as a conference speaker. One year, he was invited to address students at the Netherhall Christian Center near Largs in Ayrshire. As the students crowded in for a session, they saw a large stack of books piled up beside the speaker. That morning, Willie Still was going to explore 2 Corinthians 5:21: *"God made him who had no sin, to be sin for us, so that in him we might become the righteousness of God."*

Willie Still was well aware that this Pauline text is one of the most extraordinary in the whole of Scripture, and the books on the table represented some of the commentaries which he had consulted. He explained to the students that, in his opinion, all of these commentaries

---

1. Cf. Ferguson, "William Still," 797.

were unsatisfactory, and for a specific reason. It was because of what their authors had written about that critical verse. Many of the scholars were highly respected conservative-evangelical academics. Yet, despite their standing, Willie Still felt they were frightened to say what the verse really meant. He later wrote, "I sensed we all were afraid of what we saw."[2] He continued, "We had to ask God to give us grace to face the awfulness, and yet the wonder and the glory of the truth."

He emphasized to the students that the crucial part of the verse is the statement: *"God made him who had no sin to be sin for us,"* especially the phrase, *"to be sin for us."* He had, in fact, consulted many more commentaries than the ones displayed on the table. He explained that these were the tried and tested works which he used and relied upon, week in, week out. But, when he studied his favorite scholars on what Paul meant, he was left dissatisfied. He declared, "Not one of these scholars would stomach what Paul is obviously teaching: that Christ was made *sin* [actual sin] for us." In Still's judgment, all of them stopped short of accepting what Paul intended. It was as if they were saying: "This cannot be true," "We cannot accept this, as it is on the surface," "It is impossible," "It is too contradictory." But Willie Still felt he had to read Paul's words with what appeared to be their simple, direct, meaning. So he made his own translation, carefully crafting it to avoid implying that Jesus himself sinned. His rendering was that Jesus was made to become the *"thing of sin"* itself. He knew this was flying in the face of much scholarly opinion. All the same, he was convinced that it was a correct translation, and an unavoidable rendering of the original Greek. And, if Scripture were to be taken at face value, there had to be acceptance it actually states that Christ was *"made sin"* or *"made to become sin."* What must not be done is to water down this remarkable verse. Jesus was *made to become sin*. Or, as in his translation, *"Jesus was made to become the thing of sin itself."*

Karl Barth thought likewise. In the section of his *Church Dogmatics* which we were required to summarize during our second year at New College, Barth wrote: "All earlier theology, up to and including the Reformers and their successors, exercised at this point a very understandable reserve, calculated to dilute the offence, but also to weaken the high positive meaning of passages like 2 Corinthians 5:21, Galatians 3:13."[3] Tom Torrance was also aware that what the apostle wrote was

2. Still, *Collected Writings of William Still*, 135.
3. Barth, *CD* I/2, 153.

extraordinary and astonishing. Torrance stated: "We can only be aghast at this: nor have we any adequate categories in which to construe it."[4] And, in the *Atonement* lectures, in a section involving a brief exegesis of 2 Cor 5:21 alongside other key passages, Torrance argued that the full force of the verse had been diluted after the Council of Nicaea, as the church sought to preserve the sinlessness of Christ.[5]

If Willie Still, Karl Barth, and Tom Torrance were correct, then their interpretation of the first part of 2 Cor 5:21 has immense consequences for the interpretation of the second part. This is because the two parts mirror one another. The first part is: "*God made him who had no sin to be sin for us.*" The second part is: "*So that in him we might become the righteousness of God.*" Paul linked Christ taking our sin, with us becoming the righteousness of God. And, crucially, the manner in which Christ was made, "*to be sin*" for us, mirrors the manner in which "*we become the righteousness of God.*" As Bengel—a commentator much used by Spurgeon—wrote: "He was made sin *in the same way* as we are made righteousness. Who would have dared to speak thus, if Paul had not led the way?"[6]

## Augustine's Exegetical Time-Bomb

What Willie Still found, as he prepared for the students at Netherhall, was that the vast majority of biblical scholars were nervous of allowing the full force of Paul's words. They avoided a literal rendering. But why such reluctance? An important clue comes in Alfred Plummer's detailed and influential commentary on Second Corinthians, which appeared in 1915 in the *International Critical Commentary* series. In an important excursus, Plummer identified Augustine of Hippo's interpretation of 2 Cor 5:21 as being hugely influential on the interpretation of this verse.[7]

---

4. Torrance, *Atonement*, 126.

5. Torrance, *Atonement*, 147–49.

6. Bengel, *Gnomon of the New Testament*, 385 (italics added). Philip, *Westminster Confession of Faith*, 36, recognized that our sin was imputed to Christ *in the same way* as his righteousness was imputed to us: "The conclusion we are meant to draw is that the reckoning to us of what was his—his righteousness, his acceptability to God—is as real as was the reckoning to him of what was ours—our guilt and all that that entailed, that brought him in such agony to the cross."

7. Plummer, *International Critical Commentary on II Corinthians*. Though Plummer did not reference specific Augustinian writings, see Augustine's *Enchiridion* 42; *Reply to Faustus the Manichean* 14; *Anti-Pelagian Works On Forgiveness* 1.44; 2.37; *A Treatise Against Two Letters of the Pelagians* 3.16; *Sermon* 84; *Tractate* 41, Ch. 8;

Plummer noted that Augustine found it inconceivable that Paul meant what he seemed to say. Therefore, Paul's words had to be interpreted otherwise. And Plummer pointed out that Augustine was particularly uncomfortable with the idea that (even on the cross) Jesus, *was made sin* or, *became sin*. Plummer showed that Augustine tried to solve this difficulty by suggesting two alternative options, each based on varying meanings of *hamartia*, the Greek term for "sin" which Paul employs in 2 Cor 5:21. Augustine proposed that the statement, Jesus was *made sin* (made *hamartia*), might be interpreted in the following ways:

1. Augustine's first suggestion was that the term *sin* (*hamartia*) simply means "sin-offering." This suggestion lies behind a footnote in some editions of the New International Version.[8] However, is it valid to render *hamartia* as "sin-offering" in this context? We discuss this below.

2. Augustine's second suggestion was that the term *sin* (*hamartia*) may refer to "human nature as being liable to suffering and death" which are the penalties of sin. In other words, Paul never meant to imply that Jesus literally had been made *sin*; he only meant to teach that Jesus endured all the *consequences* of sin, including death and suffering. This also is discussed below.

In both options Augustine tried to avoid what he regarded as a huge problem. Like others after him, Augustine worried lest he might interpret the verse in a way which compromised the sinlessness of Jesus Christ. Moreover, Augustine's pre-Christian background in Neo-Platonism and Manichaeism made it difficult for him to accept that the divine Word could become sin. It was hard enough for a former Neo-Platonist to accept that the divine Word could become flesh and part of the material world. But, to go further, and to entertain the possibility that the divine Word might become sin itself, was too much. Augustine was far more at ease with the notion of Jesus becoming a sin-offering, or with the notion of Jesus suffering the consequences of sin. Hence, Augustine avoided studiously the idea that Jesus *became* sin, or was *made* sin. And it was this Augustinian interpretation which influenced a host of interpreters after him, including Thomas Aquinas, John Calvin, and John Owen.

---

*Exposition of Psalm 119*, etc. See also Appendix 4.

8. Shedd, *Dogmatic Theology*, 717, similarly inserted the words "sin offering" when quoting 2 Corinthians 5:21.

In Appendix 4 we survey some of the history of the exegesis of 2 Cor 5:21. It is this exegetical tradition which helps to explain why Willie Still found so many commentators reluctant to allow the verse to say what he thought it really said.

What of Augustine's explanations? Are they valid? Was the verse simply referring to Jesus becoming a sin offering? Or was the verse simply teaching that Jesus endured the consequences of sin? Few would dispute that both these concepts are true in themselves. Jesus *was* a sin-offering. Jesus *did* suffer the consequences of sin in our place. But, do either of these options fully represent what Paul taught in 2 Cor 5:21? On this issue, Augustine's reasoning was dissected by Plummer.

First, Plummer pointed out that the term *hamartia*, in Paul's phrase, "*he was made sin,*" cannot mean sin-offering. This is because *hamartia* does not mean sin-offering anywhere else in the New Testament.[9] More specifically, in 2 Cor 5:21 *hamartia* is used by Paul in the immediately preceding phrase to mean *sin,* simpliciter. The preceding phrase is, "*who had no sin (hamartia)*"; and, in that phrase, *sin-offering* cannot be substituted for *sin*. Plummer argued that Paul would not use the same term (*hamartia*) in such close juxtaposition but with two different meanings. Therefore, in order to have consistency within the narrow confines of the verse, *hamartia* has to be translated the same way both times. This can only be done if it is translated as *sin,* simpliciter.

Second, Plummer argued that neither can *hamartia* represent Augustine's second option: of human nature in general suffering the consequences of sin. Here, Plummer's reasoning paralleled his arguments concerning the first option. Again, the fact that *hamartia* is used by Paul in the immediately preceding phrase to mean *sin,* plain and simple, is conclusive.[10]

For Plummer, it was the phrase, "*who had no sin*" which supplies the context in which *hamartia* is to be understood for the entire verse. Thus the phrase, "*was made sin*" (*hamartia epoiesen*) must be taken to say exactly what it seems to say: namely, that Jesus was *made sin for us,* or *became sin for us,* upon the Cross. On this basis Plummer argued that we have to face up to the plain meaning of the Apostle's strong words.

---

9. For Plummer, the Septuagint has only one instance where *hamartia* is used with that meaning: Lev 4:25, 29.

10. Augustine's line was adopted by Arndt and Gingrich, *Greek-English Lexicon of the New Testament and Other Early Christian Literature*. See Appendix 4.

## Jesus as Savior

Significantly, among twentieth-century exegetes of the text Plummer's analysis has found considerable support.[11] The redoubtable Gerhard Kittel agreed with him.[12] Murray Harris, a modern scholar with impeccable conservative-evangelical credentials—having been warden of Tyndale House at Cambridge, and having gained his PhD from the University of Manchester studying under F. F. Bruce—moved in the same direction.[13] R. V. G. Tasker, writing in the conservative-evangelical Tyndale series of commentaries, came to an identical conclusion, noting that it is quite insufficient to regard the term *hamartia* in 2 Cor 5:21 as equivalent to sin-offering, since this use is not found in the New Testament. Tasker concluded that Paul's words must mean that the sinless Jesus was *made sin* by being condemned.[14]

One thing is clear. If the Greek phrase *hamartia epoiesen* did not have such radical theological implications for the person of Jesus Christ, then, on a purely linguistic basis, it would be translated with little hesitation as, *"he was made sin."* And, for Plummer, plus an increasing number of scholars, the phrase must be allowed to say exactly what it seems to say. It says that, on the cross, Jesus was *made sin for us,* or *became sin for us.* Summing up, at the close of his analysis, Plummer concluded, "We must face the plain meaning of the Apostle's strong words. In some sense which we cannot fathom, God is said to have identified Christ with man's sin, in order that man might be identified with God's own righteousness."[15] Plummer's approach to 2 Cor 5:21 is now the norm in modern biblical studies. And conservative-evangelical biblical scholarship has, by and large, adopted the radical meaning of Paul's words. But, has conservative-evangelical systematic theology kept pace?

### Symbol and Reality at the Cross of Calvary

The exegesis of 2 Cor 5:21 has major theological consequences. If Plummer, and the bulk of modern scholarship, is correct, then Jesus became much more than a sin-offering. That is not to deny that Jesus was a

---

11. Plummer, *International Critical Commentary on 2 Corinthians*, 187.

12. Kittel and Friedrich, *Theological Dictionary of the New Testament*, 295–97, 311–12 (see Appendix 4).

13. Harris, *Second Epistle to the Corinthians*, 454 (see Appendix 4).

14. Tasker, *Commentary on 2 Corinthians*, 90.

15. Plummer, *International Critical Commentary on 2 Corinthians*, 187 (italics added).

sin-offering. He indeed became all that a sin-offering was; but he transcended the essentially *symbolic* nature of a sin-offering, by becoming the *reality* to which traditional sin-offerings had but pointed. Symbols were for the Old Testament. Reality is for the New Testament. If Jesus were only a symbol, then he was on a par with an Old Testament sacrifice. Granted, he would be so as part of Adam's race, and not as an animal such as a goat or bull. Nevertheless, he would still be only *symbol* and not *reality*.

The fundamental distinction between the temple altar and the cross of Calvary, is that one was symbolic and the other was actuality. On the cross, Jesus became more than a symbol of sin. He became the reality of the "*thing of sin*" itself. In the Old Testament sin was placed symbolically on the sacrificial animal. But, at Calvary, reality supplanted the symbolic. Merely replacing an old symbol with a new symbol would leave humanity at the same place. But, in Jesus Christ, God himself took our real, actual, sin into himself and dealt with it there. Moreover, it was not just the guilt of sin which Jesus carried. It was indeed that, yet much more than that. At Calvary, Jesus became the actuality and the reality of what the Old Testament liturgy pointed to.[16] As Torrance expressed it, "In the New Testament it is no more with symbolical actions that we are concerned."[17] On the cross, Jesus *became* both sin and guilt in reality. He was *made sin* for us. And, he became an offering for sin, not by becoming a better symbol, or by becoming a better signpost, but by becoming the thing of sin itself. Like a sponge absorbs water, so, on the cross, Jesus absorbed into himself the sin of all humanity of all the ages. God took into himself all that is unrighteous. And God endured, within himself, the consequences of his own rejection of that evil on our behalf.

As the sinless lamb of God Jesus had no sin of his own; but, on the cross he was made sin. This was what Willie Still tried to convey in his translation of 2 Cor 5:21: "*Jesus became the thing of sin itself.*" Hence, Jesus suffered the penalty of sin: but not simply the penalty. And, Jesus became a sin-offering: but not simply a sin-offering. And, Jesus legally

---

16. Cf. Torrance, *Atonement*, 19: "We cannot emphasize enough then that the sacrificial and liturgical acts were regarded as *witness* and only witness to God's own action and appointment. The real agent in the Old Testament liturgy is God himself. God is not acted upon by means of liturgical sacrifice. Liturgical sacrifice rests upon God's self-revelation and answers as cultic sign to God's own word and action, which is the thing signified."

17. Torrance, *Atonement*, 83.

and forensically identified with human guilt: but not simply legally and forensically. He was all of these things: but he was also so much more. What the biblical text demands is recognition that on the cross he was *made sin*. And, it is this being *"made sin,"* and becoming the *"thing of sin itself,"* which is the true reality lying behind penal substitutionary atonement. In point of fact, it is penal substitutionary atonement unleashed in its rawest and most dreadful form. On the cross there was no symbolic substitution: but an actual substitution. On the cross there was no symbol of sin: but actual sin. And so, Jesus became the thing of sin itself in our place, and suffered the penalty of being so. On the cross Christ truly became what we are. Moreover, he became this whilst also being totally exposed to the unadulterated purity of the holiness of God, thus inevitably enduring the terrible consequence. This is penal substitutionary atonement in outrageous and shocking reality.[18]

There is another important point. It was not an innocent incarnate Son who suffered the wrath of God against sin. This is because although God is undeniably just if he pours out his wrath on *sin*, he is equally undeniably unjust if he pours it out on innocence. Thus the judgment of God at Calvary was directed towards unrighteousness, not towards purity. Hence, if God did pour out his wrath and judgment on Christ, as indeed he did, then Christ had become sin and unrighteousness, otherwise the Judge of all the earth did not act justly. Atonement did not take place because a sinless one suffered the wrath of God. Rather, atonement took place because the sinless one became sin: or, as Calvin expressed it, Christ "suffered death not because of innocence but because of sin" and "took our place and thus became a sinner and subject to the curse."[19] It was because of this being made sin that Christ suffered the wrath of God. On the Day of Atonement, under the Old Testament ritual, the goat was

---

18. Penal substitution and the wrath of God featured in Torrance's writing, though he pulled back from phrases such as, "God punished Jesus on the cross," because of some crude theology which had been built on such expressions. And, for Torrance, God's reaction to Christ becoming sin involved more than God distancing himself from such an unholy reality. Torrance alluded to God's active opposition, and to the wrath of God is unleashed on sin (cf. *Atonement*, 153–54). He rejected the idea that God has no personal anger towards sin or sinners, and that any negative consequences of sin are more an inevitable misfortune of having chosen a path in opposition to God, rather than a strong response by God himself. Torrance emphasized that not only is man in opposition to God, but God is in opposition to man. This was why atonement was necessary. And atonement involved the active outworking of the wrath of God.

19. Cf. Calvin, *Institutes* 2.16.5. Also, Calvin, *Commentary on Galatians*, 3.13.

regarded as having *become* the sin of the people; and, precisely because it had *become* the sin of the people, it suffered the exclusion from God which such sin triggers. But, significantly, without there being a becoming at some point, the symbolism loses its meaning. And, what we have in Jesus is that "some point." With Jesus, all that was previously merely symbolic became reality. Hence, he who was pure and spotless in himself, became sinner in order to bear the wrath of God in our place.[20] As Torrance emphasized, "God will not pardon apart from judgment and sacrificial expiation."[21]

As already mentioned, an important aspect of any exegesis of 2 Cor 5:21 is the connection between the two major parts of the verse. The first part is: "*God made him who had no sin, to be sin for us.*" The second part is: "*So that in him we might become the righteousness of God.*"[22] And the words "so that" imply that Jesus "becoming sin" is the *cause* of us "becoming the righteousness of God." Hence, there is a consequential symmetry in Paul's argument. If Jesus "being made sin" has to be interpreted as something which he *became* (ontologically), and not just something which he *identified with* (legally), then similar reason must be applied to our "becoming the righteousness of God." Thus, the righteousness of God is not to be understood simply in terms of it being reckoned legally to us. Much more is involved. Clearly then, no merely legal arrangement takes place at the cross on either side of the Pauline equation. Ontological realities are established both in Christ and in us. On the one hand, Jesus is made sin. On the other hand, sinners become the righteousness of God. Consequently, sinners are both *declared* to be righteous, and are *made* to be righteous. Not one without the other. Again, they can only be *declared* righteous precisely because, in Christ, they have been *made* righteous. Thus, Jesus' role in salvation consists not simply in being an agent of recompense or satisfaction, far less in being only a symbol. Instead, Christ's role lies in the very being of his person having become the

---

20. Cf. Torrance, *Atonement*, 40–42: "[In the OT liturgy] God atones only on the ground of the fulfilment of his righteousness in judgment upon the sin . . . Nowhere is there any suggestion that God will pardon or redeem apart from judgment. Therefore, God himself must 'provide the lamb,' as it were." That redemption involves Christ in an act of expiation, Torrance made clear in several passages, especially in his application of the OT *kipper* notion of redemption to Christ: e.g. Torrance, *Atonement*, 52–53.

21. Torrance, *Atonement*, 42.

22. This is clear in the Greek text. The English text reverses the order of the phrases.

act of salvation itself.²³ Hence, the underlying reality which enables God as the great Law-giver to make a forensic/legal declaration of innocence concerning a justified sinner, is the reality of the ontological exchange which took place in Jesus Christ.

On the cross Jesus was not pretending to carry the sin of the world. Nor was he a mere symbol of sin. Nor was sin reckoned to him in a purely forensic/legal manner. If any of these told the whole story then, by the same token, his righteousness would not truly have become ours, and what happened at Calvary would be insufficient for salvation. Sinners need Jesus' actual righteousness to truly become their righteousness. What we have at the cross of Calvary are ontological realities, not symbolisms. God did not treat Jesus *as if* he carried our sin. God cannot forgive us *as if* we carry his righteousness. That would be artificial. Instead, Jesus took our sin in reality. We receive his righteousness in reality. That such a Glorious Exchange can occur, is impossible to comprehend. Thankfully, it is possible for God, though at great cost.

## "He Is Our Redemption"

Torrance was well aware that a major reason why theologians, through the centuries, were reluctant to accept the brutal directness of Paul's teaching, that Jesus was "*made sin*" for us, was the fear that somehow this might compromise the personal sinlessness of Jesus Christ.[24] In face of this fear, it has taken the unswerving candor of modern biblical scholarship to face up to the full meaning of the apostle's words. Critically, the sin which Jesus became on the cross, was not his, but ours. Because he had no sin of his own, he was the sinless lamb of God, able to absorb our sin into himself and make atonement. And yet, in taking that sin of ours into himself, and in becoming that sin of ours, our sin truly became his sin. As such, he was able to take the wrath and judgment of God upon himself for us. This is the miracle of Calvary.

23. Cf. Torrance, *Preaching Christ Today*, 25: "[Think of] Paul's wonderful statement to the Corinthians: 'You know the grace of our Lord Jesus Christ, that though he was rich, yet for your sakes became poor, that you through his poverty might be rich' (2 Cor. 8:9). That is what the early Church and John Calvin called 'the blessed exchange' or 'the wondrous exchange,' and even the Roman Missal calls *mirabile commercium*. This is in fact the New Testament doctrine of *katallage*, for it is an *atoning and reconciling exchange*, in which what is ours is displaced by Christ who substitute himself in our place and yet is restored in a new way to us."

24. Torrance, *Incarnation*, 199. Cf. Torrance, *Atonement*, 150.

In 2 Cor 5:21, Paul implies that, in union with Christ, sinners actually *become* the righteousness of God. Hence, Jesus is the Gospel because he is the Gospel in his very being.[25] He is not simply teacher who communicates the Gospel through his speech. Nor is he simply agent who achieves the Gospel through his actions. In other words, he is not just the means of which the Gospel is the end. Instead, he is himself the end in his own being. And Paul alludes to this notion, that Christ is in his own person that which he accomplishes, when he states that Christ Jesus, "has become for us wisdom from God, that is, our righteousness, holiness, and redemption" (1 Cor 1:30). Christ Jesus *is* our wisdom. He *is* our righteousness. He *is* our holiness. He *is* our redemption. In other words, he *is* what he *accomplishes*. In his own being, he is what sinners need to be: and, through union with him, he is what sinners now become: namely, the righteousness of God.

On the cross Jesus cried out in anguish, "My God, my God, why have you forsaken me?" (Matt 27:46), because, in becoming the thing of sin itself he bore the consequences which that brought. But also, in him, through the Glorious Exchange, sinners become the righteousness of God.[26] And so, Jesus Christ, incarnate, crucified, risen and ascended, became in his very being our salvation. In this way, Jesus is the Gospel.

In continuity with this, Torrance pointed out that the saving work of Christ belongs to the ontological structure of the Mediator himself.[27] Moreover, and in reciprocal fashion, the ontological structure of the Mediator belongs to his saving work. And so, for Torrance, the event of incarnation could never be just a preparatory platform for the atonement. Instead, the incarnation is itself atoning reality, in which being and

---

25. Cf. Torrance, *Atonement*, 73: "We are not saved by the atoning death of Christ, far less by liturgical action, but by Christ himself who in his own person made atonement for us." In other words, it is Christ himself, through who he is and what he did, together, who is our salvation.

26. Sin involves real separation between God and humanity. When Jesus was made sin for us then that inevitably and automatically involved separation from the Father. Leon Morris: "We must connect Mark 14:36 (the cup of suffering) with the cry of dereliction on the Cross ('My God! My God! Why have You forsaken Me?') which makes the veritable descent into hell of the sinless Son of God—his descent into the Hell of utter separation from the Father, with 2 Corinthians 5:21 or Colossians 3:13" (Morris, *Cross in the New Testament*, 47). Or, as James Denney expressed it: Jesus "becoming sin" on the Cross; Jesus' cry of forsakenness on the Cross; and Jesus' experience of Hell (understanding Hell as utter separation from God), all come together when Jesus Christ, by God's appointment, dies the sinner's death (Denny, *Studies in Theology*, 112).

27. Torrance, *Space, Time and Resurrection*, 50.

act, form and content, person and work, are as one. Thus, atonement is rooted in the person of Christ. And the person of Christ is rooted in atonement. Consequently, as Torrance emphasized, the atonement has an ontological dimension which an exclusively forensic/legal interpretation falls short of expressing.

At this point choice of words is important. As we have stressed throughout, there is an irreplaceable forensic/legal aspect to the atonement. That is undeniable, and Torrance himself accepted that the atonement has forensic/legal characteristics. That must be the case, since the desired outcome of atonement is for the divine Judge to declare that sinners are now reckoned to be righteous in his sight. But these forensic/legal features require to be placed within a larger, and a more fundamental, setting. The justification of the sinner involves not only a declaration by God, but also an act of *full* and *radical* substitutionary atonement, a point which Torrance made specifically in reference to 2 Cor 5:12.[28] The legal/forensic declaration is the desired outcome of Calvary. But what makes such a declaration at all possible is the Glorious Exchange, something which affects the very ontology of Jesus Christ and of redeemed sinners.

Torrance knew why Reformed Dogmatics was hesitant about employing the phrase '*made righteous.*' And he acknowledged that the forensic/legal model was adopted by the Reformers for a very important reason. It was to avoid the disastrous pitfalls connected with the medieval notion of an infused righteousness.[29] What Torrance insisted was that God deals with ontological realities which have been forged at great cost in the person of Christ Himself. Jesus is the Gospel, precisely because something ontological happened,

> Justification becomes not only the non-imputation of sins, but the clothing of the sinner with the righteousness of Christ. Nevertheless, that would still be empty and unreal, merely a judicial transaction, unless the doctrine of justification bears in its heart a relation of real union with Christ ... We require an active relation to Christ as our righteousness. This is possible only through the resurrection—when we approach justification in this light we can see that it is a creative event in which our regeneration or renewal is already included within it.[30]

---

28. Torrance, *Atonement*, 119.
29. Cf. Torrance, *Atonement*, 224.
30. Torrance, *Space, Time and Resurrection*, 63.

Sinners are made righteous in union with Jesus Christ. They are not only declared righteous. And, on the same theme of the necessity of an ontological change as the basis for justification, Torrance strengthened his position when he wrote, "A purely forensic doctrine of justification bypasses the resurrection, and is empty without an active sharing in Christ's righteousness."[31] Behind all of this lay Torrance's conviction that, at the heart of theology, there is a coherent, unified, reality which the theologian seeks to uncover. Incarnation and atonement are one act of grace, not two.

Jesus does not simply enable the Gospel to happen, as an agent in a process (even a divine agent). Instead, Jesus *is* the Gospel in his own being. Hence, what emerges in Torrance's theology is a situation in which, when we drill down deep into Calvary, and into the meaning of Christ being made sin, we find we are at Bethlehem. And this is because, what Jesus does at Calvary in being "made sin" affects the very constitution of the nature of his person as the incarnate Son of God.

---

31. Torrance, *Atonement*, 224.

— *Chapter 12* —

# Jesus as Savior
## *Bethlehem*

ALONG WITH THE BROTHERS Basil of Caesarea and Gregory of Nyssa, Gregory of Nazianzus was one of the leading Christian thinkers of the fourth century. Collectively, the three became known as the Cappadocian Fathers, and all were formidable theologians. Nazianzus' reputation was such, that, although he belonged to the Greek Church, he has been accounted a saint in both Eastern and Western Christianity. Moreover, he is one of only three scholars in the Orthodox church to be accorded the official title of *Theologian*; the others being John the Gospel Evangelist, and the tenth-century Symeon the New Theologian.

Nazianzus worked in the wake of the 325 Council of Nicaea, influencing trinitarian theology in both East and West. But it is his work on the nature of Christ's incarnation which concerns us most. In a letter to the priest Cledonius, Nazianzus used the phrase: "That which [Christ] has not assumed he has not redeemed." Or, more literally: "That which he has not assumed he has not healed." History has abbreviated this to the concise aphorism: *"The Unassumed is the Unredeemed."* The importance of this statement by Nazianzus for Torrance's theology was such that it inspired one of the questions in our 1974, Dogmatics II, Autumn Term examination: *"Explain and comment: 'For that which he has not assumed, he has not healed; but that which is united to his Godhead is also saved.'"*

In writing to Cledonius, Nazianzus' aim was to protect Christians from heretical teachers such as Apollinarius, who denied that Jesus had a human soul or human mind. The crux of Nazianzus' argument was: because the whole of our humanity fell in Adam, then the whole of our humanity needs to be saved in Christ. Consequently, if any part of our humanity were not assumed by Christ in the incarnation, then it could not be healed by him in salvation:

> If anyone has put his trust in him as a man without a human mind, he is really bereft of mind, and quite unworthy of salvation. *For that which he has not assumed he has not healed; but that which is united to his Godhead is also saved.* If only half Adam fell, then that which Christ assumes and saves may be half also; but if the whole of his nature fell, it must be united to the whole nature of him that was begotten, and so be saved as a whole. Let them not, then, begrudge us our complete salvation, or clothe the Savior only with bones and nerves and the portraiture of humanity.[1]

Picking up on this, Torrance argued, passionately and strongly, that the principle, "*The Unassumed is the Unredeemed*," means that in the incarnation Christ assumed a *fallen* humanity rather than a *perfect* humanity. Torrance's argument was: if Christ is to save us, then he must become what we actually are, which is fallen humanity. Consequently, Christ assumed Adam's fallen and broken humanity, rather than Adam's pre-fallen and perfect humanity. Strictly speaking, Nazianzus did not state explicitly that Jesus needed to assume a *fallen* human mind and a *fallen* human soul. Nazianzus simply argued that Jesus needed to assume humanity in all of its component parts. However, Torrance, along with others, has argued that Christ's assumption of *fallen* human nature is a necessary implication of Nazianzus' thinking. This issue was discussed in detail by Jason Radcliff in a paper presented to the Second Firbush Conference in April, 2011.[2]

Did Torrance read more into Nazianzus than Nazianzus intended, especially with regard to the assumption of fallen humanity? Radcliff suggested that Torrance may indeed have been guilty of pushing the phrase further than Nazianzus envisaged. Nevertheless, whether Torrance's interpretation of Nazianzus was correct or not, what is not in dispute is that this was how Torrance construed the implications of Nazianzus' expression, and adopted them as his own. Hence, for Torrance himself, "*The Unassumed is the Unredeemed*" meant that Christ must become *fallen* humanity

---

1. Gregory of Nazianzus, *Ep.* 101, "To Cledonius the Priest Against Apollinarius" (italics added).

2. Jason Radcliff, "Vicarious Humanity in the Early Fathers"; Firbush, April, 2011. Cf. Chiarot, *Unassumed Is the Unhealed*.

in order to reach down to where humanity actually is. And that step was necessary for two substantial reasons. First, only when the Son of God became what we actually are in our fallenness—as opposed to what we were created to be in our pre-fallen perfection—could he bear the wrath of God in our place. Second, only when he truly became part of Adam's race under the curse, could he become the bridge between a holy God and a sinful humanity. In order to span a ravine any serviceable bridge has to be rooted into each side of the chasm. Hence, the Mediator not only had to be God and man, but had to be God and *fallen* man (not *abstract* man) because it is in that state of fallenness that humankind now exists.[3]

A bridge must be firmly connected to both sides of any chasm which it spans. And, in Christ, the gulf between God and humanity has been crossed from God's side of the chasm. It is uncrossable for man. But, God became Emmanuel, God with us (Isa 7:14; Matt 1:23). Hence, the otherwise impossible gulf between God and sinful humanity was overcome when God, in Christ, took our flesh in Mary's womb and was born at Bethlehem. Critically, it was because of pure grace, and not because God was in any way prompted, or acted upon, by human merit or human worthiness, that he took the initiative and bridged the gap. He came to where we are. And the astounding thing is that the place where we are, the place to which God had to come in Christ, is a place where we exist in our fallenness. Hence, the gap was only bridged when God, in Christ, made contact with humanity in its state of sin. In Torrance's mind this was axiomatic: in order to come to where we are, God must come to where sinful humanity exists.

In Torrance's thinking, the incarnation necessarily involved Jesus assuming the humanity common to men and women after the Fall, and not a humanity untouched by the Fall. Yet, doing so without any sin of his own. The core logic behind Torrance's interpretation of Nazianzus was simple. If the incarnation is necessary for atonement, and if atonement involves more than simply a forensic/legal process, then, in his incarnation, Christ had to take to himself the very humanity which needs

---

3. The implication of both the Old and the New Testaments is that sin brought a separation between God and humanity which only a mediator can bridge. An infinite qualitative gap exists between God and humanity; and for two main reasons. First: God is infinite and eternal, humanity is finite and created. Second: God is pure, humanity is impure; God is righteous, humanity is unrighteous; God is holy, humanity is unholy. Thus, separation is not only because of the finitude of human existence or intellect, but because of a moral and spiritual alienation from God himself.

salvation, and not an idealized humanity which is not the actual humanity which sinful men and women share.

This introduces an intriguing theological ambiguity. If Christ, the Son of God, assumed sinful humanity in becoming Son of Man, then the "moment" (as it were) in which he became what we are (the moment in which his divinity and humanity were conjoined) was also a "moment" in which he automatically and immediately became a man judged and rejected. Thus, under Torrance's interpretation, the Son of God became humanity under judgment, and humanity suffering the wrath of God, as "soon as" his conception by the Holy Spirit took place in the womb of Mary. Just as, at the very instant when red-hot metal touches water a volatile reaction takes place, so also, when the Son of God assumed fallen humanity, then that "touching" resulted instantaneously and immediately in that fallen humanity being judged and rejected by the all-consuming purity and holiness of the living God.

What are the implications? Does it mean that Jesus bore our sin in Mary's womb? If so, where does the cross of Calvary fit in? Does Mary's womb displace the cross? These, and similar, questions have been posed by a number of Reformed theologians. As such, they signal the disquiet which they have with Torrance. At Firbush, in November 2010, Andrew McGowan raised these very issues. Does Torrance's emphasis on atonement taking place in the person of Christ result in Bethlehem replacing Calvary? Does it, however unintentionally, downgrade the importance of the cross? If the union of God and man in the person of Christ is the fundamental mechanism which effects atonement, what more is required than Jesus being conceived in the womb of Mary? What more is needed than God and (fallen) man coming together in the hypostatic union? But where do we find this in the Scriptures? Is not the clear New Testament emphasis an emphasis on the cross and the death of Christ? Is not that the central, vital, and definitive event of atonement? And, if that is the case, is Torrance's argument at best misleading and at worst heretical? Does it empty the cross of its power? These questions flag up important issues.

This is where Torrance's theology forces us into a reversal of conceptual thinking. And our suggested solution is that it is the one event of death and resurrection, judgment and victory, humiliation and exaltation, which in fact constitutes the person of Christ in the incarnation. Or, to put it another way: Calvary made Bethlehem possible, and it was the death and resurrection of Jesus which created the very possibility of his birth—not vice versa—though all come together as one dissoluble reality.

## Christ's Humanity: Torrance

Returning to our main argument, we note how Torrance taught that the Son of God took to himself our *fallen* humanity in the womb of Mary. And, for Torrance, the Son of God's assumption of our humanity in its corrupt state was central to his understanding of Christian faith. In Torrance's mind, it was through the union of that fallen humanity with his perfect divinity that the Son of God was able to bring the reconciling healing which humanity so desperately needs but is unable to achieve for itself. Torrance commented,

> Through his incarnation, the Son of God has made himself one with us as we are, and indeed made himself what we are, thereby not only making our nature his own but taking on himself our lost condition subject to condemnation and death; all in order that he might substitute himself in our place, discharge our debt, and offer himself in atoning sacrifice to God on our behalf. Since sin and its judgment have affected the actual nature of death as we experience it, Christ has made our death and fate his own; thereby taking on himself the penalty due to all in death, destroying the power of sin and its stronghold in death, and thus redeeming or rescuing us from its dominion.[4]

Several influences lay behind Torrance's view that in the incarnation Christ assumed Adam's fallen humanity rather than Adam's original pre-fallen humanity.

First, Torrance was committed to developing a theology in which form and content were not separated. He believed that there must be unitary realities at the heart of all sciences, including theological science. This was why he referred so often in his classroom lectures to Einstein's hunch that, in a proper scientific explanation of the natural world, it must be possible to integrate the diverse principles of Quantum Theory, Relativity Theory, and Gravitational Theory, into a general unified system. Torrance carried this instinct over into theology. He was convinced that fundamental theological concepts should be explicable in terms of one doctrine, and not two or more. Thus incarnation and atonement should

---

4. Torrance, *Trinitarian Faith*, 157.

be understood as an integrated, unified, doctrine. They are aspects of one act of divine grace, not of two.

Second, this was how Torrance read the Church Fathers, not only Nazianzus but also Athanasius and many others. Heavily influenced by the Fathers, Torrance was convinced that atonement was wrought ontologically, not simply forensically or legally, and he carried that conviction over into his whole understanding of theological thought.[5] It fed his unrelenting rejection of what he saw as a mechanical and instrumental understanding of the atonement in the theology of Scottish Calvinism, an issue which he discussed at length in the introduction to his book, *The School of Faith*.

Third, Torrance believed that he was being true to the truly best elements, not only of Patristic theology, but of the Reformed tradition. He was convinced that the high-Reformers taught that atonement was achieved in Christ's *person*, and not only through his *act* upon the cross. Admittedly, sometimes he saw agreement between his thinking and that of the original Reformers where others could not detect such harmony quite so clearly. Nevertheless, Torrance was convinced that his emphasis on the relationship between incarnation and atonement existed in the teaching of all of the great Doctors of the church from Athanasius to Calvin to Barth. Moreover, in his book on Scottish theology, he identified passages in Robert Bruce, Samuel Rutherford, Erskine of Linlathen, and others, which he saw as homologating this line of thinking.[6]

Fourth, Torrance believed his approach to be biblical. When our class at New College asked him for biblical references which might undergird the soteriological significance of the life and the person of Christ, he pointed us to Romans 5:10: *"For if, while we were God's enemies, we were reconciled to him through the death of his Son, how much more, having been reconciled, shall we be saved through his life."* He argued that, even if Paul were referring to Jesus' resurrection life rather than to the days which Jesus lived in Nazareth and Galilee, Paul was still making the point that it is the *life* (and hence the person) of Christ which is fundamental to

---

5. Cf. Torrance, *Divine and Contingent Order*, 138: "The fact that God has taken the way of becoming man in allying himself with contingent existence and thereby effecting the redemption of the creation from within its ontological foundations, immediately reinforces the unique place of man in the universe." Torrance made this statement when discussing men and women's scientific role within God's creation.

6. Torrance, *Scottish Theology*.

atonement. This lay behind what Torrance later wrote, "We are justified in the resurrection."[7]

Fifth, there was the not inconsiderable influence of Karl Barth. And it was to make his students familiar with Barth's thinking on this issue that Torrance made us summarize sections of Barth's *Church Dogmatics* I/2, the term before we were asked to write our essays on, "The Relationship between the Incarnation and the Atonement." He wanted us to study that section of Barth in detail, for in it Barth dealt with the question: what kind of humanity did the Son of God take to himself in the incarnation? What we discovered in our reading was that, for Barth, the incarnation not only involved the Son of God becoming *flesh*, but becoming *sinful flesh*. In other words, it was only when the Son of God became precisely what we are, that is to say *sinful humanity*, that he was able to make atonement. In the same section, Barth made an approving reference to the early nineteenth-century Scottish theologian Edward Irving. Irving had also argued that Christ assumed *fallen* humanity, not a *perfect* humanity: hence, it was humanity as affected by Adam's Fall which Christ took to himself, rather than the unspoiled humanity which Adam had known before the Fall. Many of Irving's contemporaries saw this as implying that Christ was not sinless, an implication which Irving denied. In 1833 a heresy trial was held, and Irving was deposed from ministry in the Church of Scotland. By this date, Irving had become pastor of an independent church in London, gaining a formidable reputation as a preacher, and had founded the denomination known afterwards as the Catholic Apostolic Church.[8] Barth's reference to Irving came within the context of his own extended argument that Christ assumed *fallen* humanity and not *perfect* humanity.[9] In support of this, Barth insisted that, in the New Testament, the word "flesh" in the phrase, "The Word became flesh" (John 1:14), refers consistently to humanity in its fallenness.

Was Torrance correct in his conviction that the Son of God assumed fallen humanity? We cannot engage in an exhaustive discussion of that question, but we can tease out some of the implications which arise if it were true. This is because, if true, we have a situation in which, not only was the Savior made sin in his death, but, in a very real sense, had already been

---

7. Torrance, *Atonement*, 215.

8. Needham, "Irving, Edward," 436–37. Cf. Dorries, *Edward Irving's Incarnational Christology*.

9. Barth, *CD* I/2, 154.

made sin in his conception and birth. This pinpoints a major stress-point between Torrance's theology and that of Westminster.

## Christ's Humanity: Westminster

Westminster theology has been uncomfortable with the notion that the Son of God assumed *fallen* humanity rather than *perfect* humanity. And, within Westminster Calvinism, the fact that suspect theologians such as Karl Barth, Tom Torrance, and the idiosyncratic Edward Irving, sanction this view does little to recommend it. Over against the Irving/Barth/Torrance position, traditional Westminster theology has taught that, in the womb of Mary, the Son of God assumed the humanity of Adam as that humanity was *before* the Fall. Moreover, atonement was accomplished precisely because, clothed in that perfect, unfallen, humanity, Christ fulfilled all the obligations of the Law in our place—as Adam should have fulfilled them—before suffering for our transgressions upon the cross as the sinless, pure, unspotted, unblemished, lamb of God, to whom our guilt could be imputed legally. Only because he was innocent and untouched by sin could the Glorious Exchange be effected. Only on these grounds could God declare the sinner to be justified.

Any discussion on the nature of Christ's humanity—*fallen* or *perfect*—plays out in similar fashion to discussions surrounding 2 Cor 5:21. This is unsurprising given that the statements, "He was made sin" (2 Cor 5:21), "He became a curse for us" (Gal 3:13), "The Word became flesh" (John 1:14), and: "The Unassumed is the Unredeemed" (Nazianzus), are so closely intertwined. In each instance, Torrance rejected a purely forensic/legal interpretation, convinced that the atonement must be established on ontological grounds, and must involve Christ's being-in-his-act and his act-in-his-being. And, within this approach, there is the recognition that, at every stage, Christ must truly "become sin" in order that we might truly "become the righteousness of God."

Conversely, in Westminster theology Christ's assumption of humanity fulfils a different purpose from that envisioned by Barth and Torrance. In Westminster theology the critical issue is of the lamb of God being prepared for sacrifice. That lamb of God had to be pure and spotless in the constitution of his person, as much as in the actions of his life, if that lamb could ever be offered as an expiatory sacrifice. Thus, purity of Christ's very being, as well as purity in his actual thoughts, words, deeds, love for God, and love for neighbor, was essential. Only absolute purity, in both the *nature of his person* as well as in the *living of his life*, could create the potential for him being an acceptable offering to the Father. From this standpoint, the notion of Christ assuming *fallen* humanity strikes at the very heart of what must happen on the cross.

The two approaches, as outlined above, stem from two ways of envisioning the act of atonement. (a) In Torrance's theology, God in Christ soaks the sin of humanity into himself as a sponge soaks up filthy water. He takes it into his very being, and, in so doing, in that close contact, burns it out under his terrible wrath of judgment. And so, when human sinfulness is brought into direct contact with divine holiness within the person of Christ himself in the hypostatic union, then Christ in his very being becomes the wrath-bearer. (b) Contrariwise, in Westminster theology, atonement is made through a compensatory process in which Christ, existing apart from sin, but yet carrying the penalty of sin, judicially bears the wrath of God in our place.

In our view, what the "becoming sin" of 2 Cor 5:21 points to, is closer to the former than to the latter. Jesus *is* what he *does* (1 Cor 1:30). He *is* himself our salvation. He *is* himself our redemption. He *is* himself our sanctification. His being and his act are bound together inseparably. One does not exist without the other, though they must not be confused. Nevertheless, the *work* of Christ is part of *who* Christ is. And the *person* of Christ is what it is because of that *work*. And yet, in all of this, the New Testament is clear that the cross of Calvary, where Jesus was made the *"thing of sin itself,"* and where he bore God's judgment on sin, must remain absolutely central. The cross is at the heart of the Apostolic preaching in a way nothing else is.

⸗

For Torrance, it was precisely because the whole Easter event, of Christ's death on the cross and his resurrection from the tomb, affected the very constitution and nature of his person, that Jesus Christ is the Gospel in both his being and in his act. Reflecting this, in the *Atonement* lectures, Torrance said,

> The Christ who is proclaimed to us in the New Testament, therefore, is the Christ who is clothed with the kerygma of his *death* and *resurrection*, for they are *ontologically and structurally bound up with who he is in himself* and in his relation to the Father.[10]

---

10. Torrance, *Atonement*, 211 (italics added).

This is so important that Torrance repeated it word for word in *Space, Time and Resurrection*.[11] The wording is critical. If Torrance stated simply that Christ is "clothed with the *kerygma* of his death and resurrection," then that could be interpreted to mean that Jesus is the Gospel because he embodies his own teaching. However, Torrance said more. He specifically stated that Jesus' death and resurrection are, *ontologically* and *structurally* bound up with who he is in himself. The words *ontologically* and *structurally* are strong and significant terms. And this emphasis was elaborated further in, *Space, Time and Resurrection*:

> The union of God and man begun in the birth of Immanuel reaches throughout the incarnate life and work of Christ and *is fully and finally* achieved on man's side and on God's side in the crucifixion and resurrection of Jesus Christ.[12]

Again, we note the choice of words which Torrance used with respect to the incarnation. It is, "*fully and finally achieved on man's side and on God's side in the crucifixion and resurrection of Jesus Christ.*" Though the words *fully* and *finally* could be misinterpreted to mean that the incarnation was somehow incomplete until Jesus reached the cross, that was never Torrance's intended implication. And we return to that particular issue in our final chapter. At present, and with reference to the connection between the events of Easter and the constitution of the person of Christ in the incarnation, we note that Torrance also clearly stated,

> The resurrection is to be regarded not only as the completion of that saving work *but as belonging to the ontological structure of the Mediator himself* who stood in the gap of the *Eli, Eli, lama sabachthani*.[13]

Here again, Torrance referred to something which is normally regarded as an *event* (the resurrection), as belonging to the *ontology* of the person of Christ. Hence, what we have in Torrance's theology is a situation in which, when we drill deep into the meaning of Bethlehem and into the implications of Christ assuming our humanity, we find that we arrive at Calvary. We arrive there because his assumption of our humanity is an assumption of *fallen* humanity, which in itself brings an immediate

---

11. Torrance, *Space, Time and Resurrection*, 49.

12. Torrance, *Space, Time and Resurrection*, 66. Repeated almost exactly in Torrance, *Atonement*, 227.

13. Torrance, *Space, Time and Resurrection*, 50.

triggering of the wrath of God upon sin, a reaction which we quite properly normally associate with the cross.

For Torrance, as for Barth, the Son of God only became flesh, only became what we are, and only crossed over into our situation when he assumed our humanity in its fallenness. But we also know "where" that identification with our sinfulness fully, and completely, took place. It was at Calvary. It was at the cross that he became the sin of the world ontologically. That was where he became sin. That was where he suffered total rejection and forsakenness. Hence, in a very real sense, it was at the cross that he became what "we are." And therefore, in a very real sense—though we acknowledge that our language and modes of expression are inadequate for the task—it was at the cross that the incarnation was actualized, or, as in Torrance's words, was *fully and finally achieved.*

This brings us back to the proposition flagged up earlier. Instead of Bethlehem making Calvary possible, it is Calvary which makes Bethlehem possible. But, if so, what are the implications for Christology? And, do Torrance's presuppositions force us to say that the person of Jesus Christ is in fact generated, constituted, actualized, and created in the one, integrated, event of death and resurrection? Torrance may not have used exactly these terms; but, did his thinking necessitate them? And, how do we restructure our way of conceptualizing the Gospel to accommodate these insights?

— *Part Four* —

# Reappraisal

— *Chapter 13* —

# Christology in Reverse

RABBI DUNCAN ONCE CUT short a discussion on the atonement, saying, "I must no longer chop logic at the foot of the Cross."[1] In similar vein, Tom Torrance recalled that in the Old Testament liturgy for the Day of Atonement the most important act was done within the veil beyond human sight, meaning that the innermost mystery of atonement and intercession remained as mystery: "It cannot be spelled out, and it cannot be spied out."[2] Later in the same book he wrote: "The atonement knows no *why*, no ultimate *why* except God himself."[3] And in his lectures he often said, especially with respect to the profound mystery of the atonement, that when faced with such realities we have to put our hand to our mouth and stay silent. Nevertheless, faith seeks understanding. Consequently, though we are conscious of treading on holy ground, we attempt to work out the implications of what has been revealed, striving always to stay within the parameters set by God's Word itself.

In analyzing Torrance's theology, we have acknowledged his emphasis that, in the womb of Mary, God took to himself our fallen humanity. And yet, we are also aware that, in the very event of that hypostatic union of God and man in Jesus Christ, the fallen humanity which he assumed had to be judged and rejected. Moreover, it had to be judged and rejected *immediately*. It was impossible for the holy and the unholy to be conjoined in the person of Jesus Christ, even for a moment, without that divine reaction taking place. But the very same has to be said about the

---

1. Brown, *Life of Rabbi Duncan*, 382.
2. Torrance, *Atonement*, 2–3.
3. Torrance, *Atonement*, 88.

death of Christ on Calvary. On the cross, Christ was made the "thing of sin" itself, in a "being made" involving the same judgment, the same rejection, the same pouring out of wrath, and the same exclusion from the presence of a holy God.

This means that the logic of Torrance's theology creates a situation in which there appear to be two moments—not just one—of full-on encounter between the holiness of God and the sinfulness of humanity, each triggering immediate and inevitable consequences. One is the Bethlehem event. The other is the Calvary event. In this context, Bethlehem is shorthand for everything associated with the Son of God's assumption of our humanity, in being conceived by the Holy Spirit and born of the Virgin Mary. Similarly, Calvary is shorthand for everything associated with the passion of Easter and the death of Christ on the cross.

Two moments, not just one. Two times, not just one. Two places, not just one. At each of which, the divine holiness scorches fallen humanity. How can there be two? Did God suspend the full implications of Bethlehem until Calvary? Was a firewall introduced until Jesus hung on Calvary's cross? Was the assumption of our humanity only partial at Bethlehem, becoming complete and total only at Calvary? Did the Son of God assume our humanity in stages? But these solutions seem awkward, inelegant, artificial, even profane. Moreover, it has been axiomatic in mainstream Christian theology that Jesus Christ was truly and fully human from the very moment of his conception. And so the dilemma remains.

Both events, Bethlehem and Calvary, involve the coming together of the holy and the unholy. But the holy and the unholy are mutually exclusive. Therefore, both events trigger, unavoidably, the fullness of the divine reaction to the unholy. But if that reaction has somehow already been played out in the womb of Mary, what remains for Calvary? What is the relevance of the cross? It is certainly insufficient to state vaguely that something "deeper" happened on Calvary. How could anything "deeper" occur than that which was provoked through the coming together of fallen humanity and divine righteousness in the person of Jesus Christ? Besides, wherever, and whenever, the divine reaction to human fallenness took place, it did so as a once-for-all event. It was not something to be repeated elsewhere and at another time.

Does all of this mean that there is an unresolvable problem in Torrance's theology? Can Bethlehem and Calvary both be events in which God and sinful humanity are in full-on encounter, with the attendant implications? Can the Calvary event have any relevance if the coming together of the holy and the unholy has already taken place in Mary's womb? Or, in trying to harmonize Torrance's thinking, are we in danger of viewing Jesus Christ as a theological metaphor, rather than as a truly historical person for whom the event of Bethlehem was clearly distinguished in time and space from the event of Calvary? Is Torrance's theology able to overcome this stress-point? We believe that it can, but this requires further reflection on the relationship between Bethlehem and on Calvary.

## Calvary as the Presupposition of Bethlehem

When we drill down into the Bethlehem event, what we discover is that God's assumption of our fallen humanity inevitably, unavoidably, and immediately, results in the judgment of that humanity. From the very moment of his conception by the Holy Spirit in the womb of Mary, the sinfulness of humanity and the holiness of God are conjoined in the person of Jesus Christ, and there can be no other outcome of such a conjunction than the outpouring of God's righteous wrath. In becoming what we are, he necessarily had to endure the penalty of our sin. But yet, where was it that he truly endured the penalty of our sin? Surely it was at Calvary. What we find, therefore, is that in coming to Bethlehem we look around and find we are at Calvary. In other words, in drilling deep into the Bethlehem event we find that Calvary is the vital *presupposition* of its very possibility. In going deep into the incarnation we discover the atonement; and we do so precisely because the atonement involves the Son of God taking to himself the consequence of human sin. At the same time, Calvary was the *outcome* of Bethlehem, because it was at Bethlehem that he assumed our humanity in the womb of Mary, became what we are, and therefore became humanity under judgment on the cross.

Hence, the incarnation could not occur without the atonement. This is because, in Torrance's interpretation of Nazianzus' principle, "*The Unassumed is the Unredeemed*," the incarnation could only occur when Christ took to himself our fallen humanity, a condition only fully realized when he was made sin. Hence, in a deeply profound sense, only in being made sin could he be the incarnate one. And yet, Scripture clearly identifies his being made sin with the event of Calvary where he suffered the wrath of God, experienced abandonment, and endured hell itself in our place. It appears therefore, that his assumption of our humanity

(Bethlehem) was only possible because of his becoming sin (Calvary). Bethlehem was only possible because of Calvary.

## Bethlehem as the Presupposition of Calvary

When we similarly drill down into the Calvary event, what we discover is that God's judgment of our fallen humanity inevitably, unavoidably, and immediately, takes place precisely because of the assumption of that humanity. This is because, in Jesus being made 'the thing of sin' itself upon the cross, the sinfulness of humanity and the holiness of God clash, and clash because they are conjoined in the person of Jesus Christ. And there can be no other reason for such a reaction other than his having become what we are. What we find, therefore, is that in arriving at Calvary we look around and find we are in Bethlehem. In other words, in drilling deep into the Calvary event we find that Bethlehem is the vital *presupposition* of its very possibility. In going deep into the atonement we discover the incarnation; and we do so precisely because the incarnation involves the Son of God taking to himself the consequence of human fallenness. And yet, at the same time, Bethlehem was also the *outcome* of Calvary, because it was only on Calvary that he became sin, and therefore became that very humanity assumed in the womb of Mary.

Hence, the atonement could not occur without the incarnation. This is because, as in Torrance's interpretation of 2 Cor 5:21, the outpouring of the wrath of God on Calvary was prompted by his assumption of fallen humanity and being made sin for us. Hence, in a deeply profound sense, only in being the incarnate one could he become the rejected one. And yet, Scripture clearly identifies the moment of his becoming what we are with the event of Bethlehem where he was clothed with the same humanity as ours, and where God bridged the chasm between himself and Adam's fallen race. It appears therefore, that his bearing the sin of the world (Calvary) was only possible because of his assumption of our humanity (Bethlehem). Calvary was only possible because of Bethlehem.

What we see is that Jesus' cry of dereliction signals both atonement and incarnation. At that moment, the work of Christ is indissolubly connected with his person. As Torrance put it, "Christ is himself our redeemer in the constitution of his person."[4] In a very real sense, the Son of God only became what we are, and only crossed over into our situation, when he was made sin. But, "where" did that that truly take place? The

---

4. Torrance, *Atonement*, 54.

consistent emphasis of Scripture is to identify the cross of Calvary as the location in space and time where he became the sin of the world ontologically. The cross is uniquely central.

## The Centrality of the Cross

When we reflect on the *incarnation*, it is as if we enter a circle whose circumference is marked Bethlehem, but, when we travel to its center we find ourselves at Calvary. Similarly, when we reflect on the *atonement*, it is as if we enter a circle whose circumference is marked Calvary, but, when we travel to its center we find ourselves at Bethlehem. When we go deep into Bethlehem, we find Calvary. When we go deep into Calvary, we find Bethlehem.

Two paradoxes emerge. First, the greater we focus on the incarnation, the more we find ourselves considering the atonement. Second, the greater we focus on the atonement, the more we find ourselves considering the incarnation. The atonement undergirds the incarnation. The incarnation undergirds the atonement. Calvary lies within Bethlehem. Bethlehem lies within Calvary. It is as if Bethlehem and Calvary exist in a relationship of mutual inter-dependence, or *perichoresis*, with respect to one another.

If we were to illustrate this diagrammatically, we might draw an ellipse with two foci, one of which is Bethlehem and the other Calvary. Both foci are pivotal in defining the essential characteristics of the ellipse, and yet each is separate and distinct in space and time. However, the illustration has a flaw. Its weakness is that the image of an ellipse presents us with a too symmetric image of the mutual relationship between Bethlehem and Calvary. In contrast, what Scripture presents is asymmetry, not symmetry, with a clear centering of events on the cross and the resurrection. It is at Calvary that Jesus endures forsakenness. It is the death of Christ at Calvary, and his subsequent resurrection triumph, which drives the New Testament witness. That is what dominates the apostolic New Testament message and the apostolic understanding of salvation.

Therefore, although atonement is the presupposition of incarnation, and incarnation the presupposition of atonement, the fundamental driving force at the heart of the whole is the death and resurrection of Jesus Christ. That is the New Testament's determinative and causative principle. Calvin expressed this when—even as he acknowledged the soteriological significance of the whole life of Jesus—he noted that Scripture ascribes salvation "peculiarly and specially" to Jesus' death.[5] What this suggests is that, although incarnation lies behind atonement, and atonement lies behind incarnation, in an even deeper sense the cross and resurrection drives everything. Borrowing from C. S. Lewis's, *The Lion, The Witch, and The Wardrobe*, we might say that the cross and resurrection is the "deeper magic still" which undergirds and makes possible all else. Bethlehem could only take place when it did, because Calvary was going to occur some thirty years later. The incarnation requires the atonement, and the atonement requires the incarnation; but *both* require the underlying reality of the cross and resurrection as the fundamental driver of all else.

What this means is that the issue of Christ on the cross being made the *"thing of sin itself"* is not a minor theological detail. Instead, Jesus becoming sin belongs to the very foundations of Christian theology. It is in his becoming sin that the person of Christ is constituted; and it is within his person that both incarnation and atonement are defined.

The incarnation involves the whole downward movement through the cross to death and hell, and the whole upward movement through resurrection to glory. Thus, ontologically, the incarnation has its being in the complete movement of Christ's humiliation and exaltation. It is what it is because of that one, cohesive, event of death and resurrection, of going down to the depths and rising in triumph. The crucial issue concerning the person of Jesus Christ is the whole movement of humiliation and exaltation, of becoming sin and rising in triumph. Torrance indicated this in a dramatic passage,

> We are not to think of the humiliation and exaltation of Christ simply as two events following one after the other, *but as both involved in appropriate measure at the same time all through the incarnate life of Christ.*[6]

The humiliation and exaltation of Christ has double significance. It *constitutes* his person. And it also *fulfils* his work. This is is why it is impossible to divorce the work of Christ from the person of Christ. But, the critical center is his death and resurrection. The driver, at the heart of everything, is Jesus Christ bearing God's judgment in becoming what we are, and his

---

5. Cf. Calvin, *Institutes* 2.16.5: "From the moment when he assumed the form of a servant, he began, in order to redeem us, to pay the price of deliverance. Scripture, however, the more certainly to define the mode of salvation, *ascribes it peculiarly and specially* to the death of Christ."

6. Torrance, *Atonement*, 210 (italics added).

rising in triumph in becoming a new creation. Therefore, in this strict sense, we may even say that the person of Jesus Christ is *generated, actualized,* and *created,* in a becoming which is constituted through that event of death and resurrection. The moment when the Son of God became what we are, was also the instant he necessarily became the man judged and condemned and rejected: not prospectively so, but actually so. From the moment of conception by the Holy Spirit in the womb of Mary, he was already the man of Calvary. He could not *become* what we are, without simultaneously being the man upon the cross. In being the person of Jesus Christ, he was automatically the rejected and abandoned one.

But this whole movement of humiliation and exaltation is not to be regarded as something abstract, timeless, or non-historical. On the contrary, it is what it is because of, and only because of, the space-time specific events of Bethlehem and Calvary. These are historical events. They are not symbols of timeless ideas.[7] Hence, we speak of the Bethlehem *event,* not the Bethlehem *concept.* And we speak of the Calvary *event,* not the Calvary *concept.*[8] If they were mere concepts, then their occurring at different geographical places and in different historical times would be unimportant. If mere concepts, they would simply be illustrative of a spiritual reality which had been established independent of events at a specific place and time on earth or in history, and no more than examples of a truth which was essentially placeless and timeless. Over against this, the Christian doctrine of the incarnation involves God, in his reconciling work, interacting with real space-time and playing out the drama of salvation within real history at real places.

---

7. Cf. Torrance, *Theological Science,* 152: "This Truth [the Word made flesh] is both eternal and historical, Truth who is not timeless, for he so participates in time-relations and assumes time into himself that time is an inalienable element in his nature as incarnate Truth. Far from the historical being but the outward symbolic draping of the Truth, it belongs to his very substance." On the same page, in footnote 3, Torrance referred to Brunner, "Christian Understanding of Time," and Barth, *CD* III/2, §47.1, "Jesus the Lord of Time."

8. We reject the notion of a timeless Christ-event. Cf. Torrance, *Atonement,* 255: "[The Son of God] partook of life within the *nomistic* structure of our time and wrought his redemptive work within it in order to emancipate us from its tyranny." Cf. Torrance, *Atonement,* 326.

## Repositioning Perspective

Bethlehem is historically prior to Calvary, and, when we reflect on the relationship between *causes* and *effects*, we normally assume *causes* to be chronologically prior to *effects*. However, what happens if we move from considering *chronological* priority to considering *ontological* priority? Our argument is that time sequence and logical sequence should not be confused when dealing with issues pertaining to the boundary-conditions of reality, and Torrance himself was sharply aware of the dangers attendant on confusing temporal sequence with logical connection.[9] Therefore, though Bethlehem precedes Calvary in historical time, the argument outlined above has indicated that Calvary is ontologically prior to Bethlehem in terms of causation. But how do we deal with the intellectual challenges which this engenders? And, if the event of the death and resurrection of Christ is what makes possible the event of his assumption of our humanity, then this raises considerable issues and a radically new perspective.

The need to reposition perspective occurs frequently in the natural sciences. For example, why did Copernicus' sun-centered theory triumph over the Ptolemaic earth-centered system? After all, it is quite possible to create a set of mathematical equations which satisfy an earth-centered arrangement, rather than a sun-centered one. And though the equations may be complex, clumsy, and cumbersome, they are constructible. Hence, both earth-centered and sun-centered systems are possible from a purely mathematical perspective. Therefore, why is one system favored over the other? There are two main reasons. First, the mathematical equations for a sun-centered system are simpler and more elegant, and science has an inbuilt conviction that the simplest theories are the correct theories.[10] Second, and more importantly, the sun-centered model makes greater sense within the wider context of known fundamental laws of physics, especially the theory of gravitation. The sun-centered model fits into a more satisfying universal conceptual understanding. What this means is that an ability to construct equations which are able to account for all of the phenomena is not enough. What science really wants is an understanding of the nature of things which explains, on a more fundamental

---

9. Torrance, *Atonement*, 250: "The confusion of temporal with logical connection corresponds . . . to that between spontaneity and casual determinism in natural science . . . we can see this error recurring, for example, in notions of predestination where the free *prius* of the divine grace is converted by the scholastic mind into logico-casual relation."

10. Cf. Beck, *Simplicity of Science*.

level, why the mathematics works as it does. Thus, though it is possible on a purely theoretical basis to manufacture sets of equations supporting an earth-centered system, not only are these horribly unwieldy, but they lack any connection to a vital driving force in nature which gives rise to them. In contrast, the theory of gravitation is able to explain why the neat and stylish equations associated with the sun-centered model, actually work. In other words, the sun-centered model has an inherently more satisfying logic. It is a model, within which diverse phenomena, previously linked only by impossibly difficult mathematical systems and represented by fantastical mechanical models, are able to be brought together with an elegance of form and with a breath-taking beauty of simplicity. However, in order for that advance to be made, a change of thinking, counter-intuitive to how we thought we saw things day-by-day, had to take place. The sun does not orbit the earth: as our eyes seemed to tell us. Instead, the earth orbits the sun. It was this radical change of conceptual framework, involving the adoption of a different perspective, which enabled a better, a more natural, and a more satisfying fit of all the data and theories to emerge.

Torrance wanted a similar repositioning of perspective in Reformed theology. This was why he argued that the forensic/legal aspect of the atonement must be seen as part of something much deeper, namely an event occurring within the person of Jesus Christ himself. And he reasoned that, in viewing Christian theology from that more fundamental perspective, theologians could more easily appreciate how Jesus, as the lamb of God, bore our sin and fulfilled his mission not only legally but actually, resulting in sinners not only being declared righteous, but becoming righteous in themselves in him.[11] In this way, person and work, being and act, would be bound together. Such a repositioning of perspective would root atonement in the person of Christ in such a way that the forensic/legal aspect of atonement is seen to lie *within* this larger ontological setting,

> Justification becomes not only the non-imputation of sins but the clothing of the sinner with the righteousness of Christ. Nevertheless, that would still be empty and unreal, merely a judicial transaction, unless the doctrine of justification bears in its heart a relation of real union with Christ . . . We require an active relation to Christ as our righteousness. This is possible only through the resurrection—when we approach justification in this light

11. Torrance, *Mediation of Christ*, 94.

> we can see that it is a *creative event in which our regeneration or renewal is already included within it.*[12]

Mainstream Reformed theology has never disputed that the life of Jesus was soteriologically significant, agreeing with Calvin's emphasis on the importance of the active obedience of Christ. But Torrance wanted more. He wanted a total repositioning of perspective so that the ontology of the person of Christ would be absolutely central in all aspects of Christian theology. As such, this repositioning of perspective brings into sharp focus the nature of the relationship between Bethlehem and Calvary.

⌇

We have discussed several aspects of the question: did Torrance's rooting of the atonement in the incarnation result in Bethlehem replacing Calvary? Was that the unintended consequence of his thinking? And, if it is the union of God and man in the person of Jesus Christ which is the fundamental driver of atonement, what more is needed other than Jesus being conceived in the womb of Mary, and God and man coming together in that hypostatic union? In light of these questions, we have suggested that the apparent gulf between Torrance and traditional Reformed theology begins to fall away when we rethink Christology and allow a radically counter-intuitive understanding of what the incarnation is: namely,

> *The incarnation of the Lord Jesus Christ is constituted not simply by his conception in the womb of Mary and birth at Bethlehem; but, more fundamentally, in the one integrated event of the humiliation and exaltation of the Son of God.*

Viewed from within this perspective, we see that it is Calvary which, proleptically, makes Bethlehem possible, not vice versa. Understood in this way, Torrance's emphasis on the atonement being *in* the person of Christ and not simply *by the agency of* Christ is in no way counter to the New Testament emphasis which centers atonement on the cross. Incarnation "occurs" when Jesus becomes precisely what we are: namely, humanity in sin. And, within the mystery of the incarnation, this is at Calvary. Thus his person, as the incarnate Son of God, exists in his becoming-sin and his overcoming-it. Hence, it is the atoning action of the cross and resurrection, which enables the incarnation to occur at Bethlehem. And

---

12. Torrance, *Space, Time and Resurrection*, 63 (italics added).

all of this is without losing the distinctiveness of the historical events of Bethlehem or Calvary, and without creating a merely docetic or symbolic Christ, whose flesh and blood humanity in history was but an ephemeral manifestation of some vague spiritual reality.

The savior was not simply revealed as such at Bethlehem and Calvary. Instead, he became the savior because of, and only because of, these events. Incarnation and atonement were not timeless concepts. They were acts of God in our time and space. Thinking through these questions further involves rethinking the nature of time, in a process not dissimilar to the rethinking of time in the natural sciences. Pursuing this will enable us to see more clearly how Torrance's emphasis on atonement being *in* the person of Christ and not simply *through* the person of Christ, does not in any way neglect the Reformed emphasis on the cross.

— *Chapter 14* —

# Christology and Time

ISAAC NEWTON REGARDED TIME as something absolute. It was something which flowed serenely from an infinite past into an infinite future. It was a theatre-stage for events. But time itself was entirely disconnected from any drama taking place within it. For Newton, time and space were boxes or containers within which things happened. In contrast, what Torrance emphasized to us was that modern physics had moved away from this container-box approach. Instead, time is now understood as part of a continuum, or field, which is itself a function of events. "Time and space," Torrance wrote, "are not receptacles apart from bodies or forces, but are *functions of events* in the universe, and forms of their orderly sequence and structure."[1] With this as a springboard, he encouraged us to adopt a view of space-time in which events create and mold time and space:

> Space and time must both be conceived in *relational* terms and in accordance with the active principles or forces that move and make room for themselves in such a way that space and time arise in and with them, and their movements.[2]

For Torrance, active principles, forces, and events "move and make room" for themselves. And they do so in such a way that "space and time *arise* in and with them." In other words, at the boundary-conditions of existence, events *create* time and space, rather than occurring *within* time and space.

Torrance saw hints of this type of conceptualization in the Church Fathers. He argued that they had a view of space influenced by the Stoic

1. Torrance, *Atonement*, 289.
2. Torrance, *Atonement*, 289.

# Christology and Time

notion of space as room "forged for itself by an active agency."[3] In his opinion, this conception of space—equally applicable to time—was a decided advantage over the receptacle notion of space and time which prevailed generally in Greek thought. But why were the Fathers open to this completely different way of seeing things? In Torrance's opinion, it was because their thinking had been opened up, and profoundly reshaped, by the doctrine of the incarnation, in which they had had to think through how God had forged and created space-time for himself within human flesh. It was reflection on the incarnation which made them receptive to another way of seeing the world.[4]

In this chapter we reflect on Torrance's conviction that time is not to be envisaged as a fixed time-line onto which persons appear and disappear, like actors entering and leaving a stage. Nor is time a box within which events happen. Instead, because space-time is itself a function of events, then, without events, space-time itself cannot exist. In making this claim, Torrance was not making the obvious point that it is our awareness of events which enables us to mark, and to measure, space-time. He meant more. He meant that events themselves "forge" and "make room" for space-time. Space-time arises and exists because of boundary-condition-events. That is why and how space-time has its being. Within the disciplines of the natural sciences such a concept is challenging enough. But when, in theology, there is the added element of God's interaction with created space-time through the incarnation, then our ability to conceptualize what is involved is stretched even further.

Before launching into the heart of this chapter, there is a further point to consider. This concerns what we have referred to as boundary-condition-events. When we examine the natural world we find that, in normal circumstances, the old Newtonian way of describing things is perfectly adequate. In ordinary conditions, Newton's equations are perfectly sound and satisfactory for day-to-day purposes. It is only when we deal with the boundary-condition-events of existence which involve, for example, objects travelling near to the speed of light, that our perceptions and equations have to be based in Relativity Theory and Quantum

---

3. Torrance, *Space, Time and Incarnation*, 10, 13, 58.

4. Cf. Torrance, *Incarnation*, 218: "[The Fathers] thought of God in creation as 'containing all things by the Word of his power' and as contained by nothing, and of God coming to be with us in the realm of space and time which he created in and with the creation of the universe, yet in such a way that he did not cease to be the creator transcendent over all space and time."

Theory rather than in the classical mechanics of Newton. It is only within the context of the boundary-condition-events of existence, that unusual effects become a factor. A similar reality is true in theology. Our normal way of viewing time, history, and events, is quite workable when we deal with what may be termed the everyday aspects of faith. And so, for most day-to-day theology, we could treat time as a box or receptacle, unrelated to events taking place within it, without there being any problems. However, just as natural science has boundary-condition-events which change everything, so also does theology. In theology, the boundary-condition-events involve critical acts of God such as incarnation, cross, resurrection, and ascension. And, when we have to relate extensively to these events then everything changes because of their boundary-condition qualities. This includes how they relate to time and space. And so, for these boundary-condition-events, we do need take into account how events "forge" and "make room" for themselves, creating the very time and space in which they take place.

## Covenant and Created Time

Space-time is a created entity. As such, it has a beginning. Human language struggles with the idea of time having a "beginning," since the word "beginning" itself comes from a time-bound vocabulary. Nevertheless, until God uttered his word of creative power, space-time "was not." It came into existence when God spoke. *Deus Dixt.* From a Torrancian perspective, we may express this theologically by stating that space-time came into being as a consequence of God establishing his covenant as the basis for creation. Within the covenant relationship, space-time was fashioned to facilitate physical existence, and to be the locus of meeting and activity in the interaction between God and the created order.[5] As such, space-time has no existence in itself, but does have real existence because of this relationship. Covenant is the internal basis and the constituent principle, of creation.[6] As such, it is the covenant, established by God, which provides the very possibility of the created order, including space-time, coming into existence and having existence.

What this means is that the created order, including space-time, has existence because of the covenant, and only because of the covenant.

---

5. Torrance, *Space, Time and Incarnation*, 24.
6. Barth, *CD* III/1, 42–329. Cf. Ritchie, Personal Lecture Notes, 18–19 (Autumn, 1973).

However, precisely because of the dependency of that relationship, there are catastrophic consequences attached to the entrance of sin and evil. Because of sin and evil, the whole of creation, including space-time, has lost true being and has lost true existence. Creation's very existence had been predicated on the covenant; and so, when the covenant was broken, the ground of creation's existence was swept away. Torrance spoke of this in class. In my lecture notes for November, 1973, I recorded him saying,

> In so far as something is evil, it privates from being . . . Suppose God made the creation to have a harmonious relation to himself: then, if the link between God and the creation were broken, the creation would go into nothing . . . If there were a complete break between God and a being, then the being would go into nothing. God has to maintain the creature in being, because he has not ceased from loving it. In this way, sin and existence are brought through.[7]

The notion that God continually sustains the cosmos in existence was already a recognized concept for me. As a young Christian, it was one of the things which I had learned from my minister. Hebrews 1:3 states that God upholds the Universe by the word of his power, and so I knew that even an untarnished created order requires God's continuous sustaining power at every moment, otherwise it would fall into non-existence. But Torrance introduced a further dimension. What I had been aware of previously, was that an *unsullied* created order requires God's continuous sustaining power to *maintain* itself in being. But what we were now being told, in the Dogmatics class, was that a *fallen* created order is in a wholly different category because it has *privated* from being. Unfallen creation has legitimate being. Fallen creation has no legitimate being.

All of this raised questions. If created space-time, predicated as it is upon the covenant, has privated into non-being, how is it that we exist here and now, on earth and in history? Clearly, any answer to this question needs to be grounded in the grace of God. The time of the here and now needs to be a time of grace. And the grace of God is not a *thing*, it is a person, Jesus Christ. And so, in some way, the fallen and broken created order in which we live day-by-day has, through an act of pure grace in Christ, been granted a space-time in which to have being and existence. Thus, the cosmos retains the quality of being a place, and the cosmos retains the quality of having a history. But how?

---

7. Ritchie, Personal Lecture Notes, 17 (Autumn, 1973).

## "Old Time" and the Broken Creation

What is this space and time of grace? Concerning time in particular—though time should never be considered apart from space—what is the "here and now" granted to us and to the whole created order? Is it, somehow, the "old time" of the original creation, which, by God's grace, has been mercifully preserved, sustained, and upheld? Is it that "old time" which, somehow, has been kept from the non-existence it should relapse into? Has the executioner's axe failed to fall on "old time"? This seemed to be what Torrance was teaching us in the class lecture when he said, "If the link between God and the creation were broken, the creation would go into nothing." In his writings, this has come across as Torrance's favored approach. He held that "old time" is sustained by God's grace, even though, in having become "bad time" it should lack the very possibility of existence,

> The kind of time we have in our fallen existence is refracted time, time that has broken loose from God, as it were, and yet not time that has been allowed to slip into sheer chaos and nothingness but time that is contained, upheld, and overruled by God, within which he works out his redeeming purpose. The kind of time we have in historical events is the time of creation that has fallen from what it ought to be into disorder, and yet is contained through *nomos* from disappearing or vanishing into illusion.[8]

On this basis he wrote that the Church, "lives in two times, the time of this passing world and the time of the new creation."[9] And, when Christ comes again, he will, "change the space-time form of this fallen world (not *to eliminate it* but to change and renew it)."[10]

"Bad time" can be a synonym for "old time." And the term "bad time" certainly reflects the wording which Torrance used in class lectures, though in his books the preferred terminology has been "old time." The term "bad time" has some advantages. It conveys more of the brokenness of a sin-affected cosmos. Moreover, it powerfully expresses the notion that a fallen created order has lost the very possibility of having being and existence at all. As Torrance put it to us in class, our time is bound up with guilt:

---

8. Torrance, *Space, Time and Resurrection*, 97. Torrance, *Atonement*, 255.
9. Torrance, *Atonement*, 256; *Space, Time and Resurrection*, 98.
10. Torrance, *Gospel, Church, and Ministry*, 107 (italics added).

> Our time is not reversible; but it is recreated in the New Creation. [In heaven] the discontinuous elements that affect our time will be dealt with. We are in *refracted* time. Our time is bound up with guilt, and this is un-doable, for guilt is irreversible. When the Creator recreates time, he will recreate time going the opposite way. This is the problem of the unity of the *Parousia*. It is impossible to put the creation at a point in *bad-time*, for there is then a link with real time; similarly, with the consummation, we cannot put it in a point of *bad-time*.[11]

This extract well expresses Torrance's position. The here and now is "old time," sustained by the grace of God, but into which the "new time" of Christ's triumph penetrates every corner. And the Church exists within the tension of two times until the final consummation of all things. Jesus' cross is the death of old space and time. Jesus' resurrection is the creation of new space and time. And Jesus' ascension universalizes all the benefits of his risen humanity.

The ascension, in relation to time, was enormously important in Torrance's theology, and for two main reasons. First, the ascended Christ, as our brother, and wearing our humanity, takes that humanity into the Father's presence, presents himself eternally before the face of God, and reverses the expulsion from Eden.[12] Second, in the same risen humanity, the ascended Christ becomes present to all space and all time, in every place and in every era. Or, as Torrance expressed it, he penetrates every corner of created existence, past, present, and future. The ascension completes the saving purposes of God: first through Christ's triumphant return to the Holy of Holies; second, through "initiating" his whole heavenly ministry in the whole of history.[13] And, in particular, Torrance stressed it was through the ascension of Christ, that human time and the time of eternity were linked,

> The resurrection of the man Jesus, and his exaltation to the right hand of the Father, means the taking up of *human time* into God. In Christ the life of human beings is wedded to eternal life. The ascension also means that this time of the new creation in Christ is hidden from us, and, as it were, held back

---

11. Ritchie, Personal Lecture Notes, 18b (Autumn, 1973).
12. Torrance, *Royal Priesthood*, 14–15.
13. Dawson, *Jesus Ascended*, 133. Cf. Torrance, *Atonement*, 429–36.

until in the mercy of God Jesus Christ comes again to judge and renew all his creation.[14]

For Torrance, the resurrection and ascension, together in concert, are part of the one movement of triumph and new creation which took place in the victory of Christ; they were not two unrelated phases in the person and work of Christ. Hence, just as taking our flesh in Mary's womb, and becoming sin on the cross, are all one part of the coming down and humiliation of the Son of God; so also, his resurrection from the tomb and his ascension to the right hand of the Father, are all one part of his triumph. And, as previously indicated, it is that humiliation and that exaltation, that death and that victory, taken together, which comprises *the* event of the person of Jesus Christ.

### "New Time" and the Triumphant Lord

In Torrance's model each corner of history still includes "old time," as that "old time" is upheld by God in mercy. But, does this model satisfy all parameters? In particular, does it deal adequately with the implications of the Fall vis-à-vis the created order? Might another model serve Torrance's theology better? There is an alternative model, in which the time of grace, in the here and now, is totally "new time," freshly minted and brought into being for us, by the event of the triumph of Jesus Christ through his resurrection and ascension. In this model, the Church does not live in two times. Instead, it lives in a single time, which has been forged and made possible in Jesus Christ. As we try to describe this from our human perspective, that "new time" is seen as stretching both "back" and "forward" from the victory of Easter, making it possible for a broken created order to have a time in which to have existence. But, crucially, in this model there is no "old time" remaining for that "new time" to stretch back into. "Old time" is no more. "Old time" has privated from being. Conceptually, the situation is analogous to the "beginning" of space-time when God brought the cosmos into being, and when no time yet existed for the word "beginning" to actually make sense. Regrettably, the limitations of language mean that we are forced to use words such as "beginning," "back," "forward," despite their limitations and ambiguities.

---

14. Torrance, *Space, Time and Resurrection*, 98. Cf. Torrance, *Gospel, Church, and Ministry*, 101–10.

In Torrance's preferred model, God upholds "old time" but drives the "new time" of Christ's triumph into every corner of it. In the alternative model, God does not hold onto "old time." In Torrance's model "old time" is redeemed. In the alternative model "old time" is replaced. It has gone. In both models, God creates "new time" in and through the event of the triumph of Jesus Christ. But, in the alternative model, it is *solely* this "new time," stretched "back" and "forward" from the first Easter, which is the basis for the space-time within which humanity now lives on earth in history. And, in the alternative model, this "new time" does not interpenetrate, reclaim, or redeem, previously existing "old time." Instead, it generates, within itself, the very time—the only time—within which history occurs or can occur. In other words, under this alternative model, the time of grace in which we live, the here and now, the time of history from Adam until the Parousia, has been actualized and generated solely by the recreative power of the death, resurrection, and ascension of Jesus Christ.

In contrast, Torrance's understanding was that the work of God in Christ redeems and renews what has been distorted and broken within the created order, including space-time itself. This came out in his extended comments on an essay entitled "Logic and Grace" which I submitted to him in a series of essays I wrote on "Theology and Logic," as part of my final year specialist subject. Like most tutors, Torrance normally wrote his comments in the margin of an essay, or at the foot of its final page. On this occasion, although he agreed with much of what I had written, his reply took up two whole typed pages of foolscap, in which he argued for a positive application of the phrase "Grace perfects Nature."[15] In that reply he stated: "Grace, it is to be granted, does not merely restore this particular [current] order in nature, but *affirms creation in such a*

15. Torrance, Unpublished Response to Essay "Logic and Grace." He added: "If all creation in some way partakes of the mystery of the incarnation, then is there not a proper sense in which we must say 'yes' to the proposition that 'grace perfects nature,' provided that the terms 'grace,' 'nature,' are understood correctly and not ambiguously as appears to be the case in St Thomas Aquinas? . . .

"'Grace perfects Nature.' The problem of this statement lies in the ambiguity of nature. What is true nature is that which comes from the grace of God—then surely the statement is correct, that grace does not destroy nature but perfects it. But, if by nature is meant *fallen* nature ('nature' naturalistically conceived apart from grace) then the statement would be wrong, for it would mean that grace added to something human or natural (apart from grace) brings the latter to its perfection; but if grace also judges and corrects nature (nature as *fallen*) then some form of justification beyond 'nature' is involved" (Wording as original; but punctuation altered for clarity).

*way as to renew it*, and make good in renewal where it has been distorted: but more, it takes that up in a new and higher order in the incarnation, whereby *the order of creation is not destroyed but perfected in a transcendently new way*" (italics added). In this very full response to the thoughts of a young student, Torrance was reaffirming his belief that redemption applies to every aspect of the created order (cf. Rom 8:22), and not just to men and women. As such, redemption touches upon the very structures of the created order, including its space and time. Thus, space and time are not lost. They are redeemed through being taken up into Christ. This clarifies why Torrance preferred to speak of "old time" ("bad time") being upheld by grace, and being taken up into the "new time" of the triumph of Christ where it is *renewed*, rather than "old time" ("bad time") being lost irretrievably into nothingness when sin and evil enter the created order. However, in a covering letter which was attached to his extended comments, Torrance agreed that, "nature as we know it needs to die and be recreated."[16] Nature dies. It is not kept alive for resuscitation. It does not avoid the consequences of a Fallen created order, namely death. And so the very structures of old space and time die. And what emerges is something new, a new creation, which is actualized in and through the triumph of the risen Christ which has implications for the whole of the created order. Our conviction is that the consequences of that inevitable death of the whole created order, including space and time—which Torrance accepted—require further exploration.

Torrance's approach, in which "old time" is taken up into Christ and, through death and resurrection, is redeemed and renewed, is coherent and consistent. But it is important to explore the radical implications of the alternative model, which takes on board—in much more obvious fashion—the repercussions attending the entrance of sin and evil into the structures of creation. Because of the Fall, nature needs to die and be recreated. It cannot exist. It has lost the possibility of existence. As such, the only time which can exist now, and the only time which does exist now, is the time of Jesus Christ, crucified, risen, and ascended. And that Christ-event, affecting the boundary-condition-events of reality, has

16. Torrance, Unpublished Letter to B. Ritchie, 1976. The full extract runs: "I think that the statement 'grace does not destroy nature but perfects it' should be handled with care—as it is ambiguous, depending on what is meant by nature. If 'nature' means what comes from God in his creation, then the statement is surely sound enough—but under cover of that, it can be taken to justify naturalism by grace, which would be wrong—and it would then fail to note *that nature as we know it needs to die and be recreated.* It is best to state both sides of this when refuting the false side" (italics added).

"made room for itself." It has "forged" the very time in which, paradoxically, it can itself occur in history. Paradoxically, it is the *actuality* of the event which created the very *possibility* of the event. Normally, *possibility* precedes *actuality*. But, in any circumstance which pertains to boundary-condition-events, the order has to be reversed. And so, the event of Christ's death, resurrection, and ascension, "made room" for itself within history by creating the very possibility of the existence of the time within which its history could occur. It was Christ's triumph which enabled the very moment of history within which that triumph occurred and took place. It created the very time which itself inhabited. And, whatever connection such "new time" may have had with the original "old time" of the created order, it only gives existence to historical time in being part of the new creation in the risen Christ. Of course, this insight can apply to both models: to Torrance's model as well as to the alternative model. The possibility of the time, within which the history of Jesus Christ took place—whether that time was "old time" being renewed (as in Torrance's model), or was purely "new time" (as in the alternative model)—depends for its existence entirely upon the event of the triumph of Jesus Christ.

## Actuality and Possibility

The notion that *actuality* creates *possibility*, rather than vice-versa, was a concept which I came across at New College when reading Herbert Hartwell's book on Karl Barth.[17] Hartwell saw this as key to understanding Barth's conceptualization of profound theological entities, especially Barth's insistence on defining every theological term christologically and refusing to accept definitions from outside of a christological setting. When I read Hartwell, I was captivated by the idea that, at the boundary-conditions of existence, it is *actuality* which creates *possibility* and not vice-versa. Of course, on reflection, the concept is self-obvious. To take a simple example: if the Universe has a true "beginning," involving the "beginning" of space, time, matter, and energy, through an act of creation *ex nihilo*, then *actuality* of existence *must* occur before its *possibility* can occur. There cannot be a pre-existing abstract possibility. In other words, when dealing with ultimate issues on the very boundary of being, such as the "start" or the "beginning" of space-time, what we discover is that actuality has to create its own possibility. Event has to create the possibility of itself. That has to be. It must necessarily be the case.

17. Hartwell, *Theology of Karl Barth*.

When we apply this to theological boundary-condition-events involving God's interaction with his creation, then it requires careful reflection. In the physicist's consideration of the natural world, it is only when he or she has to deal with the boundary-condition-events of nature that he or she becomes aware of deep conceptual issues. A similar situation occurs in theology. The mighty act of God in salvation is a boundary-condition-event of theology, and that act, in all of its aspects—similar to the act of creation *ex nihilo*—is something which can only have possibility through having actuality. To elucidate further: the primal act of creation is not a possibility of existence as such; rather, it is an act whose actuality alone establishes its possibility. Expanding the principle, it also means that the actuality of of the triumph of Christ, forged in the historically-time-rooted event of his death, resurrection, and ascension, was what created the very possibility of the space-time of that event in the first place, enabling it to take place on earth and within history.

Thus, the time in which we live, the time of history, the time given for humanity to return to the living God, is a function of "new time" made possible in Jesus Christ. Our historical time has existence because of, and only because of, that event of redeeming grace. It is a time of grace. And grace occurs nowhere else than in the person of Jesus Christ. It is his time which enables historical time to exist at all. Or, to put it in Gospel terms: history, as the time granted for reconciliation with God, is a function of the event of Christ's death, resurrection, and ascension, rather than a function of the original act of creation. We have existence here and now, on earth and within history, because of the redemptive properties of that event.

We might express it in another, and more direct, fashion. Through the humiliation and exaltation of Jesus Christ a new time is created. And yet—paradoxically from our perspective—this new time is itself the time in which the very events of his incarnation, death, resurrection, and ascension occurred in the first place. In other words, the actuality of the triumph of Christ is what created the very possibility of the space-time within which that triumph could itself take place.

As the ascended Lord, Jesus Christ is present to all space and time. His time is the time enabling all events. Each day lived in human history exists as a function of the grace of God actualized in him. Each day of light and dark, each day of sunrise and sunset, each day of twenty-four hours, each day lived by Abraham, Moses, David, Paul, Timothy, Augustine, Luther, or ourselves, exists because of him and because of the "new time" of his triumph. And, even more significantly, each day of each of the years of Jesus' own life on earth—from the moment of his conception until the conclusion of his earthly ministry—existed because of that event. Crucially, what this means is that "new time," as a function of the grace of God in Christ, was the time within which the very possibility of God becoming incarnate in the womb of Mary *within time* could itself occur. All of this has implications for the relationship of Christology to historical time.

— *Chapter 15* —

# Christology and History

As part of the Christian Dogmatics final examinations in May, 1976, one of the questions set by Torrance for the paper on "Dogmatics and Logic," was, *"How far does eschatology belong to the warp and woof of Dogmatics rather than simply to its final chapters? In your answer discuss the bearing of eschatology upon the inner logical coherence of the organic structure of Dogmatics."*[1]

On the surface, the question appeared to be about eschatology in general; but behind it lay issues concerning how space-time should be understood in a theological setting. For Torrance, the ultimate coming of Jesus Christ was not to be thought of simply as a future event—though Torrance was clear that there will be a final Parousia. Nor was that ultimate coming to be understood as something realized and having already occurred, as with C. H. Dodd. Nor was it to be interpreted as a timeless principle, as with Rudolf Bultmann. Instead, for Torrance, the ultimate coming of Jesus Christ occurs historically in his incarnation, death, resurrection, and ascension, in which, and through which, the first-fruits of the new and permanent created order have been established. Torrance also insisted that such a new and reconstructed order includes a recreated space-time which now overarches *all of time*, past and present, and which, through the ascension, has been driven into every corner of history.[2] As such, both retrospectively and prospectively, this recreated space-time is the sole ground upon which existence itself has depended

---

1. See Appendix 2.
2. Cf. "Eschatology" in Walker's glossary, in Torrance, *Atonement*, 456.

ever since the entrance of sin and evil plunged the whole cosmos into a privation of existence.

Concerning the relationship of the triumph of Christ to time—whichever of the models discussed in the previous chapter is favoured—it is the overall concept of time, as understood within Torrance's eschatology, which enables us to grasp how every event in history, both before and after the historical events of Calvary and the Empty Tomb, is dependent upon that fundamental event of Christ's death, resurrection, and ascension.[3] For boundary-condition-events, actuality creates its own possibility. As such, it is the event of the triumph of Christ—as a core boundary-condition-event—which creates the very time within which that event can itself take place. And, through the benefits of the ascended Christ, who himself is Lord of time, the triumph of Christ enables all historical time to exist—not only for us, but also for Christ himself throughout his life on earth.

All of this has significance for the relationship between Bethlehem and Calvary. It means that the earthly history of Christ's incarnate life was, in fact, dependent upon, and made possible by, the event of his triumph through death, resurrection, and ascension. It was that event which enabled, actualised, generated, and made possible all else. Consequently, with this in mind, it becomes clear how Torrance's focus on Bethlehem and the incarnation never deprives Calvary or the Empty Tomb of their primary role. This is because Christ's humiliation and exaltation—his death, resurrection, and ascension—is the ultimate dynamic which lies behind all else. It is that which enables the time of all else, including Bethlehem's time, to be possible.

## Time and Existence

We can now develop these thoughts further, noting that all of them have embryonic existence in Torrance's work, though not necessarily his explicit endorsement. To begin with, we reprise our general argument, restating it in more formal terms. A Christian theology of space-time involves three propositions:

1. *Space-time is not a container within which events take place: rather, events themselves create and mold space-time.*

---

3. Torrance, *Atonement*, 304.

2. *Space-time is brought into being through the establishment of a covenant relationship between Creator and the creation.*

3. *Space-time, established by the covenant, has been shattered by the entrance of sin and evil: consequently, men and women now live in a time and space of grace brought into being in the person of Jesus Christ through the triumph of his death, resurrection, and ascension.*

*Space-time is not a container within which events take place: rather, events themselves create and mold space-time.* Torrance likened Newton's model of space and time to that of a container, or box, within which events happen.[4] But, in his lectures Torrance referred us to two moments in the history of thought which challenged this outlook.[5] First, he cited Einstein's dismissal of the receptacle notion of space-time. Second, he detected the rejection of a container view of space-time in the writings of major theologians, including several of the Church Fathers, and also Calvin and other Reformers (Lutherans excepted!).[6] In Torrance's opinion, these theologians anticipated a non-container notion of space-time, not because of any insights they had into the natural sciences, but because of the intellectual challenges thrown up by the doctrines of the Trinity and the incarnation. In class, this prompted Torrance to claim that modern science's relational understanding of space-time was in fact simply catching up with theological conceptualities. Taking this further, he used the rejection of a container view of space-time to rethink issues in Christology and sacramental theology.

---

4. Ritchie, Personal Lecture Notes, 16a (23rd November, 1973). In my notes I recorded Torrance saying: "Space and time do not exist apart from creation. (i) Greeks thought that space and time were some kind of containers. We say: 'we are *in* space or *in* time.' It is even possible to relate this to God as Newton did. Newton said that the mind of God *contained* all things. (ii) Space and time are mathematical systems in Kant's and Leibnitz's theories. In this view some would think that they are only concepts of the mind. (iii) Space and time are inherent in the Universe, and make the *order* of the Universe: this is the modern scientific idea which has caught up with the old theological idea. This is another way of saying that the Universe is a rational, intelligible, Universe, part of God's constancy. Creation is reliable because God is reliable."

5. Ritchie, Personal Lecture Notes, 16a (23rd November, 1973).

6. Torrance, *Space, Time and Incarnation*, 11, 30–32.

*Space-time is brought into being through the establishment of a covenant relationship between Creator and the creation.* Building on the first proposition, space-time is not a pre-existing framework within which a covenant relationship between God and his creation is a potential possibility. Instead, it is the event of the covenant relationship itself, brought into being *ex nihilo* by the Word of God, which establishes space-time as the theatre within which the created order is granted the possibility of existence. As such, space-time exists because of, and only because of, the covenant event. This links to Torrance's conviction that space-time is a function of events rather than being a generally existing entity within which events occur.[7] Moreover, because the covenant is the internal basis of creation, then it is the covenant which is the relentless driving force, the necessary constituent principle, and the irreplaceable dynamic reality, which alone brings space-time into existence, maintains it in being, and gives it its characteristics. However, just as we guard against regarding space-time as a *pre-existent* receptacle, so also we guard against granting space-time an independent existence *after* it has been brought into being. That is to say, we reject the notion that, once space-time has been brought into existence *through* the covenant, it gains an independent existence *apart from* the covenant. Instead, not only does space-time exist as a function of the covenant-event; but, without that covenant-event, space-time has no existence of its own.

༄

*Space-time, established by the covenant, has been shattered by the entrance of sin and evil: consequently, men and women now live in a time and space of grace brought into being in the person of Jesus Christ through the triumph of his death, resurrection, and ascension.* What is it that makes humanity's historical time possible, including the time when God became incarnate at Bethlehem, and the time within which we live day by day? Our time, historical time—which necessarily includes the years of the incarnate Son of God on earth—is itself a function of the space-time of grace. And it is this space-time of grace, and not any other, which is the space-time within which all men and women have lived by the mercy of God ever since sin and evil shattered the covenant which established original space-time in being. Hence, space-time for us now, is a space-time actualized in the person of Jesus Christ through his triumph. And,

7. Torrance, *Atonement*, 289. Cf. Torrance, *Incarnation*, 218.

ever since the entrance of sin and evil, this has been the only space-time available for life. It is the triumph of Jesus Christ which has made all historical time possible. Historical time exists in Christ as a fruit of his triumph, and as a time of grace for fallen humanity. Our time belongs to the benefits of the risen and ascended Christ, because it has come into being within that event. And, because his time bends both backwards and forwards from that first Easter, reaching into what otherwise would be the void of non-being, then historical time has been established and has been made possible.

## Time and History

As we have seen, Torrance's view of the relationship between Christ and time incorporated significant elements of what we have outlined above. He accepted that original space-time, established by the covenant, was profoundly affected by sin and evil. The way in which he expressed it was that "old time" has been held in existence alongside the "new time" of Christ Jesus because it has been taken up into Jesus Christ in the incarnation, redeemed at the cross, and renewed in his resurrection. God in his mercy upholds the fallen created order. God does not permit it to slip into nothingness. As previously quoted,

> The kind of time we have in our fallen existence is refracted time, time that has broken loose from God, as it were, and yet not time that has been allowed to slip into sheer chaos and nothingness but time that is contained, upheld, and overruled by God, within which he works out his redeeming purpose. The kind of time we have in historical events is the time of creation that has fallen from what it ought to be into disorder, and yet is contained through *nomos* from disappearing or vanishing into illusion.[8]

For Torrance, that was why the Church lives in two times,

> The church thus lives, as it were, in two times: in the time of this passing world, that is in the midst of on-going secular history and world events, the time of decay that flows down into the past and into the ashes of death; but also in the time of the risen Savior and of the new creation that is already a perfected reality in Him.[9]

---

8. Torrance, *Space, Time and Resurrection*, 97. Torrance, *Atonement*, 255.

9. Torrance, *Space, Time and Resurrection*, 99. This introduces the notion of an "eschatological pause" in the midst of event, which could be seen as a model for the 'pause' of Jesus' life in the midst of the one event of cross and resurrection. Torrance

Our emphasis is on the death of "old time"—a reality acknowledged by Torrance—and we view historical time as being entirely a function of the grace of Christ's death, resurrection, and ascension, rather than being the result of God tenaciously holding on to "old time," and stopping it from vanishing into nothingness. Hence, whereas Torrance preferred to speak of "old time" being upheld by God's mercy in order that men and women can have existence in historical time, it is also possible to describe historical time as something which exists within, and only within, the hard-won benefits of the risen and ascended Christ. In reality, the two approaches are not widely divergent, and represent alternative emphases rather than different concepts.

Torrance's emphasis corresponded to his softening of the early Barth's total and absolute rejection of the notion that "Grace perfects Nature." Over against that stark "No" of the early Barth, Torrance saw the created order—even in its fallenness—as being taken up into Christ through the incarnation, and in Christ being redeemed and renewed. But, importantly, its fallenness is not affirmed, ignored, or "baptized." Instead, in Christ it dies and then is recreated. Thus "old time" is not patched-up, or kept indefinitely on a life-support system. In Christ, as part of the fallen created order, it dies. But in Christ it is also recreated. In Christ it is "new time." In this way Torrance regarded all of the created order here and now, including space-time, as dependent upon the triumph of the risen Christ.

This "new time" bends backwards and forwards from that first Easter, not to connect with an "old time" existing in parallel with it, but to create a historical time within which life can be lived, and to cancel the nothingness of non-being. As such, it is "new time" which has created the possibility of history, and which has underpinned all human existence from Adam to the Parousia.[10]

---

wrote in *Atonement*, 303: "The ascension thus introduces, as it were, an eschatological pause or interval in the heart of the Parousia which makes it possible for us to speak of a first advent and a second or final advent of Christ." Torrance taught that, ontologically, there is only one parousia. In November, 1973, I recorded him stating: "The New Testament never uses *Parousia* in the plural. The 'final' Advent is not 'another' Advent, but still the one Advent. The final judgment is the same as that judgment on the cross. The judgment is not tagged on at the end of time. New Testament eschatology is both a relation between the New and the Old, the Present and the Final. The final coming is presented as both now and then, to show this idea of the *one* Parousia." Cf. Torrance, *Atonement*, 429–30.

10. At Easter of 2020, during the coronavirus (COVID-19) lockdown—when

In other words, the time in which all humanity has lived since the Fall, and the time in which Jesus himself lived in the days of his flesh upon earth, is a time which has being in and through—and only in and through—the incarnate and risen Jesus Christ himself. It is this time of the new creation which has created the very possibility of historical time, which, in God's mercy, enables us to live on earth at all. There is no grace outside of the person of Jesus Christ. Consequently, there is no time outside of Christ in which we can have existence. We live in him. Our time is in him. And our time has been actualized in the event which constitutes his person: namely, his humiliation and exaltation.

The mind-bending aspect of this is that such time, made possible in him, and existing in him, is also itself the historical time within which he was himself born at Bethlehem, within which he lived out his years, and within which he died and rose again. Hence, all of his time, and all of the events of his time, are functions of his death, resurrection, and ascension. His triumph—itself an event *in time*—was what made possible the very time within which itself took place. Torrance moved towards stating this when he wrote: "The church lives and works in the time that is established by the ascension for the proclamation of the gospel to all nations and ages. *God has established a time in the midst of history* in which he waits to be gracious, allowing time and history to run on its course in order that the world may be given time to repent and believe."[11]

In our suggested refinement of Torrance's approach, there exists no space-time *apart from* that which was brought into being through the event of the death, resurrection, and ascension of Christ. He is in himself that new covenant which is the internal basis and presupposition of the new creation. The risen and ascended Christ upholds our time in being because our time has its existence in him. Hence, the years from BC 4 to AD 30 were not part of an historical sequence left over from "old time" onto whose ruptured time-line the incarnate Son of God could step. Rather, these years only had substance because they were created within the event of his triumph. His years in history were themselves part of

---

much of the editing of this book took place—my friend Alastair Morrice wrote the following on Facebook: "[On the day following the crucifixion] the disciples went into a kind of lockdown. But was nothing happening? Nothing the human eye could see, but Peter gives a hint that some kind of preaching was taking place. I Peter 3:18–22: a mysterious passage indeed, but suggesting that the dying of Jesus *had implications reaching way back into the past as well as into the future*" (italics added).

11. Torrance, *Atonement*, 304.

the fruit of that "new time." And, that particular day in Nazareth, during the course of which he was conceived by the Holy Spirit in the womb of Mary, was a day which existed in history as the fruit of that "new time" which would be created through his triumph. That "new time" is the presupposition of all historical time.

From the normal perspective of a human observer, the specific boundary-condition-event of death, resurrection, and ascension, as an event in history, occurred several years *after* Bethlehem. But, ontologically, it was that event which drove everything, which "forged" and "made room" for itself, and which created the very possibility of the space-time which itself would occupy as an historical event in time. It was "new time" which created the moment in history when the Son of God's assumption of our humanity in the womb of Mary could take place. And there are echoes of this in Torrance: "The whole life of Jesus, the Word made flesh, is creative life within our fallen and corrupt existence: it is therefore re-creative."[12]

What this means is that when Jesus said, "I am the resurrection and the life" (John 11:25), he was not just anticipating what he would *become* after Calvary. Instead, he was describing what and who he *was* every moment of his life on earth. He lived the years from Bethlehem to Calvary *because of* the reality of his triumph, not simply in *anticipation* of it. His resurrection life was what gave substance to that life he led on earth. The whole ministry of Jesus—including his miracles—played out in historical time what he achieved in his resurrection.[13] Certainly, in class, Torrance stressed that it was because of the triumph of Christ that, "God is renewing creation all the time, though war, evil, etc., blind us to this reality."[14] Elsewhere, Torrance touched on the fact that the death and

---

12. Torrance, *Atonement*, 235.

13. Cf. Torrance, *Atonement*, 205: "The use of *egeiro* in the New Testament to speak of the raising up of the sick is an indication that the miraculous acts of healing are regarded as falling within the orbit of the resurrection, and as belonging to the creative and recreative activity of God in incarnation and resurrection. In these miracles the resurrection is already evidencing itself beforehand in signs and wonders." Cf. Torrance, *Space, Time and Resurrection*, 62.

14. Ritchie, Personal Lecture Notes, 18 (Autumn, 1973). My full notes record Torrance saying: "The idea of millenarianism, of Christ coming to reign for one thousand years on an unrenewed earth, is . . . an affront to the power of the resurrection and of the meaning of Christ coming and renewing the world. The millennium begins with *alpha* and ends with *omega*. It is a symbolic entity. God is renewing creation *all the time*, though war, evil, etc., blind us to this renewing."

resurrection of Christ disturbs the accepted ontology of time, especially its irreversibility,

> We recall that redemption is an act of *anakephalaiosis* or recapitulation with a dual movement. On the one hand it involves a penetration backwards in time and existence into the roots of human involvement in sin and evil, even into death and hell. We can discern something of the profound implications of that when we think of the descent into hell as a descent into the *irreversibility* of time and memory and guilt.[15]

⸻

In refining Torrance's model of the relationship between Christ and time, we have seen that all historical time has been possible only in and through the triumph of Christ. Jesus' own historical life on earth was possible only as part of the fruit of that "new time" which itself is part of his being. But what must be stressed is that these years when the Son of God trod the earth in our humanity were true years in real history. They were not phantasm. They were not illusion. They were not in appearance only. It was not a docetic Christ.[16] The Son of God was truly born of Mary. He truly lived. He truly suffered under Pontius Pilate. He truly died and was buried. All within real time and space.

What this means—and again our language is ill-fitted to express such realities—is that the Son of God was able to become flesh in the womb of Mary at a moment in historical time, only because of what would be actualized at Calvary and on Easter Day. The very "time" in which each of these events took place was itself created within his resurrection triumph. The constituent principle of the person of Jesus Christ is his becoming sin and his being raised in glory. He is who is he because of that event. As such, it was that event which "made room" for the historical

---

15. Torrance, *Atonement*, 243. Cf. Torrance, *Space, Time and Resurrection*, 86. For Torrance the creative power was especially linked to the resurrection. He wrote: "It is this conjunction of atoning death and recreation in the resurrection which means that out of the Cross there goes forth into the world the creative, saving, Word of God Almighty, so that all things, visible and invisible, fall under its purpose and sway" (*Space, Time and Resurrection*, 59).

16. In relation to the danger of Docetism, one of the questions in the Dogmatics II Autumn Term examination in 1974 was: "How may the concepts 'enhupostatos' and 'anhupostatos' be constructively combined in Christology? Is it true that the use of 'anhupostatos' implies lingering Docetism?"

time when Mary heard the angel's voice. It was that which "made room" for the historical time when she carried Christ in her womb. All the years of grace, from Bethlehem to Jerusalem, from Adam to the Last Trumpet, were "made room for," and created in, the person of the crucified, risen, and ascended Lord.

As Torrance put it, Christ's death and resurrection "are ontologically and structurally bound up with who he is in himself and in his relation to the Father."[17] What this means is that during every moment he was what he was precisely because of the cross and resurrection. It was that event which enabled him to be a physical, historical, person in time. And it was that event which made room for, created the possibility of, and established the actuality of, his time on earth. Without his humiliation and exaltation, there could not be, either ontologically or historically, the person of Jesus Christ, Jesus of Nazareth. He could not exist as a physical human person in time apart from existing as the humiliated and exalted one.

In the *Atonement* volume, Torrance made a revealing statement about what it is that constitutes the ontology of the person of Jesus Christ. He wrote: "The resurrection is to be understood not only as the completion of that saving work but as belonging to the *ontological structure of the mediator himself.*[18] This was closely replicated in a passage in *Space, Time and Resurrection*: "The resurrection is to be regarded not only as the completion of that saving work *but as belonging to the ontological structure of the Mediator himself* who stood in the gap of the *Eli, Eli, lama sabachthani.*"[19] What Torrance was emphasizing in these passages was that Christ's very being is what it is because of his *forsakenness* and because of his *resurrection triumph*. His person was formed and actualized, in the conjunction of the humiliation of his death and the triumph of his resurrection.

In Jesus Christ time is redeemed and recreated. Hence, all time and all history exists as a function of that resurrection victory. All history depends for its existence on the death and resurrection of Easter. It is there that time and space are forged and given substance. Consequently, the incarnation did not make the atonement possible as a future event in time. Instead, it was "new time," established in Christ's new humanity of the resurrection, and bent backwards and forwards from that first Easter,

---

17. Torrance, *Atonement*, 211.

18. Torrance, *Atonement*, 212 (italics added); also, 235. Torrance appeared to weaken this strong statement when he described the resurrection as that which "holds firm" the hypostatic union rather than as that which "establishes and actualizes it" (216).

19. Torrance, *Space, Time and Resurrection*, 50 (italics added).

which enabled the historical time of Bethlehem and of Calvary to be possible. This is why Bethlehem can never empty Calvary of significance. The opposite is the case. Bethlehem is ontologically dependent upon, and rooted in, the humiliation and exaltation of Jesus Christ.

— *Chapter 16* —

# Christology and Gospel

DID TORRANCE'S EMPHASIS ON Bethlehem diminish the importance of Calvary? This question has reappeared throughout our discussions. Consideration of the issues has led us to affirm that Calvary is the presupposition of Bethlehem, that Bethlehem is the presupposition of Calvary, and that the cross and the resurrection is the foundational reality which undergirds and empowers everything. The whole movement of the Son of God, through humiliation to exaltation, is the driver for the saving act of God. And the crucial moment of that action is coincident with the lowest place to which Christ went, namely, hell, abandonment, forsakenness, the moment of his awful cry of dereliction from the cross, his becoming sin for us. Consequently, it was because of what happened on Calvary, that Bethlehem was ever possible, both in terms of being an event in space and time, and in terms of its theological significance.

Pursuing this argument has necessitated the development of a christological understanding of time. Usually, ontological possibility tracks the same linear sequence as historical chronology. Over against this, our model points to the one integrated event of cross and resurrection, the Son of God's complete downward and upward movement to hell and to glory, making possible both the time and the reality of his conception, birth, and historical life. The person of Jesus Christ was generated and constituted in the womb of Mary, precisely *because of* the event of his humiliation and exaltation. It was the twin event of Calvary and Easter morning, of becoming sin and becoming a new creation, which made possible all else. He did not live his historical life in order, at some point, to become the Savior. Rather, it was because in his death and resurrection he was the Savior, that he was able to live his life on earth. The theologically cosmic boundary-condition-event of the triumph of his death, resurrection, and ascension, is what enabled the Son of God to be Jesus of Nazareth on earth in our history.

This inversion of perspective enables an understanding of incarnation and atonement in which each is truly dependent on the other, and yet avoiding the serious criticism that Torrance's incarnational soteriology strips the cross of its centrality, necessity, and supremacy. Such an inference is nullified because, in what we have outlined, there can be no incarnation without the cross undergirding it. The incarnation occurs and has its being, precisely because the person of Jesus Christ was constituted in his becoming sin in the forsakenness of Calvary, and in his becoming a new creation in the resurrection. Apart from the cross Christ cannot become sin: hence, consequently, neither can he assume our broken humanity in order to redeem it. Thus the ontology of Christology moves in reverse to that of the chronology of history. In a profound sense, the incarnation took place through the portal of the cross.

## Solidarity with Sinners

Crucially, the incarnation did not occur in two stages. Jesus was not partially incarnate at Bethlehem, and then fully incarnate at Calvary. Instead, within real historical time Jesus lived out the ontological reality of his being, itself constituted in his humiliation and exaltation. The humanity borne at Calvary was the humanity born at Bethlehem.

It is true in a literal sense—and not simply in a poetic or metaphorical sense—that Jesus Christ *is* the dying and rising one, *is* the abandoned and justified one, and *is* the resurrection and the life. Moreover, he was so from the moment of his birth, and continued as such throughout through his ministry. The gift of myrrh was brought to the infant Christ because he was already, in his being, the one who dies and rises again. In the same way, it was the power of the resurrection which made his healing miracles possible. Not a power granted in *prospect* of a future event. But a power which was present because he was *already*, in his being, the first fruits of the new creation which were now breaking in upon all history as the benefits of his triumph were bent both backwards and forwards from the first Easter.

With this in mind, we can clarify some of Torrance's expressions. One of his themes was that Jesus, throughout his life and ministry, had

## Christology and Gospel

an "increasing solidarity" with sinners as he identified ever more deeply with the human condition, and as he grew from a babe, to a boy, to a youth, to a man (cf. Luke 2:52). This ever-increasing solidarity with sinners meant that, from the moment of his assumption of our humanity, he was engaged in sanctifying our human nature. In Torrance's words, from the moment of assuming our humanity, the Son of God' "began to pay the price" of our sin.[1] What Torrance was trying to express was how the whole life of Jesus, issuing from the nature of his person, was involved in the process of redemption. As he stated in *Space, Time and Resurrection*, "The union of God and man begun in the birth of Immanuel reaches throughout the incarnate life and work of Christ and *is fully and finally* achieved on man's side and on God's side in the crucifixion and resurrection of Jesus Christ."[2] This is repeated almost exactly in the *Atonement* volume. In these extracts we pay close attention to Torrance's choice of words. The incarnation is, "*Fully and finally achieved on man's side and on God's side in the crucifixion and resurrection of Jesus Christ.*"[3] But what does "fully and finally" mean?

There is no doubt that Torrance's emphasis on Jesus' "increasing solidarity" with sinners, as Jesus penetrated ever more deeply into the human condition, is a pastorally helpful concept. But, though homiletically arresting, might the chosen wording be injudicious? The problem—if there is a problem—lies in the vocabulary employed. Words and phrases such as "began," "increasing," "fully," "finally" are potentially ambiguous. We have no desire to be pedantic in this matter, nor to be over literal, but some clarification is required. This is because the word "began" implies that a process is to be completed, which is as yet incomplete. But was that the case for the incarnation? Similarly, the phrase "increasing solidarity" implies that Jesus, at a given point, had *less* solidarity with sinners than he would have in the future. And also, "fully and finally" could be read as implying that, in some manner, there may be stages to the incarnation.

Concerning the word "began," Torrance could insist quite justifiably that there is good biblical precedent for stating that the work of Christ was "completed" on the cross: at least as viewed from a human, time-bound, perspective. But what must not be overlooked is that the work was already complete in Christ throughout his life *because* of the

---

1. Torrance, *Atonement*, 128.

2. Torrance, *Space, Time and Resurrection*, 66 (italics added). Cf. Torrance, *Atonement*, 62.

3. Torrance, *Atonement*, 227.

cross. All through his life, Jesus lived out the consequences of what he actualized in his death, resurrection and ascension. This is what Torrance meant, though his chosen terminology was capable of misunderstanding. Similar points could be made with respect to the "fully and finally" of the hypostatic union of the incarnation.

To be clear, there was, in fact, no time at which the incarnate Son of God lacked total ontological solidarity with those for whom he came. Of course, as one who was fully human, and who grew in understanding (Luke 2:52), his awareness and practical experience of that ontological solidarity was something which developed day by day and year by year. However, it was the *full* work of the cross, the *complete* achievement of Calvary, which he expressed all though his ministry. Importantly, what this means is that in the womb of Mary his fundamental assumption of our broken humanity was not partial, but total. And all of what happened in him, and through him, flowed from what he was, and from what he became, on Calvary's cross. Torrance never intended to give the impression that at Bethlehem the incarnation was partial whereas at Calvary it was total. Only a superficial reading could allow such an interpretation.[4] The Christ born at Bethlehem was not a human being waiting for his humanity to be completed on the cross later in his life. Rather, at Bethlehem he was fully the incarnate one who was made sin for us. But, he was so precisely because of what happened on the cross.

## The Gospel and the Person of Jesus Christ

There are passages in Torrance's writings which allude strongly to our fundamental proposition that it is the death and resurrection of Jesus Christ, his humiliation and exaltation, which constitutes his person. As we have already seen, in an important passage in the *Atonement* lectures Torrance used the term "ontological" in a context in which he taught that the person of the New Testament Christ can never, at any point, be divorced from the person of the risen Christ.

> The Christ who is proclaimed to us in the New Testament, therefore, is the Christ who is clothed with the kerygma of his *death* and *resurrection*, for they are ontologically and

---

4. Ambiguity also appears in Torrance, *Atonement*, 10: "[The covenant promise to Israel] is remarkably fulfilled in the incarnation of Jesus as the seed of Abraham although that circumcision is *entirely fulfilled*, as Paul puts it, *only* in the total circumcision, that is the crucifixion of the body of Christ on the cross" (italics added).

structurally bound up with who he is in himself and in his relation to the Father.⁵

This is repeated word for word in *Space, Time and Resurrection*.⁶ For Torrance, Jesus' death and resurrection were, "*ontologically and structurally bound up with who he is in himself.*" In stating this, Torrance was not referring simply to the person Jesus "became" after the first Easter, but to the person whom he always was from his birth of Mary.

Elsewhere, when Torrance wrote in terms of Christ's death and resurrection as a revelatory event, he stated, "It is in the resurrection that we have the unveiling of the mystery of the incarnation." He then added, "The birth and resurrection of Jesus belong inseparably together and have to be understood in the light of each other."⁷ Going further, Torrance pointed out that, alongside the *revelatory* significance of the death and resurrection of Christ, lies the *ontological* significance of the cross and empty tomb for the person of Christ,

> What Jesus Christ is in his resurrection; he is in himself . . . The resurrection was not just an event that happened to Christ, for it corresponded to the kind of person he was in his own being . . . the whole life of Jesus Christ, together with his resurrection, was the manifestation among mankind in time and history of the *ultimate* and *original* and *final* creative activity of God.⁸

There are other extracts which indicate how Torrance understood Jesus' death and resurrection in relation to the time of Jesus' ministry here on earth; a time chronologically preceding the decisive events of Calvary and Easter. For example, in *Atonement*,

> The teaching of the New Testament makes it clear that we cannot isolate the resurrection from the whole redeeming purpose of God, *or from the decisive deed of God in the incarnation of his Son that ran its full course from the birth of Jesus to his crucifixion and triumph over the powers of evil* . . . We are not to think of the humiliation and exaltation of Christ simply as two events following one after the other, *but as both involved in appropriate measure at the same time all through the incarnate life of Christ*.⁹

5. Torrance, *Atonement*, 211 (italics added).
6. Torrance, *Space, Time and Resurrection*, 49.
7. Torrance, *Atonement*, 218.
8. Torrance, *Atonement*, 221 (italics added).
9. Torrance, *Atonement*, 209–10 (italics added).

In these words, Torrance linked the death and resurrection of Christ to his entire life. Incarnation and atonement are not two events, but one reality. And that one reality is the person of Jesus Christ himself. It is through the resurrection and ascension that the person of Christ is actualized in time. And it is the Christ of the cross and resurrection who creates, and makes possible, the time of his whole life, ministry, existence here on earth.

⁓

I had not seen or spoken to Tom Torrance for some years until the Church of Scotland General Assembly of 2001. At that Assembly, now frail, he came to hear his son Iain present one of the Reports. In November of the same year I took up a post at Zomba Theological College in Malawi, teaching Systematic Theology. How would a theology learned in Edinburgh apply in Central Africa? And yet, as I became aware of issues arising at the interface between African Traditional Religion and the Gospel, these very issues prompted me to write my lectures with Torrance and Barth's christologically-centred principles very much in mind. The aim was to try and remove ideas from my own thinking, and from my students' thinking, which were imbued with non-biblical content from our respective cultures. This was what Barth had tried to do after 1914. And it had also been what Torrance resolved to put into practice in both his Alyth manse and his New College classroom. Each word, each idea, had to be redefined from a christological centre. The aim of this discipline was to allow the object of our enquiry—God himself—to dictate the meaning of each word for us. What do we mean by the word "God"? We tried to redefine it from within a christological perspective, rather than from within a particular cultural context—whether that culture is Eastern, Western, or African. What do we mean by the word "sin"? Again, we tried to redefine it from a christological perspective. And so on. We did this across the whole range of theological language, concepts, and imaging, constantly re-examining terms such as "salvation," "humanity," "spirit" etc. And the aim of the exercise was to allow, as far as we could, the being and the act of God in Jesus Christ to re-inhabit each word used in in theological speech. And what I found, as I wrote my theology lectures for students who were training to be ministers of the Gospel in an African context, was that this approach crossed so many cultural barriers because it helped all of us—teacher and student alike—to root our thinking more fully in Jesus Christ. It was our way of trying to allow the object of our study, namely God as he comes to us in Jesus Christ, attested in Holy Scripture, to remold and to recreate the way we thought.

It was during my time in Malawi that Tom Torrance became ill, unable to write more, and needing nursing care. Even during these difficult and constrained years, his passion for the Gospel remained strong. One of his visitors, who had been on a visit to China, was able to bring news of families whom Tom Torrance's father and mother had influenced for Christ so many years beforehand. That gave him great joy. Then, on the second of December, 2007, Thomas Forsyth Torrance passed to glory and into the nearer presence of the Lord whom he had sought to serve. When I heard the news I was now in Dingwall in the north of Scotland, involved both in parish ministry and teaching at Highland Theological College. It so happened that that week I led College prayers, and I spoke to the students about TFT, and about the utter centrality of Jesus Christ in both his personal faith and academic calling.

At New College, Tom Torrance had given us, his students, something more than an ordinary theological education. He had given us a different way to think. He had made us reflect on what it means to truly put Christ at the centre of both form and content in theology. And that momentous series of lectures which he delivered in the autumn of 1973, during the opening term of our studies, made an indelible mark on our whole understanding of theology, and profoundly influenced our personal Christian faith.

In this book we have concentrated on a specific point of tension between Torrance's theology and the tradition of Westminster Calvinism. There are other areas of divergence, but our attention has been occupied by this one, important, aspect. And we have suggested a way in which this stress-point may be overcome. The fact that there are stress-points at all, should neither surprise nor distress. Sharp disagreement does not mean that one, or both, of the opposing parties are far from the truth. It is not unusual in the sciences for stress-points to emerge, especially when two lines of thought both begin to home in on the true nature of the reality under examination. That is the case in the tension between Relativity Theory and Quantum Theory. Both systems apprehend something beyond their total grasp. Both are feeling their way towards deep-rooted facets of the truth. And similar situations occur in theological science,

What we have emphasized throughout is that, in Torrance's theology, the Christian Gospel is not a thing, a teaching, a concept, an ideal.

Instead, the Christian Gospel is a person. *He* is the one we proclaim (Col 1:28). Thus, Jesus Christ is the Gospel in his very being. "Jesus is the Gospel." In working through that principle, Torrance's theology signals that Calvary is the presupposition of Bethlehem, that Bethlehem is the presupposition of Calvary, and—most importantly and fundamentally—that the cross and resurrection is the ultimate reality undergirding and underpinning everything. Absolutely everything. It is Easter which feeds us with the logic of all theology. And it is the crucified, risen, and ascended Christ who makes the grace of God a reality in time and space, and in the souls of men and women.

— *Appendix 1* —

# The Dogmatics Course

THE FOLLOWING LIST REFERS to the bulk of the Guidance Notes, Reading Lists, Seminar Programs, and Class Handouts which were issued to students. The Reading Lists for Dogmatics I, II, and III, were augmented for final year Honors. In class Torrance commented, line-by-line, on most of the printed handouts on soteriology and ecclesiology.

## Dogmatics I: Initial Reading List

Athanasius, *Contra Gentes; De Incarnatione.*
D. M. Baillie, *God Was In Christ.*
Karl Barth, *Dogmatics in Outline: Church Dogmatics,* I/1, 8–18.
F. J. Sheed, *Theology and Sanity.*
D. Bonhoeffer, *The Cost of Discipleship.*
E. Brunner, *Truth as Encounter.*
G. S. Hendry, *The Gospel of the Incarnation.*
H. R. Mackintosh, *The Christian Experience of Forgiveness.*
James Orr, *The Progress of Dogma.*
L. Berkhoff, *The History of Christian Doctrine.*
W. Pannenberg, *The Apostles' Creed.*
J. Burnaby, *The Belief of Christendom.*
T. F. Torrance, *The School of Faith*
    (Introduction & Calvin's Geneva Catechism)
A. W. Wainwright, *The Trinity in the New Testament.*

## Dogmatics I: Honors Augmented Reading List

Anselm, *Truth, Freedom and Evil.*
John Hick, *Evil and the God of Love.*
Augustine, *On the Trinity* (XII–XV).
Hilary, *On the Trinity.*
Karl Barth, *Church Dogmatics,* I/2, 19–24; II/1, 25–28;
    III/1, 40–41; III/2, 43–47.
Paul Tillich, *Systematic Theology* I.
Henri Bouillard, *The Knowledge of God.*
Edward Schillebeeckx, *Revelation and Theology.*
Karl Rahner, *The Trinity.*
T. F. Torrance, *Theological Science; God and Rationality.*
C. Welch, *The Trinity in Contemporary Theology.*
L. Hodgson, *The Doctrine of the Trinity.*
E. Brunner, *Dogmatics* 2 (part 1, Creation); *Man in Revolt.*
K. Heim, *The Transformation of the Scientific World View.*
A. Mackinnon, *Falsification and Belief.*
Peter Baelz, *Providence and Prayer.*

## Dogmatics I: Assignment

"The Significance of Matthew 11:27 (Luke 10:22) for the Doctrine of the Person of Christ." To be handed in no later than Monday 11th February, 1974.

## Dogmatics I: 1973 Autumn Term Seminar Text

Karl Barth, *Dogmatics in Outline.*

## Dogmatics II: Initial Reading List

Anselm, *Cure Deus Homo?*
D. M. Baillie, *God Was in Christ.*
Karl Barth, *Church Dogmatics,* I/2, 15; IV/1, 57–59; IV/2, 64.
D. Bonhoeffer, *Christology* (seminar text).
Emil Brunner, *The Mediator.*
John Calvin, *Institutes,* II:1–2, 9–17.

S. Cave, *The Doctrine of the Person of Christ.*
R. H. Fuller, *Foundations of New Testament Christology.*
E. R. Hardy and C. C. Richardson, *Christology of the Later Fathers.*
J. McLeod Campbell, *The Nature of the Atonement.*
J. K. Mozley, *The Doctrine of the Atonement.*
T. F. Torrance, *Theology in Reconstruction,* 7–10;
   *Space, Time, and Incarnation; Theology in Reconciliation.*

## Dogmatics II: Honors Augmented Reading List

T. H. Bindley and F. W. Green, *The Ecumenical Documents of the Faith.*
G. L. Prestige, *God in Patristic Thought; Fathers and Heretics.*
Athanasius, *Against the Arians.*
Anselm, *Epistle on the Incarnation.*
W. Kunneth, *The Theology of the Resurrection.*
R. S. Franks, *The Work of Christ.*
W. Pannenberg, *Jesus, God and Man.*

## Dogmatics II: Assignment 1

"Summarize, in no more than 2,500 words, Section 15 of Karl Barth's *Church Dogmatics,* I/2, entitled 'The Mystery of Revelation'."

## Dogmatics II: Assignment 2

"Write a 2,500-word essay on the 'The Relationship between the Incarnation and the Atonement.' To be submitted by Monday 3rd Feb, 1975."

## Dogmatics II: 1974 Autumn Term Seminar Text (Thursdays)

Bonhoeffer, *Christology* (Fontana edition).

| | | |
|---|---|---|
| 10th Oct | 27–40 | Introduction. |
| 17th Oct | 43–48 | The Present Christ—The *Pro Me.* |
| 24th Oct | 49–61 | The Figure of Christ. |
| 31st Oct | 61–67 | The Place of Christ. |
| 7th Nov | 71–77 | Access to the Historical Christ. |
| 14th Nov | 77–88 | Critical or Negative Christology |

| | | | |
|---|---|---|---|
| 21st Nov | 88–106 | | Heresies. The Contribution of Critical Christology. |
| 28th Nov | 106–18 | | Positive Christology. |
| 5th Dec | | | Revision |

## Dogmatics II: 1975 Spring Term Seminar Texts:

Hilary, *On the Trinity*
John Calvin, *Institutes*, II:1–2, 9–17.

## Dogmatics III: Initial Reading List

Anselm, *On the Procession of the Holy Spirit.*
Athanasius, *Letters on the Spirit to Serapion* (seminar text).
Karl Barth, *Church Dogmatics*, I/1, 12; I/2, 15; IV/1, 62; IV/2, 67.
Basil, *On the Holy Spirit.*
R. Bruce, *The Mystery of the Lord's Supper.*
John Calvin, *Institutes*, I:13; III:1–3,6–10; IV:1–2,14–18.
Church of Scotland, *The Biblical Doctrine of Baptism;*
    *The Doctrine of Baptism.*
Oscar Cullman, *Salvation in History.*
Cyril of Jerusalem, *Lectures on the Sacraments* (seminar text).
Hans Kung, *The Church.*
L. Newbiggin, *The Household of God.*
A. M. Ramsay, *The Gospel and the Catholic Church.*
John V. Taylor, *The Go-Between God.*
T. F. Torrance, *God and Rationality*, 6–8; *Theology in Reconstruction*,
    11–15; *Theology in Reconciliation.*
J. J. von Allmen, *The Lord's Supper.*
G. Wainwright, *Eschatology and Eucharist.*
Vatican II, *Lumen Gentium.*

## Dogmatics III: Honors Augmented Reading List

Robert F. Evans, *One and Holy: The Church in Latin Patristic Thought.*
V. Lossky, *The Mystical Theology of the Eastern Church.*
Cyprian, *On the Unity of the Church.*

William Milligan, *The Ascension of our Lord*.
L. Newbiggin, *The Reunion of the Church*.
Hans Kung, *Structures of the Church*.
E. L. Mascall, *The Mystery of the Lord's Supper*.
D. Bonhoeffer, *Communio Sanctorum*.
D. M. Baillie, *The Theology of the Sacraments*.
Killian McDonnell, *Calvin's Doctrine of the Church and Eucharist*.
G. S. Hendry, *The Holy Spirit in Christian Theology*.
Origen, *De Principiis*, I:3.
Gregory of Nazianzus, *Oration*, 31 (5th Theological Oration)
Augustine, *Homily 99 on St. John; De Trinitate*, XV:27–51;
    *On the Spirit, Letters*.
Aquinas, *Summa Theologica*, I: qq. 36–38

## Dogmatics III: 1975 Autumn Term Seminar Text (Fridays)

Athanasius, *Letters to Serapion, mainly on the Holy Spirit*.

| | | |
|---|---|---|
| 10th Oct | I:1–2 | The heresy of the "Tropici" |
| 17th Oct | I:3–14 | Their exegesis of Amos 4:13 and 1 Timothy 5:21. |
| 24th Oct | I:15–21 | Their argument: "Either Son or creature." |
| 31st Oct | I:22–27 | Athanasius' arguments for the divinity of the Spirit. |
| 7th Oct | I:28–33 | The Trinity in the Church's tradition. |
| 14th Nov | II:1–9 | The Son is not a creature. |
| 21st Nov | III:1–7 | The Spirit is not a creature. |
| 28th Nov | IV:1–7 | "Either Son or creature" again refuted |

## Dogmatics III: 1976 Spring Term Seminar Text

Cyril of Jerusalem, *Lectures on the Sacraments*.

## Dogmatics III: Assignments

For honors students, no set titles were given. Instead, each student was expected to write a short essay each week for submission to one of the tutors and to be discussed with them, either on a one-to-one basis or in a group. The essay topics were of the student's own choosing, but should engage with the whole range of theology covered by the Dogmatics course. The following is a record of the essays which I submitted, with approximate dates and the initials of the tutor they were submitted to.

| | |
|---|---|
| 14th Oct, 1975 | "Revelation" (TFT) |
| 27th Oct, 1975 | "Reason" (TFT) |
| 10th Nov, 1975 | "Faith" (TFT) |
| 12th Nov, 1975 | "Logic" (TFT) |
| 17th Nov, 1975 | "Symbolization" (TFT) |
| ? Dec, 1975 | "Logic and Evil" (TFT) |
| 9th Jan, 1976 | "Logic and Grace" (TFT) |
| 25th Feb, 1976 | "Gödel's Theorem and Dogmatics" (TFT) |
| 13th Oct, 1975 | "God is Love" (JBT) |
| 31st Oct, 1975 | "Basil's *De Spiritu Sancto*" (JBT) |
| 13th Nov, 1975 | "Anselm's *Cur Deus Homo?*" (JBT) |
| 26th Nov, 1975 | "Baptism in the Spirit, and Baptism in Water" (JBT) |
| 8th Dec, 1975 | "Sonship and the Image of God" (JBT) |
| 14th Jan, 1976 | "The Penal Aspect of the Atonement" (JBT) |
| 26th Nov, 1975 | "Holy Spirit in Tertullian's *Adversus Praxean*" (AICH) |
| ? Dec, 1975 | "God as Three and God as One" (AICH) |
| ? Dec, 1975 | "Epistemological Significance of the Holy Spirit" (AICH) |
| 20th Jan, 1976 | "Anhypostasia-Enhypostasia" (AICH) |
| 17th Feb, 1976 | "Worship and the High-Priesthood of Christ" (AICH) |

⁓

## Dogmatics IV, Series 1:
### "Scottish Theology from 1560 to 1843" (JBT)

| | |
|---|---|
| 5th Jan, 1976 | The Covenant concept in Biblical and Reformed thought. |
| 6th Jan, 1976 | The Marrow Controversy (1717–1722) |
| 8th Jan, 1976 | Federal Theology: The Westminster Documents; The Sum of Saving Knowledge; Thomas Boston (1676–1732) |

| | |
|---|---|
| 9th Jan, 1976 | The Rise of Federal Theology—from Scots Confession to Westminster Assembly (1560–1643) |
| 12th Jan, 1976 | Theological Background: Musculus; Szegedin; Dudley Fenner; William Perkins; Robert Rollock; Ames; Cocceius. |
| 13th Jan, 1976 | Political Background: The Development of Contractarian Ideas. |
| 15th Jan, 1976 | Covenant and Contract of Government: The Historical Argument: Major; Boece; Knox; George Buchanan's *De Iure Regni apud Scotos* (1579) |
| 16th Jan, 1976 | Covenant and Contract of Government: The Biblical Argument: Duplessis Mornay; *Vindiciae Contra Tyrannos* (1579) |
| 19th Jan, 1976 | Covenant and Contract of Government: Samuel Rutherford, *Lex Rex* (1644) |
| 20th Jan, 1976 | Covenant and Contract of Government: Robert Douglas and the Coronation at Scone of Charles II (1651) |
| 22nd Jan, 1976 | The Covenant Concept in Federal Theology—Covenant or Contract? |
| 23rd Jan, 1976 | SEMINAR I |
| 26th Jan, 1976 | Atonement and Federal Theology: The Headship of Christ: David Dickson; Thomas Erskine; William Symington. |
| 27th Jan, 1976 | John McLeod Campbell (1800–1872): The Nature and Extent of Atonement and the unconditional freeness of Grace. |
| 29th Jan, 1976 | Edward Irving (1792–1834): The Incarnation and Baptism of the Spirit. |
| 30th Jan, 1976 | SEMINAR II |

**Dogmatics IV, Series 2:**
**"Protestant Theology in the Nineteenth Century." (JBT)**

# Appendix 1

## Printed Class Handouts

*All but the last item in the following list of class handouts was written by T. F. Torrance. The one exception was by J. B. Torrance.*

"Hugh Ross Mackintosh: Theologian of the Cross." *SBET*, Vol. 5/2, 1987, 160–73.
"The Integration of Form in Natural and in Theological Science."
"The Church in the New Era of Scientific and Cosmological Change."
"The Place of Michael Polanyi in the Modern Philosophy of Science."
"The iItegration of Form in Natural and Theological Science."
"Revelation and Religion."
"Hermeneutics, or the Interpretation of Biblical and Theological Statements according to Hilary of Poitiers."
"Priestly Aspect of Atonement."
"The Priesthood of Christ."
"Range of Redemption."
"The Old Israel and the Incarnation."
"The Understanding of Redemption in the Early Church."
"The Kingdom of Christ and Evil."
"The Continuous Union in the Historical life and Obedience of Jesus."
"Atoning Justification."
"The Resurrection of Jesus Christ."
"The Resurrection and the Person of Jesus Christ."
"The Resurrection and the Atoning Work of Christ."
"The Nature of the Resurrection Event."
"The Ascension of Jesus Christ."
"The Resurrection and the Ascension."
"Jesus Christ the Servant-Son."
"The Life and Faithfulness of the Son toward Man."
"The One Church of God."
"The Doctrine of the Church."
"The Foundation of the Church."

"The One Baptism Common to Christ and his Church."
"A Neglected Aspect of the Doctrine of Baptism."
"The Contribution of McLeod Campbell to Scottish Theology" (JBT).

— *Appendix 2* —

# The Dogmatics Exams

**Dogmatics I: Autumn Term Exam (13 Dec, 1973).** *(THREE Questions to be answered).*

1. Examine the implications for theological method of the principle that we know things in accordance with their nature.//
2. Write a short essay on "the knowability of God": OR, How would you distinguish between *revelation* and *discovery* as used respectively in theological science and in natural science?
3. Discuss the relation between knowing God and being reconciled to him.
4. Examine carefully the claim that since knowledge of God arises only on the ground of his interaction with the world, true knowledge of God is not without empirical correlates in space and time; OR, Discuss the bearing upon theological interpretation and formulation of radical change in our cosmological outlook.
5. How would you answer the question "Who is God?"
6. Offer a theological analysis of the statement "God is love."
7. Expound what is meant by the Creed in confessing faith in "God the Father Almighty."
8. Explain what Barth means by speaking of man as "the creature of the boundary between heaven and earth."
9. What is meant by *creation out of nothing*? How does this affect our understanding of the intelligibility of created and contingent existence?

10. How do you react to the Augustinian teaching that evil is merely a "defection from the good" and a "privation of being"?

---

**Dogmatics I: Degree Exam (6 June, 1974).** *The General Theology Paper for the yearly Degree examination was in two sections: Divinity and Dogmatics. (FIVE questions to be answered with at least TWO from each section). The following questions comprised the Dogmatics component of the examination.*

1. "Science universally proceeds on the assumption that something on the subject dealt with can be known, and that, if right methods are employed, sure results may be expected." How far is this applicable to Christian theology?

2. Consider the claim that the act of faith is incipient theology. OR: What is the nature of biblical statements? How are they related to dogmatic statements? Is the same mode of verification applicable to both?

3. Comment upon the statement that true and proper fatherhood resides in God and that from the Fatherhood of God what we know as fatherhood among us is derived.

4. Offer a critical analysis of the view advanced by Basileides that we cannot know what God is but only what he is not.

5. "Worship is the gift of participating through the Spirit in the Son's communion with the Father." Elucidate this statement and show its applicability to the Christian understanding of God. OR: Elucidate the statement that there is an inner polarity in the Person of Christ which is fundamental for our understanding of Christian doctrine.

6. Our Anglo-Saxon word "atonement" is a good word to translate the New Testament word *katallage* (reconciliation). Evaluate this statement.

7. Jesus' life of communion with the Father did not begin at Bethlehem, nor did it end on the Cross. Discuss.

8. Explain why the Council of Nicaea chose the term *homoousious* (of *one* or the *same* substance) instead of the term *homoiousios* (of like substance) to express the essential divinity of Christ.

9. How far would you agree with Athanasius or Karl Barth that the doctrine of the Trinity sums up the Gospel? OR: How far would you agree with the following statement by R. Gregor Smith? "The real question is not what Jesus is, or what the Spirit is, or what God the Father is: but the question is how are we to understand ourselves in relation to the realities indicated by these names."

***

**Dogmatics II: Autumn Term Exam (10 Dec, 1974).** *(Answer Question One and TWO further Questions).*

1. Briefly explain and comment on TWO of the following:
   a. "He stood before Pilate and sat by the Father; he hung on the cross and supported the universe" (Melito of Sardis).
   b. "He passed through each stage of life, restoring to each age fellowship with God" (Irenaeus).
   c. "We have always believed in one only God, yet subject to the 'dispensation' (which is our translation of 'oikonomia')" (Tertullian).
   d. "It is an eternal and ceaseless generation, as radiance is generated from the light" (Origen).
   e. "The Word is from above; Jesus Christ is man from hence" (Paul of Samosata).
   f. "Before he was begotten, he was not" (Arius).
   g. "It is not lawful to say that the fountain is dry, or that the light has no ray, or that God has no Word" (Athanasius).
   h. "Humanity would not have been deified if the Word who became flesh had not by nature derived from the Father, and his true and proper Word" (Athanasius).
   i. "If God had bound himself together with a man, one complete reality with another complete reality, then there would be two—one, Son of God by nature, and one, assumed" (Apollinarius of Laodicea).
   j. "For that which he has not assumed, he has not healed; but that which is united to his godhead is also saved" (Gregory of Nazianzus).

2. Outline the main developments in Christology in the early church up to the Council of Chalcedon. How far can a constant pattern be traced through them all?

3. "A good heresy never dies away: it merely reappears in another form." Discuss, with reference to Docetism OR Arianism OR Apollinarianism.

4. "The doctrinal decisions of Nicaea and Chalcedon are primarily negative." Discuss. OR: "Chalcedon asks the question 'How?', but in answering it, shows the impossibility of the question." Discuss.

5. Comment on the epistemological implications of Tertullian's remark: "The Son of God was born: shameful and therefore there is no shame. The Son of God died: absurd and therefore utterly credible. He was buried and rose again: impossible and therefore a fact."

6. "When a subject is obscure and requires to be brought within our understanding, not only do diverse but even quite contradictory illustrations convey the meaning sought for" (Dionysius of Alexandria). Comment, with reference to the use of such models as Logos, Image, Radiance and Son in the second, third and fourth centuries.

7. "Had Arianism conquered, the church would have retreated into mythical polytheism, abandoning alike the knowledge of God in Christ and the hope of salvation through Christ." Discuss. OR: "The Arians say that what they cannot understand cannot be true." Why does Athanasius make this accusation?

8. How may the concepts "enhupostatos" and "anhupostatos" be constructively combined in Christology? Is it true that the use of "anhupostatos" implies lingering Docetism?

9. "In both Luther and Calvin, the grace of God in Christ is re-established at the center of theology." Explain and discuss. OR: "Where Luther stresses our confrontation with God in Christ, Calvin emphasizes the Son's participation in our humanity." How far does this contrast: (i) resemble similar differences of approach in the early church and (ii) lead to the divergent Lutheran and Reformed emphases in Christology? To what dangers is each open?

# Appendix 2

**Dogmatics II: Degree Exam (29 May, 1975).** *(FIVE Questions to be answered).*

1. How does scientific questioning operate in theological inquiry? What do we learn about this from the relation of the disciples to Jesus?

2. Assess the importance of *empirical* and *theoretical* components in developing a doctrine of Christ, and show its relevance to the Church's rejection of *Adoptionism* and *Docetism*.

3. "Christ is the eternal communication center who makes possible the holy conversation between God and man, between God and the world" (Karl Rahner). Elucidate and discuss.

4. Compare and contrast the Logos Christology of the Apologists with Origen's understanding of the "eternal generation" of the Son. How far may Origen's position be regarded as an advance?

5. State, defend, and criticize the position of EITHER Arius or Apollinarius of Laodicea.

6. In what sense may the *Symbol of Chalcedon* be regarded as normative for Christology today?

7. Write a short essay on the Christology of *one* of the following: Athanasius, Calvin, Barth, Bonhoeffer.

8. Give an account of the *communicatio idiomatum* in Patristic, Lutheran and Reformed theology.

9. Comment upon the following citation from John Calvin: "He received what is ours in order to give us what is his, making that which is his by nature become ours by grace." OR: Comment upon the theological importance of the patristic principle that *the unassumed is the unhealed*.

10. How would you relate the *dramatic* to the *ontological* aspects of redemption through Christ?

11. Explain the place of the merit and voluntary obedience of Christ in St. Anselm's answer to the question why God became man.

12. Discuss McLeod Campbell's appeal to the doctrine of the vicarious humanity of Christ to safeguard the Gospel of grace. OR: Give an account of the priestly ministry of Christ, with a reference to *prayer*, *penitence*, and *propitiation*.

13. Comment on the view that in the pragmatism of the West we have too often given priority to the How? Question over the Who? Question in our approach to soteriology.
14. Christology points to a historical event that took place at a certain time and in a certain place. At the same time Christology claims that this event is relevant to all people at all times and places. Discuss the significance of Pneumatology and Ecclesiology in an understanding of this claim.
15. Expound the nature of the resurrection of Christ and show its organics connection with his reconciling work.
16. Write a short essay on the eschatological import of redemption through Christ, with special reference to his Ascension and final Parousia.

**Dogmatics III: Autumn Term Exam: (18 Dec, 1975).** *(Answer Question One and TWO further Questions).*

1. Briefly explain and comment upon ANY TWO of the following quotations from Athanasius" *Letters to Serapion*:
    a. "The holy and blessed Triad is indivisible and one in itself."
    b. "God is not as man, that we should dare to ask human questions about him."
    c. "As the Father is fountain and the Son is called river, we are said to drink of the Spirit."
    d. "In regard to order and nature, the Spirit bears the same relation to the Son as the Son to the Father."
    e. "The creatures were not: but God has 'being', and the Spirit is from him."
    f. "If the Father, through the Word, in the Holy Spirit, creates and renews all things, what likeness or kinship is there between the Creator and the creature?"
    g. "The Holy Spirit, being in God, is incapable of change, variation, and corruption."
    h. "Is God Triad or dyad?"

2. Compare and contrast the approaches of Irenaeus and Origen to the placing of the Spirit in relation to the Father and the Son. What are their respective strengths and weaknesses?

3. "Where the Church is, there is the Spirit of God; and where the Spirit of God is, there is the Church and every kind of grace" (Irenaeus). "The Church will indeed remit sins, but it will be the Church of the Spirit, by the agency of a spiritual man, not the Church as a number of bishops" (Tertullian). What issues are involved in these affirmations, and how do Irenaeus and Tertullian differ?

4. "We would now say something concerning the Holy Spirit, not to declare his being, for that would be impossible, but to speak of various mistakes of some concerning him . . . in order to block up the paths of error, that we may journey on the king's highway" (Cyril of Jerusalem). Discuss the implications of this approach.

5. Sketch in outline the position of the Tropici. Why does Athanasius compare it with Arianism, when it attempts to be orthodox on the Son?

6. "And in the Holy Spirit, the Lord and Life-giver, who proceeds from the Father, who with the Father and the Son is worshipped and glorified, who spake by the prophets." Briefly indicate the force of the elements in this formula.

7. In what sense must Christian theology regard the Holy Spirit as not only the Spirit *of God*, but in particular as the Spirit *of Christ*? OR: Briefly summarize the different ways of understanding the Trinity in East and West which underlie the conflict over the *filioque*.

8. "The work of the Spirit is constantly in danger of being objectified in gifts or institutions. When that happens, the Spirit himself disappears from view." Discuss and illustrate from the New Testament or subsequent history.

9. How does Calvin relate the *"internal testimony of the Holy Spirit"* to the objective Word of God in Scripture, and so deny the conflict seen by some contemporaries between the freedom of the Spirit and the "dead letter"?

# The Dogmatics Exams

**Final Honors BD: First Paper (25 May, 1976). Dogmatics I: Dogmatic Science, Knowledge of God, the Trinity.** *(Not more than FIVE Questions to be answered).*

1. Consider the claim of Christian Dogmatics to engage in "scientific inquiry." How far, in your view, does it develop an appropriate method of its own? OR: Examine the relation between: *questioning, understanding,* and *explaining* in theological inquiry.

2. "Those who propose to inquire what the essence of God is, only delude us with frigid speculations . . . it being much more our interest to know what kind of being God is, and what things are agreeable to his nature" (John Calvin). Elucidate and discuss.

3. How far would you agree with the statement that "Revelation is not a special way in which we know; it is a special way in which God makes himself known." OR: Write a short essay discussing the interrelations between reason and revelation.

4. "Natural theology (*theologia naturalis*) is included and brought into clear light in the theology of revelation (*theologia revelata*); in the reality of divine grace is included the truth of the divine creation. In this sense, it is true that 'Grace does not destroy nature but completes it (*gratia non tollit naturam sed perficit*).' The meaning of the Word of God becomes manifest as it brings into full light the buried and forgotten truth of creation" (Karl Barth). Explain what is meant here and assess its significance.

5. "He who does not believe will not understand. For he who does not believe will not have experience of it; and he who does not have experience will not know" (Anselm). Elucidate this statement, and express in your own way the relation between experience, faith and knowledge, in respect of our knowledge of God.

6. What do you consider to be the implication of the personal character of God for a theological epistemology? OR: How would you describe the role of the Holy Spirit in our knowledge of God? Does this imply a non-cognitive element in revelation or a non-conceptual element in faith?

7. "Knowledge of God involves a God-world-man or a God-Man-world relation, not just a God-Man or a man-God relation." How far would you agree? OR: What is the bearing of the *imago Dei* on our knowledge of God?

8. "Many of the things relating to God that are dimly understood cannot be put into fitting terms, but on things above us we cannot do else than express ourselves according to our limited capacity; as for instance when we speak of God we use terms like *sleep* and *wrath* and *regardlessness*; *hands* too, and *feet,* and such like expressions" (John of Damascus). What does this imply about the character of theological language? Express in your own way the status of human words used of God. OR: Discuss the use of "models" or "analogies" in theological formulation, and assess the role of negative or *apophatic* elements in their construction and employment.

9. Offer an account of Holy Scripture as Word of God, and discuss whether the distinction/relation between form and content is applicable here.

10. "We come to the Trinity by no other way than by an analysis of the concept of Revelation." Explain what Karl Barth means by this statement and examine his claim that Revelation is the root and ground of the doctrine of the Trinity.

11. How are we to relate the Economic Trinity to the Immanent (or Ontological) Trinity? OR: Draw out the significance of the teaching of Athanasius and/or Barth about the mutual inherence of God's Act and his Being.

12. Would you agree that it is in the doctrine of the Holy Trinity that we have to do with "the basic grammar of theology"? Discuss in this connection with the problem created by the separation (since Aquinas) of the doctrine of the One God from the doctrine of the Triune God, with special reference to the thought of Barth and Rahner. OR: Offer an account of the creation as the act of the Triune God.

13. Explain what is meant by *creation out of nothing*. What does this imply about God's relation to *space and time* and to *order* in the created universe.

14. Write a short essay on the Love of God and show its epistemological importance for all true knowledge of God. OR: How would you meet the charge that evil must be allowed to count against belief in the love of God?

15. "The image of the Trinity is one Person, but the supreme Trinity himself is three Persons." Expound the idea St. Augustine expresses here, and draw out its significance.

16. How would you express the relation between *knowing* God and *worshipping* God? What does this imply for the structure of dogmatic formulation?

⁓

**Final Honors BD: Second Paper (26 May, 1976). Dogmatics II: Christology and Soteriology.** *(Not more than FIVE Questions to be answered.)*

1. Assess the importance of empirical and theoretical components in developing an adequate doctrine of Christ, and show the relevance of this to the Church's rejection of both Adoptionism and Docetism. OR: Examine the problems raised by a phenomenalist and observationalist approach to the historical Jesus.

2. What is meant by the *Incarnation*? How would you relate it to the interaction of God with the creaturely world, and the interaction of the Word with historical Israel? OR: Write a succinct essay on the relation of the Incarnation to *space and time*.

3. How far, in your view, did the christological heresies from Gnosticism to those disposed of by Chalcedon operate with *dualist assumptions*? Relate your answer to a fuller account of one of them. OR: Offer a careful account of Arianism and its antecedents.

4. Compare and contrast the Antiochene and Alexandrian approaches to Christology, and show the dangers of extremism in their respective emphases. OR: Explain carefully what is meant by *"the communication of properties."*

5. Comment upon the following citation from Apollinarius: "Christ is not man but like man, since he is not *homoousios* with man in the supreme governing principle of his existence." "Christ is man titularly (*homonumos*) for he is divine spirit united to human flesh." "The Logos became flesh without assuming a human mind, for a human mind is changeable and subject to impure thoughts; but he has a divine mind, changeless and heavenly."

6. "He who was sent in the likeness of the flesh of sin, bearing indeed sin in his flesh but our sin" (Hilary, *De Trinitate* 10.47). "The very virgin from whom his manhood was taken was conceived in iniquities, and in sins did her mother conceive her, and with original sin was she born" (Anselm, *Cure Deus Homo* 2.16). Discuss.

7. "His understanding of Jesus Christ not as God *in man*, but as God *as man*, meant that Athanasius had to understand the humanity of Jesus Christ in a profoundly *vicarious manner*." Elucidate and discuss. OR: Write a succinct essay on the saving obedience of Jesus Christ as man.

8. Explain carefully what is meant by the compound concept of *anhypostasia* and *enhypostasia* and discuss its application to the saving work of Christ.

9. "In the Person of the Mediator we witness both a God-manward and a man-Godward movement." What is the import of this for our understanding of the "threefold office of Christ"? OR: How would you relate the objective to the subjective aspects of the atonement?

10. Offer a critical account of ONE of the following: (a) The unassumed is the unredeemed; (b) The Christology of Chalcedon; (c) The influence of Kant on nineteenth-century Christology; (d) Bonhoeffer's distinction between the question "Who?" and the question "How?"

11. Write an essay expounding the interrelation between Incarnation and atonement with special reference to ONE of the following: Athanasius; Calvin; Barth. OR: Offer an analytical account of the satisfaction theory of atonement as represented by St. Anselm.

12. Offer arguments in defense and criticism of the concept of penalty in a doctrine of atonement. OR: Write an essay examining the notions of *expiation* and *propitiation* in atoning reconciliation through Christ.

13. Give a brief account of the teaching of John McLeod Campbell on the nature of the atonement, with an extended discussion on "legal" and "filial" aspects of his thought.

14. Consider what light the resurrection of Christ, and the doctrine of the hypostatic union, throw upon our understanding of his birth of the Virgin Mary. OR: Characterize the epistemological relevance of the *homoousion*.

15. Discuss the place of spatial and temporal ingredients in our statement of the Ascension.

16. How far is the "empty tomb" integral to the resurrection? What is the inner soteriological connection between the resurrection and the crucifixion? OR: How would you expound the relation between redemption and consummation?

**Final Honors BD: Third Paper (24 May, 1976). Dogmatics III: Doctrine of the Spirit, the Church and Sacraments.** *(Not more than FIVE Questions to be answered).*

1. "It behoved Jesus Christ to be God that he might give his Spirit to men, for only God can give God. It behoved Christ also to be man, that he might receive the Spirit of God in our human nature and mediate it to his brethren through himself." Elucidate and discuss.

2. "The Spirit is God himself even though he be given to no one, for before he was given to anyone he was God coeternal with the Father and the Son. Nor because they gave and he is given is he less than they. For as God's gift he is given in such a way that he is himself God the Giver" (St. Augustine, *De Trinitate* 15.36). Elucidate and explain the theological significance of this. OR: "While God remains ultimately ineffable, beyond all created being, he is not closed to us, but makes himself accessible and knowable by us through his Word and in his Spirit." Expound and draw out the implications of this statement.

3. "Through the Holy Spirit and only through the Holy Spirit can man be there for God, be free for God's work on him, believe, be a recipient of this revelation, the object of divine reconciliation... Through the Spirit it becomes really possible for the creature, for man, to be there and to be free for God" (Karl Barth). Explain what Barth intends by this statement, and offer a brief account of his doctrine of the Holy Spirit.

4. Give an account of the agency of the Holy Spirit in *creation*. How far is this to be distinguished from the agency of the Father and of the Son?

5. Consider the relation between the work of the Holy Spirit and the work of the Son in incarnation and redemption. OR: Elucidate and discuss the following statement: "Ecclesiology must avoid any kind of division in the Trinity; it must avoid isolating Christ. But neither must it eliminate the christological aspect of Pentecost and so isolate the Spirit, which leads to a spiritual and sectarian ecclesiology based on emotionalism" (N. A. Nissiotis).

6. Write a short essay on ONE of the following: (a) The patristic conception of the "economy of the Spirit"; (b) Tertullian's linking of the Spirit with the Father and the Son; (c) Athanasius' defense of the divinity of the Spirit; (d) The place of the Holy Spirit in Calvin's theology.

7. Comment upon the following citations: (a) "And we speak also of the Spirit of the Son, not as through proceeding from him, but as proceeding through him from the Father. For the Father alone is cause." (John of Damascus, *De Fide Orthodoxa* 1:13); (b) "If the Son has the same deity as the Father, it is impossible to understand how the Holy Spirit proceeds from the deity of the Father *through* the deity of the Son, but not *from* the deity of the Son" (Anselm, *De Processione Spiritus Sancti* 9).

8. What do the formulae: "*From the Father, through the Son, and in the Spirit*," and: "*In the Spirit, through the Son, and to the Father*," tell us about the activity of the Spirit (a) in the life of the Church, and (b) in the celebration of the Sacraments? OR: "The Word and the Spirit are never divided." Bring out the significance of this axiom with special reference to (a) the doctrine of Holy Scripture, and (b) the celebration of the Sacraments.

9. What are the *creedal* marks of the Church? Give a fuller account of ONE of them.

10. Explain carefully what is meant when the Church is called the *Body of Christ*. OR: Discuss the relation of the Christian Church to Israel in the light of St Paul's principle that the branches do not bear the trunk, but the trunk the branches.

11. Relate the Baptism of Christ to the Baptism of the Church by the Spirit of Christ at Pentecost. OR: Comment upon the following passage from Calvin's *Institutes*: "He dedicated and sanctified baptism in his own body that he might have it in common with us: and so St Paul proves that we are sons of God from the fact that we put on Christ in baptism. Thus we see that the fulfillment of baptism is in Christ, and even call him for this reason 'the proper object of baptism.'"

12. Write a short essay on the relation between baptism and faith. OR: offer a justification of infant baptism.

13. Explain the inner connection between the Eucharist and (a) The vicarious life and passion of Jesus, and (b) the heavenly ministry of the glorified Lord.
14. Show the importance of the unity of the Person and Work of Christ for (a) the real presence, and (b) the Eucharistic sacrifice.
15. What is the eschatological reference of baptism and the Lord's Supper?

---

**Final Honors BD: Fifth Paper (28 May, 1976). Dogmatics V (a): Dogmatics and Logic.** *(Not more than FIVE Questions to be answered).*

1. Explain carefully, and with historical references, what is meant by "dogmatic thought", and show the significance of its application to Dogmatic science.
2. "Theology is the science which systematizes the doctrines prevalent in the Christian Church at a given time" (Schleiermacher). "Theology is the self-test to which the Church puts herself in respect of the content of her peculiar language about God" (Barth). Compare these different views on the character and function of dogmatics.
3. Examine the relation between theological science and natural science, and show their similarities and differences.
4. How would you distinguish between "the truth of statement" and "the truth of being"? Discuss the relevance of this distinction for theological inquiry. OR: What criteria are to be employed in determining the truth and falsity of dogmatic statements?
5. Examine the relation between the "logic of existence-statements" and "the logic of coherence-statements." What help does this offer us in assessing the logical status of biblical statements?
6. "As the Word of God incarnate in our human existence Jesus Christ gives decisive content and structure to our knowledge of God and constitutes the objective center by reference to which Christian theology clarifies and develops its own *inner logic*." Discuss.
7. How far would you agree with the thesis of Karl Rahner that the essential difference between Protestant and Catholic theology is to be found in the fact that for the Catholic theologian the "logical

explanation" of the words of Scripture by the Church can become a statement of faith, un unchangeable dogma, even although "logical explanation" unlike "ontic explanation" has to do only with statements and not with states of affairs? (*Trinity*, 54).

8. Consider whether it is possible, and/or hopeful, with the aid of "fluid axioms" to treat dogmatics as "an axiomatic science."

9. Discuss the application of *Gödel's theorem* to dogmatic formulation. OR: Assess the value of *modal logic* in establishing and justifying valid theological connections.

10. "Theology attempts to throw light on the reality of revelation in its inner intelligibility" (E. Schillebeeckx). Interpret this statement and assess the significance of this view for a modern Roman Catholic dogmatics. OR: Discuss carefully Karl Barth's distinction between *dogma* and *dogmas*, that is: between dogma as the objective meaning and norm of all true dogmas, the truth which they intend as they fulfil their function in directing the Church to apprehend and appropriate God's self-revelation. How far would you agree that here in Christian dogmatics *dogma* takes the place of the basic logical concept or the ultimate unity and simplicity, which we strive to reach in other fields of inquiry, while dogmas take the place of the accepted scientific principles with which we operate in the construction of theoretical models through which we advance our knowledge of the intrinsic nature of things?

11. Give an account of the different levels of *ratio veritatis* with which St Anselm operated in theological investigation, and show how they are coordinated in the service of the *Suprema Veritas*. Does this bear any relation to the modern concept of "logical levels"?

12. Consider how far a rigorous scientific theology requires a new logical or theoretical instrument in its own field, similar in its function to that our four-dimensional geometries in field-physics, to be able to give adequate formulation of such basic statements as "God created the world" or "the Word became flesh."

13. "If God is good he must want to abolish all evil; if he is ultimately powerful he must be able to abolish it" (John Hick). "We cannot know sin as a fact; we cannot place it in intelligible correlation with other things except *per accidens* . . . The mysteries of faith are mysterious to us only because of their excess of intelligibility; but the

*mysterium iniquitatis* is mysterious in itself and objectively, because of a defect of intelligibility" (Bernard Lonergan). Compare these two approaches, and discuss the application of logical argumentation to the problems of evil and sin.

14. Draw out the epistemological implications of *justification by grace alone*. OR: Write a short essay on "*the logic of grace.*"

15. How far does *eschatology* belong to the warp and woof of dogmatics rather than simply to its final chapters? In your answer discuss the bearing of eschatology upon the inner logical coherence of the organic structure of dogmatics.

16. What contribution can rigorous scientific inquiry make toward an *ecumenical* dogmatics? OR: Consider the role played by the Ecumenical Councils in the formulation and development of basic doctrine?

**Final Honors BD: Sixth Paper (27 May, 1976). Dogmatics VI: Essay.** *(Write an essay on ONE of the following themes).*

1. "The Visible is more persuasive than the Audible."
2. Theology and Worship.
3. Love and Justice in God and man.
4. Miracles
5. Models.
6. Mission.

— *Appendix 3* —

# The Firbush Conferences

THE FOLLOWING LIST OF speakers and papers is as accurate as I have been able to establish. As in conference submissions, titles often changed from first proposal, to advertised title, to what the speaker preferred when he or she presented the paper.

### FIRBUSH I: 16–18 Nov, 2010

Robert T. Walker, (i) *"Christology: The Person and Work of Christ; Incarnation and Atonement."* (ii) *"The Holy Spirit: The Completion of Atonement and the Apostolic Foundation of the Church."* (iii) *"Resurrection, Ascension, and Eschatology."*

David W. Torrance, (i) *"The Vicarious Humanity of Jesus."* (ii) *"The Word of God, the Church, and Worship."*

Andrew T. B. McGowan, *"Participation in Christ."*

Bruce Ritchie, *"Torrance and Universalism."*

### FIRBUSH II: 25–27 April, 2011

Robert T. Walker, (i) *"Torrance and Vicarious Humanity."* (ii) *"Jesus Christ's Vicarious Bearing of Human Sin."*

David W. Torrance, (i) *"Vicarious Humanity and Baptism."* (ii) *"Preaching the Book of Revelation."*

Douglas Kelly, *"The Active Obedience of Christ."*

Jason Radcliff, *"Vicarious Humanity in the Early Fathers."*

Adam Nigh, "*Torrance on the Doctrine of Scripture.*"

Geordie Ziegler, "*Vicarious Humanity and New Creation in Christ.*"

## FIRBUSH III: 8–10 Nov, 2011

Robert T. Walker, "*Incarnation, Atonement, Election, Christocentrism in Torrance.*"

Andrew T. B. McGowan, "*Adam and Christ.*"

David W. Torrance, "*Covenant, Israel, and Atonement.*"

John Ferguson, "*Atonement.*"

Dick Eugenio, "*T. F. Torrance's trinitarian Soteriology.*"

## FIRBUSH IV: 11–13 April, 2011

Robert T. Walker, (i) "*The Spirit in the Theology of T. F. Torrance.*" (ii) "*Word and Spirit in Torrance.*"

Jason Radcliff, "*The Holy Spirit in the Church Fathers and Torrance.*"

Vanessa Platek, "*The Mission of the Spirit in Torrance's Theology.*"

Alan Torrance, "*The* Homoousion *of the Son and Spirit.*"

Peter Donald, "*Torrance: The Spirit and the Unity of the Church.*"

Geordie Ziegler, "*Christology and the Spirit.*"

Alexandra Stuart-Lee, "*T. F. Torrance and Pentecostal Theology.*"

## FIRBUSH V: 6–8 Nov, 2012

Robert T. Walker, "*Resurrection, Ascension, and New Creation in the Theology of T. F. Torrance.*"

John Miller, "*T. F. Torrance and His Legacy.*"

David Fergusson, "*Torrance as a Scottish Theologian.*"

Gary Deddo, "*T. F. Torrance on the Continuing Humanity and Priesthood of Christ.*"

Joanna MacDonald, "*The New Creation and the Holy Spirit in the Work of T. F. Torrance.*"

David W. Torrance, "*Origins and Meaning of Communion.*"

## FIRBUSH VI: 19–21 June, 2013

Robert T. Walker, "*The Gospel in the Theology of T. F. Torrance.*"

Gary Deddo, (i) "*Theological Education and Equipping the Church to Share in the Ministry of Christ.*" (ii) "*Preaching and Teaching Christ: Forks in the Road.*"

David W. Torrance, "*Preaching Christ: Grace, Faith, and Assurance.*"

Peter Donald, "*Preaching Ministry, Eldership and Diaconate.*"

Peter Kimber, "*Preaching Christ to Children and Reaching Out to the Young.*"

Kevin Navarro, "*Christ in Prayer and Worship*'

Geordie Ziegler, "*The Lord's Supper in the Theology of T. F. Torrance.*"

## FIRBUSH VII: 5–7 Nov, 2013

Robert T. Walker, (i) "*The Trinity and Judgment.*" (ii) "*The Trinity in Christian Life.*"

Bruce Ritchie, "*Christology in Reverse.*"

Thomas A. Noble, "*A Centenary Reminiscence and Assessment.*"

David W. Torrance, (i) "*The Vicarious Humanity of Christ and the Christian Life.*" (ii), "*The Christian Nurture of Children.*"

John Miller, "*The Role of Dogma in Preaching the Trinity.*"

## FIRBUSH VIII: 18–20 June, 2014

Robert T. Walker, "*Worship in the Theology of T. F. Torrance.*"

Robin Parry, (i) "*Ancient-Future Worship I: The Gospel Embodied in Worship.*" (ii) "*Ancient-Future Worship II.*"

David W. Torrance, "*Prayer and the Trinity.*"

Bill Steele, "*Reformed Worship: Principles and Practice.*"

Jennifer Floether, "*Reflections on Anglican Worship.*"

## FIRBUSH IX: 5–7 Nov, 2014

Robert T. Walker, "'*Worship, Preaching, Diaconate: Jesus' Ministry and Human Response.*"

Joey Sherrard, "*Church, Ministry, and Mission, in T. F. Torrance.*"

David W. Torrance, (i) "*What Is the Gospel?*" (ii) "*To the Jew First . . .*"
Jonathan Lett, "*Worship and Mission: Yet Not I, but Christ.*"
Neil Meyer, "*Worship, Mission, and Congregational Participation.*"

## FIRBUSH X: 17–19 June, 2015

Robert T. Walker, "*The Gospel and Evangelism in T. F. Torrance.*"
Baxter Kruger, (i) "*The Message of the Gospel: I.*" (ii) "*The Message of the Gospel, II.*"
Jennifer Floether, "*The Task and Difficulty of Preaching.*"
Richard Begg, "*Leadership and Rural Ministry.*"
Thomas A. Noble, "*Teaching Nicene Theology Today.*"
Angus Morrison, "*Memories and Appreciation of T. F. Torrance.*"

## FIRBUSH XI: 11–13 Nov, 2015

Robert T. Walker, "*T. F. Torrance on Word and Spirit in the Life of Jesus.*"
Andrew Torrance, "*Christ and the God of the Gaps.*"
David J. Torrance, "*Ephesians 1: A theological commentary.*"
David W. Torrance, "*John 7–9.*"
Thomas A. Noble, "*Torrance's 'The Mediation of Christ', Chapters 1 &2.*"
Robin Brodie, "*Congregational Participation.*"

## FIRBUSH XII: 15–17 June, 2016

Robert T. Walker, "*Ministry in the Bible, and in T. F. Torrance.*"
Thomas A. Noble, "*The Person of the Mediator: Ch. 3: 'The Mediation of Christ'.*"
Alan Torrance, "*Recovering the Sole Priesthood of Christ.*"
David W. Torrance, "*The High Priestly Ministry of Christ: John 17.*"
Alan Hamilton, "*Lay Training and Education.*"

## FIRBUSH XIII: 2–4 Nov, 2016

Robert T. Walker, "*The Centrality of the Sacraments in T. F. Torrance.*"
Bruce Ritchie, "*A Theology of Response in Torrance's 'Mediation of Christ'.*"

Lance Stone, "*Bonhoeffer, the Secular, and the Humility of Christ.*"
David J. Torrance, "*Baptism in T. F. Torrance.*"
Angus Morrison, "*Eucharist and Renewal in the Church.*"
Jennifer Floether, "*Congregational Understanding of the Eucharist.*"

### FIRBUSH XIV: 14–16 June, 2017

Robert W. Walker, "*Creation and New Creation in T. F. Torrance.*"
David W. Torrance, "*The New Creation: Romans 8 and 2 Corinthians 5.*"
Thomas A. Noble, "*Christ and Human Response: Ch. 4 of 'Mediation of Christ'.*"
David Thistlewaite, "*Beauty in Creation and Christian Faith.*"
Trevor Hart, (i) "*Creation, Eucharist, and New Creation: I.*" (ii) "*Creation, Eucharist, and New Creation: II.*"

### FIRBUSH XV: 1–3 Nov, 2017

Robert T. Walker, "*T. F. Torrance on New Creation by Incarnation, Word, and Spirit.*"
Robin Brodie, "*Becoming What We Are: Relating Torrance's Theology to Everyday Life as a Christian.*"
David W. Torrance, "*The Centrality of Covenant in the Bible.*"
Stephen May, "*The Redemption of Physical Creation.*"
Steve Chaffee, "*Mind, Body, and Spirit, in Transformation.*"
Jennifer Floether, "*Life under Covenant Faithfulness.*"

### FIRBUSH XVI: 13–15 June, 2018

Robert T. Walker, "*Torrance and the Incarnation of the Word.*"
Jeremy Begbie, "'*Music and Theology*" (4 lectures).
Gary Deddo, "*Creation and Incarnation.*"
Seminar, "*The Relation between Theology and other Subjects.*"

### FIRBUSH XVII: 31 Oct–2 Nov, 2018

Robert T. Walker, "*Gospel and Mission in T. F. Torrance.*"
David W. Torrance, "*Preaching Jesus Christ.*"

Jennifer Floether, *"Christ as the Fulfilment of the Law."*

Sandy Forsyth, *"Mission in Scotland."*

Bruce Ritchie, *"Jesus is the Gospel."*

Tomas Kodacsy, *"The Work of the Holy Spirit in the Preaching of the Gospel today."*

Donald Walker, *"Key Points of Forty Years of Ministry."*

## FIRBUSH XVIII: 12–14 June, 2019

Robert T. Walker, *"Torrance on the Cross, Resurrection, and New Creation."*

Gerrit Dawson, *"Three Days: Good Friday, Holy Saturday, Easter Sunday"* (3 lectures).

Geordie Ziegler, *"Spiritual Formation."*

Kerry Magruder, *"Torrance, Science, and New Creation: Did the Resurrection Change the Order of Nature?"*

Myk Habets, *"Torrance as a Preacher: His Sermons in Context."*

David W. Torrance, *"Preaching, and Preaching the Ascension."*

## FIRBUSH XIX: 30 Oct–1 Nov, 2019

Robert T. Walker, (i) *"Torrance on Word, Spirit, and Evil in Creation."* (ii) *"The Significance of the Incarnation for the Relation between God, Man, and Theology."*

Bruce Ritchie, (i) *"Devils, Demons, and Deliverance: Aspects of Early Christian Theology in Scotland."* (ii) *"Studying Dogmatics under T. F. Torrance."* (iii) *"How Do We Do Theology? T. F. Torrance's Methodology."*

Sandy Forsyth, *"Pioneer Ministry and Church Planting."*

David W. Torrance, *"Ephesians 6: The Conflict with Evil."*

— *Appendix 4* —

# The Historical/Theological Exegesis of 2 Corinthians 5:21

TORRANCE ARGUED THAT THE interpretation of 2 Cor 5:21 changed following the Council of Nicaea in 325; after which, the full force of the verse was diluted in order to avoid any notion that Christ was not sinless.[1] How have major theologians dealt with this crucial verse? The following selection is not intended to prove a majority of opinion on either side of the issue. However, the quotations do give a flavor of the debate through the centuries. At the same time, it should be borne in mind that the questions which we ask of the text were not necessarily the questions uppermost in a particular scholar's thinking. Citations from the Church Fathers are from the appropriate volumes of the *Ante-Nicene Christian Fathers* and *Post-Nicene Christian Fathers* series.

∽

**ORIGEN OF ALEXANDRIA (185–254).** *Origen was concerned that if 2 Cor 5:21 were translated as "was made sin" then some may read that as meaning that, in some sense, darkness and evil have come into Jesus Christ and become part of him. Origen was prepared to accept the possibility of this misunderstanding.*

"We will now, however, go a step further than we did before, and add that if God made Christ who knew no sin to be sin for us, then *it could not be said of Him that there was no darkness in him.* For if Jesus was in the likeness (Romans 8:3) of the flesh of sin, then it cannot be said of

---

1. Torrance, *Atonement*, 147–49.

# The Historical/Theological Exegesis of 2 Corinthians 5:21

him absolutely and directly there was no darkness in him. We may add that "He took our infirmities and bore our sicknesses," both infirmities of the soul and sickness of the hidden man of our heart. On account of these infirmities and sicknesses which he bore away from us he declares his soul to be sorrowful and troubled (Matthew 26:38), and he is said in Zechariah to have put on filthy garments (Zechariah 3:4) which, when he was about to take them off, are said to be sins: 'Behold it is said, I have taken away thy sins'" (Origen, *Commentary on John* 2.21; cf. *Commentary on Matthew* 14:7).

⸎

**ATHANASIUS OF ALEXANDRIA (c. 296–373).** *Athanasius discussed 2 Cor 5:21 within the context of the troublesome Prov 8:22 which states (concerning Wisdom): "The Lord created me at the beginning of his works." Arians had argued that because Wisdom is the Son of God, then the Son of God was created. In the following extract Athanasius deliberated on the use of symbolic language.*

"For as by receiving our infirmities, he is said to be infirm himself, though not himself infirm, for he is the Power of God, and he became sin for us and a curse, though not having sinned himself, but because he himself bare our sins and our curse, so, by creating us in him, let him say, he created me for the works, though not himself a creature." (Athanasius, *Orations Against the Arians* 2.20.55).

⸎

**GREGORY OF NYSSA (c. 335–95).** *Gregory, one of the three Cappadocian Father, wrote extensively on 2 Cor 5:21.*

"For it was when he came in the form of a servant to accomplish the mystery of redemption by the cross, who had emptied himself, who humbled himself by assuming the likeness and fashion of a man, being found as man in man's lowly nature—then, I say, it was that he became obedient, even he who 'took our infirmities and bare our sicknesses,' healing the disobedience of men by his own obedience, that by his stripes he might heal our wound, and by his own death do away with the common death of all men,—then it was that for our sakes he was made obedient, even as he became 'sin' and 'a curse' by reason of the dispensation on our behalf, not being so by nature, but becoming so in his love for man" (Gregory of Nyssa, *Against Eunomius* 2.11).

"Since then it was impossible that our life, which had been estranged from God, should of itself return to the high and heavenly place, for this cause, as saith the Apostle, he who knew no sin is made sin for us, and frees us from the curse by taking on him our curse as his own; and having taken up, and, in the language of the Apostle: 'slain' in himself 'the enmity' which by means of sin had come between us and God (in fact sin was 'the enmity') and *having become what we were*, he, through himself again, united humanity to God. For having by purity brought into closest relationship with the Father of our nature that new man which is created after God, in whom dwelt all the fullness of the Godhead bodily, he drew with him into the same grace all the nature that partakes of his body and is akin to him. And these glad tidings he proclaims through the woman, not to those disciples only, but also to all who up to the present day become disciples of the Word—the tidings, namely, that man is no longer outlawed, nor cast out of the kingdom of God, but is once more a son, once more in the station assigned to him by his God" (Gregory of Nyssa, *Against Eunomius* 12.1).

"But to those who quote from the Proverbs the passage: 'the Lord created me,' and think that they hereby produce a strong argument that the Creator and Maker of all things was created, we must answer that the only-begotten God was made for us many things. For he was the Word, and was made flesh. And he was God, and was made man. And he was without body, and was made a body. And besides, he was made 'sin,' and 'a curse,' and 'a stone,' and 'an axe,' and 'bread,' and 'a lamb,' and 'a way,' and 'a door,' and 'a rock,' and many such things: not being by nature any of these, but being made these things for our sakes, by way of dispensation. As, therefore, being the Word, he was for our sakes made flesh, and as, being God, He was made man, so also, being the Creator, He was made for our sakes a creature; for the flesh is created" (Gregory of Nyssa, *On the Faith*).

᠅

**GREGORY OF NAZIANZUS (c329–90).** *Nazianzus was aware of the theological implications of 2 Cor 5:21. He viewed the phrase "He was made sin" as equivalent to "The Word was made flesh" (John 1:14), and as equivalent to Paul's teaching that on the Cross Jesus became "a curse for us" (Gal 3:13). Conscious of the radical nature of 2 Cor 5:21, Gregory wrote:*

"In no other way was it possible for the love of God toward us to be manifested than by making mention of our flesh, and that for our sake he descended even to our lower part. For, that flesh is less precious than soul, everyone who has a spark of sense will acknowledge. And so the passage: 'the Word was made flesh' seems to me to be equivalent to that in which it is said that he was 'made sin,' or 'a curse' for us; not that the Lord was transformed into either of these, how could he be? But, because by taking them upon him, he took away our sins and bore our iniquities. This, then, is sufficient to say at the present time for the sake of clearness and of being understood by the many. And I write it, not with any desire to compose a treatise, but only to check the progress of deceit" (Gregory of Nazianzus, *Ep.* 101, "To Cledonius Against Apollinarius").

*Nazianzus was ambiguous. On the one hand he admitted the full force of the verse's implications. On the other hand, he was wary of saying too much. Nevertheless, like Origen, Gregory did not translate "αμαρτια" as meaning anything other than simply "sin." He did not give it an alternative meaning such as "sin-offering."*

☙

**BASIL OF CAESAREA (329–79).** *Basil discussed the issue of figurative expressions. In this extract, it is unclear whether Basil regarded "made sin" as literal or figurative.*

"As is said through Solomon the Wise in the Proverbs: 'He was created', and he is named 'Beginning of ways' of good news, which lead us to the kingdom of heaven. He is not in essence and substance a creature, but is made a 'way' according to the economy. Being made, and being created, signify the same thing. As he was made a way, so was he made a door, a shepherd, an angel, a sheep, and again a High Priest and an Apostle, the names being used in other senses. What again would the heretics say about God unsubjected, and about his *being made sin* for us? For it is written, 'But when all things shall be subdued unto him, then shall the Son also himself be subject unto him that put all things under him.' Are you not afraid, sir, of God called unsubjected? For he makes thy subjection his own; and because of thy struggling against goodness he calls himself unsubjected. In this sense too he once spoke of himself as persecuted: 'Saul, Saul,' he says: 'why persecutest thou me?' on the occasion when Saul was hurrying to Damascus with a desire to imprison the disciples. Again he calls himself naked, when any one of his brethren is naked. 'I was naked,' he says: 'and ye clothed me'; and so when another is in prison he speaks of himself as imprisoned, for he himself took away our sins and bare our sicknesses." (Basil of Caesarea, *Letter VIII:8 to the Caesareans*).

---

**HILARY OF POITIERS (c. 310-67).** *The early Latin theologian Hilary of Poitier made firm connections between being "made flesh" and "being made sin."*

"For the reasons mentioned, he was esteemed 'stricken, smitten and afflicted.' He took the form of a servant. And 'man born of a virgin' conveys to us the idea of one whose nature felt pain when he suffered. But, though he was wounded, it was for our transgressions. The wound was not the wound of his own transgressions: the suffering not a suffering for himself. He was not born man for his own sake, nor did he transgress in his own action. The Apostle explains the principle of the divine plan when he says: 'We beseech you through Christ to be reconciled to God. Him, who knew no sin, he made to be sin on our behalf.' To condemn sin through sin in the flesh, he who knew no sin was himself made sin; that is, by means of the flesh to condemn sin in the flesh, he became flesh on our behalf but knew not flesh: and therefore was 'wounded because of our transgressions'" (Hilary, *On the Trinity* 10.47).

---

**JOHN CHRYSOSTOM (c. 349-407).** *Many of Chrysostom's comments came in the contexts of sermons and homilies, rather than in formal theological discourses. He usually interpreted 2 Cor 5:21 to mean that Christ suffered the curse, or penalty, of sin.*

"We find [Paul] saying: 'We were made righteousness in him'; in these words: 'Him who knew no sin he made to be sin for us that we might be made the righteousness of God in him' (2 Cor. 5:21.); but now he saith: 'He hath been made righteousness unto us; so that whosoever will may partake plentifully.' For it is not this man or that man who hath made us wise, but Christ." (Chrysostom, *Homily 5*).

"If he himself also sinned, how shall he die for other sinners? But if for others' sins he died, he died being without sin: and if being without sin he died, he died not the death of sin (for how could he, being without sin?) but the death of the body. Wherefore also Paul did not simply say: 'he died,' but added: 'for our sins': both forcing these heretics against

# The Historical/Theological Exegesis of 2 Corinthians 5:21

their will to the confession of his bodily death, and signifying also by this, that before death he was without sin: for he that dies for others' sins, it followeth must himself be without sin. Neither was he content with this, but added: 'according to the Scriptures,' hereby both again making his argument credible, and intimating what kind of death he was speaking of, since it is the death of the body which the Scriptures everywhere proclaim . . . setting forth his slaughter in the flesh and that he was slain for our sins . . . But if thou dost not endure the Old Testament, hear John crying out and declaring both, as well his slaughter in the body, as the cause of it: thus: 'Behold,' saith he: 'the lamb of God, who taketh away the sin of the world': (John 1:29) and Paul saying: 'For him who knew no sin, he made to be sin on our behalf, that we might become the righteousness of God in him" (2 Cor. 5:21); and again: 'Christ redeemed us from the curse of the law, having become a curse for us' (Gal. 3:13); and again: 'having put off from himself principalities and powers, he made a show of them openly, triumphing over them' (Col. 2:15); and ten thousand other sayings to show what happened at his death in the body because of our sins. Yea, and Christ himself saith: 'for your sakes I sanctify myself' and: 'now the prince of this world hath been condemned,' showing that having no sin he was slain" (Chrysostom, *Homily 38*).

"'For him who knew no sin he made to be sin on our account.' I say nothing of what has gone before, that you have outraged him (him that had done you no wrong; him that had done you good) that he exacted not justice, that he is first to beseech, though first outraged; let none of these things be set down at present. Ought you not in justice to be reconciled for this one thing only that he has done to you now? And what has he done? *'Him that knew no sin He made to be sin, for you.'* For had he achieved nothing but done only this, think how great a thing it were to give his Son for those that had outraged him. But now he has both well achieved mighty things, and besides, has suffered him that did no wrong to be punished for those who had done wrong. But he did not say this, but mentioned that which is far greater than this. What then is this? *'Him that knew no sin,'* he says, him that was righteousness itself: *'He made sin,'* that is suffered as a sinner to be condemned, as one cursed to die. *'For cursed is he that hangeth on a tree'* (Galatians 3:13.) For to die thus was far greater than to die; and this he also elsewhere implying, saith: *'Becoming obedient unto death, yea the death of the cross'* (Philippians 2:8). For this thing carried with it not only punishment, but also disgrace. Reflect therefore how great things he bestowed on you. For a great thing indeed it were for even a sinner to die for any one" (Chrysostom, *Homily 11 on 2 John, Ver. 21*).

**THEODORETUS, BISHOP OF CYRUS (c.393–58).** *In his Dialogues, written as a theological conversation between Orthodoxos and Eranistes, Theodoretus discussed 2 Cor 5:21 and similar passages. The latter part of this extract belongs to a discussion on the immutability of the divinity of Christ: Theodoretus was reluctant to state that Jesus was made the "nature of sin," i.e., the "thing of sin itself."*

"*Orthodoxos*: The expression of John 'the Word was made flesh' has this interpretation (so far as can be discovered from the similar passage which we find in St. Paul): Christ was 'made a curse for us.' *It is not because he was made a curse but because he received the curse on our behalf* that he is said to have been made a curse; and so it is not because he was turned into flesh, but because he took flesh on our behalf, that he is said to have been 'made flesh.'[2] So far the divine Athanasius. Gregory, too, whose glory among all men is great . . . wrote to Cledonius against the specious fallacies of Apollinarius . . . [Gregory] says: 'the expression he was made flesh' seems to be parallel to his being said to have been made sin and a curse; not because the Lord was transmuted into these (for how could he?) but because he accepted these when he took on him our iniquities and bore our infirmities. . . . [Also] Ambrosius says in his work concerning the faith: 'It is written that the Word was made flesh. I do not deny that it is written, but look at the terms used; for there follows "and dwelt among us," that is to say "dwelt in human flesh."' You are therefore astonished at the terms in which it is written that the Word was made flesh, on the assumption of flesh, by the divine Word, when also concerning sin which he had not: it is said that he was made sin, that is to say, not that he was made the nature and operation of sin, but that he might crucify our sin in the flesh. Let them then give over asserting that the nature of the Word has undergone change and alteration; for he who took is one and that which was taken other" (Theodoretus, *Dialogues*).

**AMBROSE OF MILAN (340–97).** *Ambrose was highly influential on Augustine.*

"Who, then, is he by the wound of whose stripes we are healed, but Christ the Lord? Of whom the same Isaiah prophesied his stripes were

---

2. Theodoretus argued that Christ was "made sin" in the same way as he was "made flesh."

our healing; of whom Paul the Apostle wrote in his epistle: '*Who knew no sin, but was made sin for us.*' This, indeed, was divine in him, that his flesh did no sin, nor did the creature of the body take in him sin. For what wonder would it be if the Godhead alone sinned not, seeing it had no incentives to sin? But if God alone is free from sin, certainly every creature by its own nature can be, as we have said, liable to sin." (Ambrose, *On the Holy Spirit* 1.9, 111).

"What, then, is the reason that you prefer saying that God or Christ is glorified *in* the Spirit rather than *with* the Spirit? Is it because, if you say *in* the Spirit, the Spirit is declared to be less than Christ? Although your making the Lord greater or less is a matter which can be refuted. Yet since we read: 'For Christ was made sin for us, that we might be the righteousness of God in Him,' he is found chiefest in whom we are found most low. So, too, elsewhere you read: 'For in him all things consist,' that is, in his power. And the things which consist in him cannot be compared to him, because they receive from his power the substance whereby they consist." (Ambrose, *On the Holy Spirit* 2.8, 80)

"It is profitable to me to know that for my sake Christ bore my infirmities, submitted to the affections of my body; that for me, that is to say, for every man, *he was made sin*, and a curse; that for me and in me was he humbled and made subject; that for me he is the Lamb, the Vine, the Rock, the Servant, the Son of a handmaid, knowing not the day of judgment, for my sake ignorant of the day and the hour" (Ambrose, *Exposition of the Christian Faith* 2.9, 93).

"But if you should ask how he was made subject in us, he himself shows us, saying: 'I was in prison, and you came to me; I was sick, and you visited me: Inasmuch as you have done it unto one of the least of these you have done it to me.' You hear of him as sick and weak, and are not moved. You hear of him in subjection, and are moved, though he is sick and weak in him in whom he is in subjection, *in whom he was made sin and a curse for us*. As, then, *he was made sin and a curse not on his own account but on ours*, so he became subject in us not for his own sake but for ours, being not in subjection in his eternal nature, nor accursed in his eternal nature. For 'cursed is every one that hangs on a tree.' Cursed he was, for he bore our curses; in subjection, also, for he took upon him our subjection, but in the assumption of the form of a servant, not in the glory of God. So that whilst he makes himself a partaker of our weakness in the flesh, he makes us partakers of the divine nature in his power. But neither in one nor in the other have we any natural fellowship with the heavenly generation of Christ; nor is there any subjection of the Godhead in Christ. But, as the Apostle has said, that on him through that flesh which is the pledge of our salvation, we sit in heavenly places, though certainly not sitting ourselves, so also he is said to be subject in us through the assumption of our nature" (Ambrose, *Exposition of the Christian Faith* 5.14, 177–78. *The context is a discussion of how is Christ, as man, made subject to the Father*).

"Interpreting which truth, the Apostle says: 'For God, sending his own Son in the likeness of sinful flesh, and for sin condemned sin in the flesh, that the righteousness of the Law might be fulfilled in us.' He does not say 'in the likeness of flesh,' for Christ took on himself the reality not the likeness of flesh; nor does he say 'in the likeness of sin,' for he did no sin, but was made sin for us.[3] Yet he came 'in the likeness of sinful flesh,' that is, he took on him the likeness of sinful flesh, the likeness, because it is written: 'He is man, and who shall know him?' He was man in the flesh, according to his human nature, that he might be recognized, but in power was above man, that he might not be recognized, so he has our flesh, but has not the failings of this flesh" (Ambrose, *Concerning Repentance* 1.3, 12).

"Shall any one, then, follow this law, whereby the Council of Ariminum is confirmed, wherein Christ was said to be a creature? But say they: 'God sent forth his Son, made of a woman, made under the law.' And so they say 'made,' that is: 'created.' Do they not consider these very words which they have brought forward: that Christ is said to have been made, but of a woman; that is: he was 'made' as regards his birth from a virgin; [but] who was begotten of the Father as regards his divine generation? Have they read also to-day: '*that Christ redeemed us from the curse of the law, being made a curse for us*'? Was Christ a curse in his Godhead? But why he is called a curse the Apostle tells us, saying that it is written: '*Cursed is every one that hangs on a tree*,' that is, he who in his flesh bore our flesh, in his body bore our infirmities and our curses, that he might crucify them. For he was not cursed himself, but was cursed in you. So it is written elsewhere: '*Who knew no sin, but was made sin for us*,' for he bore our sins, that he might destroy them by the Sacrament of his Passion" (Ambrose, *Sermon against Auxentius* 25).

---

3. This may indicate a radical interpretation.

**AUGUSTINE (354-430).** *As discussed in our main text, Augustine read 'hamartia' in 2 Cor 5:21 as either "sin-offering" or "human nature liable to death." His reluctance to adopt a more literal meaning of Paul's words may have been due to several reasons, including a fear of implying that Christ had sinned or was not sinless.*[4]

"Christ, who was himself free from sin, *was made sin for us*, that we might be reconciled to God. Begotten and conceived, then, without any indulgence of carnal lust, and therefore bringing with him no original sin, and by the grace of God joined and united in a wonderful and unspeakable way in one person with the Word, the only-begotten of the Father, a son by nature not by grace, and therefore having no sin of his own; nevertheless, on account of the likeness of sinful flesh in which he came, he was called sin, that he might be sacrificed to wash away sin . . . For, under the old covenant, sacrifices for sin were called sins. And he, of whom all these sacrifices were types and shadows, was himself truly made sin. Hence the apostle, after saying: 'We pray you in Christ's stead, be ye reconciled to God,' forthwith adds: *'for he hath made him to be sin for us who knew no sin; that we might be made the righteousness of God in him.'* He does not say, as some incorrect copies read: 'He who knew no sin did sin for us,' as if Christ had himself sinned for our sakes; but he says: 'Him who knew no sin,' that is, Christ, God, to whom we are to be reconciled: 'hath made to be sin for us,' that is, hath *made him a sacrifice for our sins*, by which we might be reconciled to God. He, then, being made sin, just as we are made righteousness (our righteousness being not our own, but God's, not in ourselves, but in him); He being made sin, not his own, but ours, not in himself, but in us, showed, by the likeness of sinful flesh in which he was crucified, that though sin was not in him, yet that in a certain sense he died to sin, by dying in the flesh which was the likeness of sin; and that although he himself had never lived the old life of sin, yet by his resurrection he typified our new life springing up out of the old death in sin" (Augustine, *Enchiridion* 41)

"He had no sin at all; and therefore became a true sacrifice for sin because he himself had no sin . . . [sacrifices] are called sins by the law . . . such sin then, that is, such a sacrifice for sin, was our Lord Jesus

---

4. In Augustine's *Faith, Hope, and Love* 14.13, he wrote: "(Paul) does not say, as we read in some defective copies: 'He who knew no sin did sin for us,' as if Christ himself committed sin for our sake. Rather, he says: 'He [Christ] who knew no sin, he [God] made to be sin for us.' The God to whom we are to be reconciled hath thus made him the sacrifice for sin by which we may be reconciled."

Christ made "who knew no sin." (Augustine, *On the Gospel of St. John*, Tractate 41, 5ff.).

"[God] has made him to be sin for us: that is to say a sacrifice by which our sins may be remitted" (Augustine, *On Original Sin* 37)

"How do we tolerate what is said "He made him sin'? They who are acquainted with the Scriptures of the Old Testament recognize what I am saying. For it is not an expression once used, but repeatedly, very constantly, sacrifices for sins are called 'sins'" (Augustine, *Sermons on New Testament Lessons*, Sermon 84, 5).

*(The notion that "sin" refers to human nature liable to death comes out strongly in Augustine's anti-Manichean writings. The following is an example)* "He takes away death by death, and sin by sin. In the words 'cursed is everyone that hangeth on a tree,' there is no more blasphemy than in the words of the apostles 'he died,' or 'our old man was crucified along with him,' or 'by sin he condemned sin,' or 'he made him to be sin for us who knew no sin,' and in many similar passages. Confess then, that when you exclaim against the curse of Christ you exclaim against his death" (Augustine, *Reply to Faustus the Manichean* 14.12; see also, Augustine, *Against Two Letters of the Pelagians* 16).

﹌

**PETER ABELARD (c. 1079–1142).** *Abelard interpreted 'hamartia' in 2 Corinthians 5:21 as equivalent to "sin-offering." He also promulgated the Moral Influence theory of the atonement, which emphasizes the ability of the cross, as a demonstration of the love of God, to evoke the response of repentance and love.[5] However, this quotation from his works shows that Abelard also held to a traditional interpretation of the work of Christ alongside his theory of moral influence.*

"A victim for sin is also called 'sin' as when the apostle speaks of Jesus Christ as having been 'made sin.' The penalty of sin is also called 'sin' or 'a curse', as we say that sin is forgiven, meaning that the penalty is remitted, and that the Lord Jesus Christ 'bore our sins', meaning that He endured the penalty for our sins, or the penalties springing from them" (Abelard, *Ethics* 14).

﹌

---

5. See Walker's glossary in Torrance, *Atonement*, 459.

# The Historical/Theological Exegesis of 2 Corinthians 5:21

**THOMAS AQUINAS (1225-1274).** *Aquinas followed Augustine, illustrating Augustine's dominance in the Latin West. Aquinas first interprets "αμαρτια as "sin-offering", before expounding Augustine's second option of "vulnerable humanity."*

"God "made Christ to be sin", not by making Him a sinner, but by making Him a victim for sin. There is a parallel here in Hosea where the people are said to feed on the sin of my people (Hosea 4:8), because, according to the Law they would eat the victim offered for sin. In the same sense we have in Isaiah, 'The Lord has laid on Him the iniquity of us all', meaning that He gave Him up to be a victim for the sins of all men." (Aquinas, *Summa Theologiae*, 3a, XV, 1:4).

"Or: 'made Him to be sin' could mean "in the likeness of sinful flesh as in *Romans 8:3*. And this would be because of the vulnerable and mortal body which He took on." (Aquinas, *Summa Theologiae*, 3a, XV, 1:4).

⌇

**JOHN CALVIN (1509-1564).** *Calvin followed Augustine, Abelard, and Aquinas. He emphasized that Christ was sinless, and argued that "sin" in this context means the "guilt of sin" in becoming a sacrifice for us.*

"[Paul] says, then, that Christ, while he was entirely exempt from sin, was *made sin for us*. It is commonly remarked, that sin here denotes an expiatory sacrifice for sin, and in the same way the Latins term it, *piaculum*. Paul, too, has in this, and other passages, borrowed this phrase from the Hebrews, among whom μça (*asham*) denotes an *expiatory sacrifice* as well as an *offense* or *crime*. But the signification of this word, as well as the entire statement, will be better understood from a comparison of both parts of the antithesis. *Sin* is here contrasted with *righteousness*, when Paul teaches us, that we were made the righteousness of God, on the ground of Christ's having been made sin. Righteousness, here, is not taken to denote a quality or habit, but by way of imputation, on the ground of Christ's righteousness being reckoned to have been received by us. What, on the other hand, is denoted by *sin*? It is the guilt, on account of which we are arraigned at the bar of God. As, however, the curse of the individual was of old cast upon the victim, so Christ's condemnation was our absolution, and '*with his stripes we are healed*' (Isaiah 53:5)" (Calvin, *Commentary on 2 Corinthians 5:21*).

For Calvin, 2 Cor 5:21 did not imply necessarily that sin was ontologically imputed to Jesus Christ. Nevertheless, Calvin noted the connection between *our sin being imputed to Jesus Christ and his righteousness being imputed to us. At this point we would like Calvin to go further. Calvin drew on the notion of a legal/forensic imputation, as introduced by Melanchthon. However, this means that Jesus on the cross was simply a symbol in the same way as the scapegoat in the Old Testament was a symbol. But, as we argued in our main text, in contrast to the symbolic atonement of the Old Testament sacrificial system, on the cross reality breaks in when true atonement takes place. It has sometimes been claimed that Calvin described Jesus as becoming a sinner in our place. What he did say of Jesus was that he represented "the person of a sinner"; this is indicative of something deeper in his exegesis of 2 Cor 5:21 than Jesus merely being the "sin-bearer":*

"When we hear that Christ was led from the judge's seat to death and hanged between thieves, we possess the fulfillment of the prophecy to which the Evangelist referred: 'He was reckoned among the transgressors' (Mark 15:28, Vulg.; cf. Isa. 53:12). Why so? Surely that he might die in the place of the sinner, not of the righteous or innocent man. For he suffered death not because of innocence but because of sin . . . Thus we shall *behold the person of a sinner and evil-doer* represented in Christ, yet from his shining innocence it will at the same time be obvious that he was burdened with another's sin rather than his own" (Calvin, *Institutes* 2.16.5).

"It follows, therefore, either that he was crucified in vain, or that our curse was laid upon him that we might be delivered from it. Now, [Paul] does not say that Christ was cursed, but something more, that he was a curse, signifying that the curse of all was placed on him . . . But how does it happen, someone may object, that a beloved Son is cursed by his Father? I reply, there are two things to be considered, not only in the person of Christ, but even in His human nature. The one is that he was the unspotted lamb of God, full of blessing and grace. The other is that he took our place *and thus became a sinner* and subject to the curse, not in Himself indeed, but in us; yet in such a way that it was necessary for Him to act in our name" (Calvin, *Commentary on Galatians*).

*In the above extract there is the suggestion that to be identified with the curse is synonymous with identification with sin itself. Calvin also wrote:*

"Hence, when Christ is hanged upon the cross, he makes himself subject to the curse which (on account of our sins awaited us, or rather lay upon us) might be lifted from us, while it was transferred to him . . . Now it is clear what the prophet's utterance means: 'The Lord has laid on him the iniquity of us all' (Isa. 53:6). That is, he who was about to cleanse the filth of those iniquities was covered with them by *transferred imputation.* The cross, to which he was nailed, was a symbol of this, as the apostle testifies: 'Christ redeemed us from the curse of the law, when he became a curse for us'" (Calvin, *Institutes* 2.16.6).

~

**JOHN OWEN (1616-1683).** *The Puritan John Owen interpreted 2 Cor 5:21 in terms of forensic imputation. From many references in his writings, the following have been selected.*

"'He made him to be sin for us, who knew no sin; that we might be made the righteousness of God in him.' The adjunct in both places is put for the subject, as the opposition between his being made sin and our being made righteousness declareth. 'Him who knew no sin'—that is, who deserved no punishment—'him hath he made to be sin,' or laid the punishment due to sin upon him. Or perhaps, in the latter place, sin may be taken for an offering or sacrifice for the expiation of sin, *hamartia* answering in this place to the [Hebrew text of] the Old Testament, which signifieth both sin and the sacrifice for it."[6]

"'*He made him to be sin for us*': how could that be? Are not the next words: '*He knew no sin*'? Was he not a Lamb without blemish, and without spot? Doubtless: 'he did no sin; neither was guile found in his mouth.' What then is this: '*God made him to be sin*'? It cannot be that God made him sinful, or a sinner by any inherent sin; that will not stand with the justice of God nor with the holiness of the person of our Redeemer. What is it, then: '*He made him to be sin who knew no sin*'? Why then, clearly, by dispensation and consent, he laid that to his charge whereof he was not guilty. He charged upon him, and imputed unto him, all the sins of all the elect, and proceeded against him accordingly. He stood as our surety, really charged with the whole debt, and was to pay the utmost farthing, as a surety is to do if it be required of him; though he borrow not the money, nor have one penny of that which is in the obligation, yet if he be sued to an execution, he must pay all. The Lord Christ (if I may so say) was sued by his Father's justice unto an execution, in answer whereunto he underwent all that was due to sin; which we proved before to be death, wrath, and curse.'"[7]

---

6. Owen, *Works of John Owen*, 10:172.
7. Owen, *Works of John Owen*, 10:285; cf. 210, 294.

*In his influential book on the Doctrine of Justification, Owen devoted a major section (332–38) to a detailed theological exegesis of 2 Cor 5:21.*[8] *The whole of Owen's scholarly discussion is important, but too extensive to quote in full. The following extracts give a flavor of Owen's meticulous work, as he followed Augustine's line.*

"To set out the greatness of the grace of God in our reconciliation by Christ, he describes him by that paraphrasis . . . 'who knew no sin' or 'who knew not sin.' He knew sin in the notion or understanding of its nature, and he knew it experimentally in the effects which he underwent and suffered; but he knew it not—that is, was most remote from it—as to its commission or guilt. So that 'he knew no sin,' is absolutely no more but 'he did no sin, neither was guile found in his mouth,' as it is expressed (1 Peter 2:22); or that he was 'holy, harmless, undefiled, separate from sinners' (Hebrews 7:26). Howbeit, there is an emphasis in the expression, which is not to be neglected: . . . and the observation of it is not to be despised . . . 'He has made him to be sin.' 'That is' say many expositors: 'a sacrifice for sin.' . . . And I shall not contend about this exposition, because that signified in it is according unto the truth. But there is another more proper signification of the word: *hamartia* being put for *hamartolos*, 'sin' for a 'sinner' (that is, *passively*, not *actively*; not by inhesion, but imputation); for this the phrase of speech and force of the antithesis seem to require. . . . And if this be the interpretation of the Greek scholiasts, as indeed it is, Luther was not the first who affirmed that Christ was made the greatest sinner—namely, by imputation. But we shall allow the former exposition, provided that the true notion of a sin-offering, or expiatory sacrifice, be admitted: for although this neither was nor could consist in the transfusion of the inherent sin of the person into the sacrifice, yet did it so in the translation of the guilt of the sinner unto it; as is fully declared (Leviticus 16:20, 21)."[9]

"The only inquiry is, how God did make him to be sin? 'He has made him to be sin' so that an act of God is intended. And this is elsewhere expressed by his 'laying all our iniquities upon him', or causing them to meet on him (Isaiah 53:6). And this was by the imputation of our sins unto him, as the sins of the people were put on the head of the goat, that they should be no more theirs, but his, so as that he was to carry them away from them. Take sin in either sense before mentioned, either

---

8. Owen, *Doctrine of Justification by Faith*.
9. Owen, *Doctrine of Justification by Faith*, 332.

of a sacrifice for sin, or a sinner, and the imputation of the guilt of sin antecedently unto the punishment of it, and in order whereunto, must be understood. For in every sacrifice for sin there was an *imposition of sin* on the beast to be offered, antecedent unto the sacrificing of it, and therein its suffering by death. Therefore, in every offering for sin, he that brought it was to 'put his hand on the head of it' (Leviticus 1:4). And that the transferring of the guilt of sin unto the offering was thereby signified, is expressly declared (Leviticus 16:21). Wherefore, if God made the Lord Christ a sin-offering for us, it was by the imputation of the guilt of sin unto him antecedently unto his suffering. Nor could any offering be made for sin, without a typical translation of the guilt of sin unto it . . . But a sacrifice for sin without the imputation of guilt there could not be. And if the word be taken in the second sense—namely, for a sinner, that is, by imputation, and in God's esteem—it must be by the imputation of guilt; for none can, in any sense, be denominated a sinner from mere suffering. None, indeed, do say that Christ was made sin by the imputation of punishment unto him, which has no proper sense; but they say sin was imputed unto him as unto punishment: which is indeed to say that the guilt of sin was imputed unto him; for the guilt of sin is its respect unto punishment, or the obligation unto punishment which attends it. And that any one should be punished for sin without the imputation of the guilt of it unto him, is impossible; and, were it possible, would be unjust: for it is not possible that any one should be punished for sin properly, and yet that sin be none of his. And if it be not his by inhesion, it can be his no other way but by imputation. One may suffer on the occasion of the sin of another that is no way made his, but he cannot be punished for it; for punishment is the recompense of sin on the account of its guilt. And, were it possible, where is the righteousness of punishing any one for that which no way belongs unto him? Besides, imputation of sin, and punishing, are distinct acts, the one preceding the other; and therefore the former is only of the guilt of sin: wherefore, the Lord Christ was made sin for us, by the imputation of the guilt of our sins unto him."[10]

"Unless the *guilt of sin* was imputed unto Christ, sin was not imputed unto him in any sense, for the punishment of sin is not sin; nor can those who are otherwise minded declare what it is of sin that is imputed. But the Scripture is plain, that "God laid on him the iniquity of us all" and: "made him to be sin for us" which could not otherwise be but by imputation."[11]

10. Owen, *Doctrine of Justification by Faith*, 334; see also, 337.
11. Owen, *Doctrine of Justification by Faith*, 196.

**KARL BARTH (1886-1968).** *Barth adopted a literal reading of 2 Cor 5:21. He accepted that Christ was truly made sin on the Cross. This cut across traditional interpretations of the verse. Barth denied that this compromised the personal sinlessness of Jesus Christ: Christ became sin: but it was our sin that he became, he had no sin of his own. At the same time, Barth accepted that Jesus is also a sin-offering. That must be so. However, he is such, not by a symbolic transference of sin or guilt, but by taking real sin into himself.*

"All earlier theology, up to and including the Reformers and their successors, exercised at this point a very understandable reserve, calculated to dilute the offence (but also to weaken the high positive meaning of passages like 2 Corinthians 5:21, Galatians 3:13)" (Barth, *CD* I/2, 153).

"'He has made him to be sin for us' does not mean that he made him a man who also sins again—what could that signify for us!—but that he put him in the position of a sinner by way of exchange (*katalasson* in the sense of the Old Testament sin-offering)" (Barth, *CD* I/2, 156).

**GERHARD KITTEL (1888-1948).** *Kittel, in his ground-breaking theological dictionary of the New Testament, Vol. 1, 295–97, pointed out that, in classical Greek, and in Plato, 'hamartia' simply denoted the defective nature of man; however, under Hebrew and Old Testament influence, 'hamartia' in the Septuagint and the New Testament means 'human nature in hostility to God.' Commenting on 2 Corinthians 5:21, Kittel wrote that the verse 'shows hamartia to be a pregnant expression for the whole sinful nature of man.'*

"At this point Paul differs from Judaism. For Paul, sin does not consist only *in the individual act*. Sin is for him an *all-embracing state* which embraces all humanity . . . It is in this reality that the Christ event strikes man. This event is the overcoming of sin . . . The aim of Christ's sending by God is to judge and destroy sin. This is the meaning of the incarnation. Paul states this graphically [in 2 Corinthians 5:21] . . . The sinlessness of Jesus is the presupposition of His mission. According to Paul's description of the mystery of the Christ event, *this sinless Jesus became sin* . . ."[12]

---

12. Kittel and Friedrich, *Theological Dictionary of the New Testament*, 311–12.

# The Historical/Theological Exegesis of 2 Corinthians 5:21

**W. F. ARNDT (1880–957) and F. W. GINGRICH (1901–1993).** *Augustine's line was adopted by Arndt and Gingrich in their Greek-English Lexicon. Their work was based on the fourth German edition (1949–1952) of Walter Bauer's Greek-German lexicon. Arndt & Gingrich adopted Augustine's weaker interpretations of hamartia. Arndt & Gingrich cited Plummer but did not make clear that Plummer strongly rejected the possibility that hamartia only means "liable to death" or "sin-offering.*

"(God) has made Him to be sin (i.e., subject to death) who knew no sin, for our sakes. Or, *hamartia* means 'sin-offering' here as in Leviticus 4:24 (cf. Plummer ICC ad. Loc.) Or Jesus is viewed as representative and bearer of the world's sin."[13]

~

**ROBERT L. REYMOND (1932–2013).** *Robert Reymond had BA, MA, and PhD degrees from Bob Jones University, and held a traditional Reformed position on 2 Cor 5:21.*[14] *For Reymond, forensic imputation was seen as adequately describing the transaction which took place on Calvary. Reymond rejected the notion that a forensic imputation creates a legal fiction.*

"Paul was viewing the reconciliatory work as a past, objective and forensic event and not as a subjective ongoing operation in men's hearts."[15]

"The Scriptures make it clear that Christ died not a potentially but an actually *sacrificial* death on the cross, becoming there both sin and curse as the substitute for others, as the substitute in behalf of others, as a substitute in the stead or place of others, thereby paying the penalty, bearing the curse, and dying the death for all those for whom he died."[16]

"Justification refers to God's *wholly* objective, *wholly* forensic [italics are Reymond's] judgment concerning the sinner's standing before the law, by which forensic judgment God declares that the sinner is righteous in hs sight because of the imputation of his sin to Christ, on which ground he is pardoned, and the imputation of Christ's perfect obedience to him, on which ground he is constituted righteous before God."[17]

---

13. Arndt and Gingrich, *Greek-English Lexicon of the New Testament*, 43.

14. Reymond, *Systematic Theology*. See also Oden, *Systematic Theology*, 2:384, 412; 3:113, 320.

15. Reymond, *Systematic Theology*, 647.

16. Reymond, *Systematic Theology*, 680.

17. Reymond, *Systematic Theology*, 742.

"Romes urges, as do also Sanday and Headlam, that if justification is only forensic 'the Christian life is made to have its beginning in a fiction.'" But this objection is due to a failure to realize that God does not treat the justified sinner *as if* he were righteous before him when actually he is not. To the contrary the justified sinner is in fact righteous in God's sight because of the 'in Christ' relationship in which he stands (2 Corinthians 5:21) in which relationship the righteousness of Christ is actually imputed to him."[18]

**MURRAY J. HARRIS (1939–).** *In his commentary on the Greek text of 2 Corinthians, the conservative-evangelical biblical scholar Murray Harris, engaged in an extended analysis of 2 Cor 5:21. His work requires comment as well as citation.*

"We conclude that in v. 21 Paul is not saying that at the crucifixion the sinless Christ became in some sense a sinner, yet he is affirming more than that Christ became a sin-offering or even a sin-bearer. In a sense beyond human comprehension, God treated Christ as "sin" aligning him so totally with sin and its dire consequences that from God's viewpoint he became indistinguishable from sin itself."[19]

"With the next phrase 'he [God] made himself [Christ] to be sin' we penetrate to the center of the atonement and stand in awe before one of the most profound mysteries in the universe ... The meaning here is not 'God made the sinless one into sin' but 'God *caused* the sinless one *to be* sin.'"[20]

*Harris then discussed when Christ's identification with sin took place? At the incarnation? At the crucifixion? He noted that supporters of the "incarnational view" point to Rom 8:3, but he rejected that interpretation. Though 2 Cor 5:21 makes no explicit reference to the death or the cross of Christ, Harris argued that the three references to the death of Jesus in verses 14 and 15 give the context for verse 21. After a more detailed discussion than that of Plummer on whether* hamartia *might simply mean "sin-offering" he concluded it meant more.*

---

18. Reymond, *Systematic Theology*, 753. Reymond allowed the notion of an ontological imputation of righteousness to the sinner. He did not allow the notion of an ontological imputation of sin to Christ. Reymond's argument is unconvincing, though he did realize that imputation of righteousness must be ontological.

19. Harris, *2 Corinthians*, 454.

20. Harris, *2 Corinthians*, 451.

"It remains true that *hamartia* does not bear the meaning "sin offering" anywhere else in Paul or the NT."[21]

Harris felt that Paul may well have construed hamartia *in a more personal, inter-relational, sense than is represented by "sacrifice for sin" or "victim for sin." Significantly, Harris brought out the parallel between* hamartia *and the 'righteousness of God':* "If hamartia is parallel to *dikaiosune Theou* it is more likely to bear a judicial or forensic sense than a sacrificial or cultic meaning."[22] *He then discussed three possible meanings of* hamartia: Sinner, Sin-Bearer, or Sin. *It was the third which he focused on most:* "This total identification of the sinless one with sinners at the cross, in assuming the full penalty and guilt of their sin, leaves no doubt that substitution as well as representation was involved."[23]

*This reveals a concern of Harris' entire exegesis. He wanted to clarify that Jesus was not simply representing sinners before God, but was involved in atonement through substitution. To protect the doctrine of penal substitution he used the forensic/legal model. And yet, Harris was aware that Paul's phrase not only gives an exegetical foundation for penal substitution, but points further:* "Yet [Paul] is affirming more than that Christ became a sin-offering or even a sin-bearer."[24]

☙

**ALISTER E. McGRATH (1953-).** *Alister McGrath's* Iustitia Dei: A History of the Christian Doctrine of Justification *(Cambridge: CUP, 2020) dealt at length with patristic, medieval, and reformation understanding of the doctrine, and discussed forensic/ontological categories. Elsewhere, he wrote the following.*

"Whereas Augustine taught that the sinner is made righteous in justification, Melanchthon taught that he is counted as righteous or pronounced to be righteous. For Augustine: 'justifying righteousness' is imparted; for Melanchthon, it is imputed in the sense of being declared or pronounced to be righteous. Melanchthon drew a sharp distinction between the event of being declared righteous and the process of being made righteous, designating the former 'justification' and the latter 'sanctification' or 'regeneration.' For Augustine, these were simply different aspects

---

21. Harris, *2 Corinthians*, 453.
22. Harris, *2 Corinthians*, 453.
23. Harris, *2 Corinthians*, 453.
24. Harris, *2 Corinthians*, 454.

of the same thing . . . The importance of this development lies in the fact that it marks a complete break with the teaching of the church up to that point. From the time of Augustine onwards, justification had always been understood to refer to both the event of being declared righteous and the process of being made righteous. Melanchthon's concept of forensic justification diverged radically from this. As it was taken up by virtually all the major reformers subsequently, it came to represent a standard difference between Protestant and Roman Catholic from then on. In addition to differences regarding how the sinner was justified, there was now an additional disagreement on what the word 'justification'designated in the first place. The Council of Trent, the Roman Catholic church's definitive response to the Protestant challenge, reaffirmed the views of Augustine on the nature of justification, and censured the views of Melanchthon as woefully inadequate . . . the concept of forensic justification actually represents a development in Luther's thought."[25]

---

25. McGrath, *Reformation Thought: An Introduction*, 108–9.

# Bibliography

Arndt, William F., and F. Wilbur Gingrich. *A Greek-English Lexicon of the New Testament and Other Early Christian Literature*. Grand Rapids: Zondervan, 1968.
Barrett, Matthew, ed. *The Doctrine on Which the Church Stands or Falls: Justification in Biblical, Theological, Historical, and Pastoral Perspective*. Wheaton: Crossway, 2019.
Barth, Karl. *Church Dogmatics*. Translated by G. T. Thomson et al. Edinburgh: T. & T. Clark, 1936–77.
———. *Evangelical Theology*. Translated by Grover Foley. London: Collins/Fontana, 1963.
———. *Fragments Grave and Gay*. Translated by Eric Mosbacher. London: Collins, 1971.
———. *The Göttingen Dogmatics: Instruction in the Christian Religion*. Vol. 1. Translated by Geoffrey W. Bromiley. Grand Rapids: Eerdmans, 1991.
———. *The Knowledge of God and the Service of God: According to the Teaching of the Reformation, Recalling the Scottish Confession of 1560*. Translated by J. L. M. Haire and Ian Henderson. 1938. Reprint, Eugene, OR: Wipf & Stock, 2005.
———. *Letters of Karl Barth, 1961–1968*. Edited by Jürgen Fangmeier and Hinrich Stoevesandt. Translated by Geoffrey W. Bromiley. Edinburgh: T. & T. Clark, 1981.
———. *The Word of God and the Word of Man*. Translated by Douglas Horton. London: Hodder & Stoughton, c. 1930.
Beck, Stanley D. *The Simplicity of Science*. London: Lutterworth, 1960.
Bengel, J. A. *Gnomon of the New Testament*. Vol. 3, *Romans–2 Corinthians*. Edinburgh: T. & T. Clark, 1858.
Bonar, Andrew. *Diary*. London: Banner of Truth, 1960.
Brown, David. *The Life of Rabbi Duncan*. 1872. Reprint, Glasgow: Free Presbyterian Publications, 1986.
Brunner, Emil. "Christian Understanding of Time." *SJT* 4.1 (1951) 1–12.
———. *The Mediator*. Translated by Olive Wyon. London: Lutterworth, 1934.
Busch, Eberhard. *Karl Barth: His Life from Letters and Autobiographical Texts*. Translated by John Bowden. London: SCM, 1976.
Calvin, John. *Commentary on the Epistle of Paul to the Galatians*. Translated by T. H. L. Parker. Edinburgh: St Andrew's, 1965.
———. *Geneva Catechism, 1541*. Translated and edited by T. F. Torrance. The School of Faith. London: Clarke, 1959.
———. *The Institutes of the Christian Religion*. Vol. 1. Translated by F. L. Battles. The Library of Christian Classics. Philadelphia: Westminster, 1960.

Cameron, Nigel M. de S., ed. *Dictionary of Scottish Church History and Theology.* Edinburgh: T. & T. Clark, 1993.

Campbell, J. McLeod. *The Nature of the Atonement.* 1856. Reprint, London: Clarke, 1959.

Chiarot, Kevin. *The Unassumed Is the Unhealed: The Humanity of Christ in the Christology of T. F. Torrance.* Eugene: Pickwick, 2013.

Church of Scotland. *The Biblical Doctrine of Baptism.* Edinburgh: The Saint Andrew Press, 1958.

Crowe, Brandon. *The Last Adam: A Theology of the Obedient Life of Jesus in the Gospel.* Baker, 2017.

———. "Passive and Active Obedience of Christ." In *The Doctrine on Which the Church Stands or Falls: Justification in Biblical, Theological, Historical, and Pastoral Perspective,* edited by Matthew Barrett, 443–46. Wheaton: Crossway, 2019.

———. "Two Benefits of Justification." https://faculty.wts.edu/posts/two-benefits-of-justification/.

Dawkins, Richard. *Unweaving the Rainbow: Science, Delusion and the Appetite for Wonder.* London: Penguin, 2006.

Dawson, Gerrit Scott. *Jesus Ascended: The Meaning of Christ's Continuing Incarnation.* Phillipsburg, NJ: P&R Publishing, 2004.

Denny, James. *Studies in Theology: Lectures given in Chicago Theological Seminary.* London: Hodder & Stoughton, 1895.

Dorries, David W. *Edward Irving's Incarnational Christology.* Fairfax, VA: Xulon, 2002.

Duncan, George. *Jesus, Son of Man: Studies Contributory to a Modern Portrait.* London: Nisbet, 1947.

Ferguson, Sinclair B. "William Still." In *DSCHT* 797.

Ferguson, Sinclair B., ed. *The Collected Writings of William Still.* Vol. 2, *Studies in the Christian Life.* Edinburgh: Rutherford House, 1994.

Green, Lowell C. *How Melanchthon Helped Luther Discover the Gospel.* Fallbrook: Verdict, 1980.

Harnack, Adolf von. *Das Wesen des Christentums.* 1901. Reprint, Tübingen: Mohr Siebeck, 2012.

———. *What Is Christianity?* Translated by T. B. Saunders: London: Williams and Norgate, 1901.

Harris, Murray J. *The Second Epistle to the Corinthians: A Commentary on the Greek Text.* Grand Rapids: Eerdmans, 2005.

Hart, Trevor, and Daniel Thimell. *Christ in Our Place: The Humanity of God in Christ for the Reconciliation of the World: Essays presented to Professor James Torrance.* Princeton Theological Monograph Series. Princeton: Pickwick, 1991.

Hartwell, Herbert. *The Theology of Karl Barth: An Introduction.* London: Duckworth, 1964.

Heron, Alasdair I. C. *A Century of Protestant Theology.* Cambridge: Lutterworth, 1980.

———. "Homoousios with the Father." In *The Incarnation: Ecumenical Studies in the Nicene-Constantinopolitan Creed A.D. 381,* edited by Thomas F. Torrance, 58–87. Edinburgh: Handsel, 1981.

———. "James Torrance: An Appreciation." *Participatio* 3 (2014) 23–29.

Heron, Alasdair I. C., ed. *The Westminster Confession in the Church Today.* Edinburgh: St. Andrew Press, 1982.

Jaki, Stanley L. *The Relevance of Physics.* Chicago: Chicago Press, 1966.

———. *The Road of Science and the Ways to God*. Edinburgh: Scottish Academic Press, 1978.
Kittel, Gerhard, and Gerhard Friedrich, eds. *Theological Dictionary of the New Testament*. Vol. 1. Translated by Geoffrey W. Bromiley. Grand Rapids: Eerdmans, 1985.
Lessing, Gothold. "On the Proof of the Spirit and of Power." In *Lessing's Theological Writings: Selections in Translation*, by Gothold Lesson, edited by Henry Chadwick, 51–55. London: A. & C. Black, 1956.
Mackintosh, Hugh Ross. *The Christian Apprehension of God*. London: Nisbet, 1929.
———. *Types of Modern Theology: From Schleiermacher to Barth*. London: Nisbet, 1937.
McConnachie, John. *The Barthian Theology and the Man of Today*. London. Hodder & Stoughton, 1933.
———. *The Significance of Karl Barth*. London: Hodder & Stoughton, 1931.
McGrath, Alister E. *Iustitia Dei: A History of the Christian Doctrine of Justification*. Cambridge: Cambridge University Press, 2020.
———. *Reformation Thought: An Introduction*. Oxford: Blackwell, 1988.
———. *T. F. Torrance: An Intellectual Biography*. Edinburgh: T. & T. Clark, 1999.
Miller, John. *A Simple Life: Roland Walls and the Community of the Transfiguration*. Edinburgh: Saint Andrew, 2014.
Morris, Leon. *The Cross in the New Testament*. Exeter: Paternoster, 1965.
Needham, Nicholas R. "Irving, Edward." In *DSCHT* 436–37
Noble, Thomas A. "Torrance, Thomas Forsyth." In *DSCHT* 823–24.
Oden, Thomas C. *Systematic Theology*. 3 vols. Massachusetts: Hendrickson, 2006.
Owen, Huw P. *The Christian Knowledge of God*. London: Athlone, 1969.
Owen, John. *The Doctrine of Justification by Faith: Through the Imputation of the Righteousness of Christ Explained, Confirmed, and Vindicated*. N.p.: Christian Classics Ethereal Library, n.d.
———. *The Works of John Owen*. 16 vols. Banner of Truth edition. Edinburgh: Banner of Truth, 1968.
Paul, Iain. *Science, Theology, and Einstein*. Belfast: Christian Journals Limited, 1982.
Philip, James. *The Westminster Confession of Faith: An Exposition*. Edinburgh: Holyrood Abbey Church, 1966.
Plummer, Alfred. *International Critical Commentary on 2 Corinthians*. Edinburgh: T. & T. Clark, 1915.
Reymond, Robert L. *Systematic Theology*. Nashville: Nelson, 1998.
Ritchie, Bruce. "Theology and Logic." *SBET* 4.2 (1986) 109–22.
———. *Unpublished Manuscript Lecture Notes, 1973–1976*. Ritchie Personal Papers.
———. *Unpublished Manuscript Seminar Notes, 1973–1976*. Ritchie Personal Papers.
Robinson, John A. T. *But That I Can't Believe*. London: Fontana, 1974.
———. *Honest to God*. London: SCM, 1963.
———. *Re-Dating the New Testament*. 1976. Reprint, Eugene, OR: Wipf & Stock, 2001.
———. "Universalism—A Reply." *SJT* 2.4 (1949) 378–80.
———. "Universalism: Is It Heretical?" *SJT* 2.2 (1949) 139–55.
Rumscheidt, H. Martin. *Revelation and Theology: An Analysis of the Barth-Harnack Correspondence of 1923*. *SJT* Supplement 1. Cambridge: Cambridge University Press, 1972.
Schleiermacher, Friedrich. *The Christian Faith*. Translated by J. S. Stewart. Edinburgh: T. & T. Clark, 1928.

Shedd, W. G. T. *Dogmatic Theology*. 3rd ed. Edited by A. W. Gomes. Phillipsburg: P&R Publishing, 2003.
Still, William. *The Collected Writings of William Still*. Vol. 2, *Studies in the Christian Life*. Edited by Sinclair B. Ferguson. Edinburgh: Rutherford, 1994.
Stuart, Moody. *Recollections of the Late John Duncan, LL.D*. Edinburgh: Edmonston and Douglas, 1872.
Tasker, R. V. G. *Commentary on 2 Corinthians*. London: Tyndale, 1958.
Torrance, David W. *The Reluctant Minister*. Edinburgh: Handsel, 2015.
———. "The Vicarious Humanity of Christ, Incarnate, Crucified, Risen and Ascended." Unpublished paper presented at Firbush, November 2010.
Torrance, J. B. "Christ in our Place." In *A Passion for Christ: The Vision that Ignites Ministry*, edited by Thomas F. Torrance et al., 35–52. Edinburgh: Handsel, 1999.
———. "The Vicarious Humanity of Christ." In *The Incarnation: Ecumenical Studies in the Nicene-Constantinopolitan Creed A.D. 381*, edited by T. F. Torrance, 127–47. Edinburgh: Handsel, 1981.
Torrance, Thomas F. *The Apocalypse Today*. London: Clarke, 1960.
———. *Atonement: The Person and Work of Christ*. Edited by R. T. Walker. London: Paternoster, 2009.
———. *Divine and Contingent Order*. Oxford: Oxford University Press, 1981.
———. *Divine Interpretation: Studies in Medieval and Modern Hermeneutics*. Thomas F. Torrance Collected Studies 2. Edited by Adam Nigh and Todd Speidell. Eugene, OR: Pickwick, 2017.
———. *The Doctrine of Grace in the Apostolic Fathers*. 1948. Reprint, Eugene, OR: Wipf & Stock, 1996.
———. *God and Rationality*. London: Oxford University Press, 1971.
———. *Gospel, Church, and Ministry*. Thomas F. Torrance Collected Studies 1. Edited by J. Stein. Eugene, OR: Pickwick, 2012.
———. "Hugh Ross Mackintosh: Theologian of the Cross." *SBET* 5.2 (1987) 160–73.
———. *Incarnation: The Person and Life of Christ*. Edited by R. T. Walker. London: Paternoster, 2008.
———. "Intuitive and Abstractive Knowledge from Duns Scotus to John Calvin." In *De doctrina Ioannis Duns Scoti, Acta Congressus Scotistici Internationalis Oxonii et Edimburgi 11–17 Sept. 1966: Scotismus decursu saeculorum*, 291–305. Studia Scholastico-Scotistica 4. Rome: Societas Internationalis Scotistica, 1968.
———. *Karl Barth: An Introduction to His Early Theology 1910–1931*. London: SCM, 1962.
———. *The Mediation of Christ*. Grand Rapids: Eerdmans, 1984.
———. *Preaching Christ Today*. Musselburgh: Handsel, 1994.
———. *Royal Priesthood*. SJT Occasional Papers 3. Edinburgh: Oliver & Boyd, 1955.
———. *The School of Faith: The Catechisms of the Reformed Church*. London: Clarke, 1959.
———. *Scottish Theology: From John Knox to John McLeod Campbell*. Edinburgh: T. & T. Clark, 1996.
———. *Space, Time and Incarnation*. Oxford: Oxford University Press, 1969.
———. *Space, Time and Resurrection*. Edinburgh: Handsel, 1976.
———. *Theological Science*. London: Oxford University Press, 1969.
———. *The Trinitarian Faith: The Evangelical Theology of the Ancient Catholic Church*. Edinburgh: T. & T. Clark, 1988.

———. "Universalism—or Election." *SJT* 2.3 (1949) 310–18.

———. *Unpublished Letter to B. Ritchie, 1976*. Ritchie Personal Papers.

———. *When Christ Comes and Comes Again*. London: Hodder & Stoughton, 1957.

Torrance, Thomas F., ed. *The Incarnation: Ecumenical Studies in the Nicene-Constantinopolitan Creed A.D. 381*. Edinburgh: Handsel, 1981.

Torrance, Thomas F., et al., eds. *A Passion for Christ: The Vision that Ignites Ministry*. Edinburgh: Handsel, 1999.

Walker, R. T. "Introduction." In *Atonement: The Person and Work of Christ*, by T. F. Torrance, edited by R. T. Walker, xxxv–lxxxiv. London: Paternoster, 2009.

Zellweger-Barth, Max. *My Father-in-Law: Memories of Karl Barth*. Eugene, OR: Pickwick, 1986.

# Index

Abelard, Peter, 258, 259
Allmen, J. J. von, 220
Alyth, 4, 37, 214
Ambrose of Milan, 254–56
Anderson, George W., 15–17, 26, 59, 110
Anderson, Hugh, 15–17, 59, 110
Anselm of Canterbury, 31, 218–22, 230, 233, 235, 236, 238, 240
Apollinarius of Laodicea, 161–62, 228, 230, 235, 251, 254
Aquinas, Thomas, 45–46, 70–72, 81, 151, 193, 221, 234, 259
Arius of Alexandria, 82, 228, 230
Argyll, Duke of, 121
Arndt, William F., 152, 265
Athanasius of Alexandria, 20, 29, 31, 33, 74, 78, 82, 90, 140, 166, 217, 219–21, 228–32, 234, 236, 238, 249, 254
Auburn, 4, 51
Augustine of Hippo, 14, 33, 55, 150–53, 196, 218, 221, 234, 237, 254, 257–59, 262, 265, 267–68

Baelz, Peter, 218
Baillie, Donald M., 3, 29, 217, 218, 221
Baillie, John, 3
Barclay, William, 3
Basel, 4, 19, 122, 137
Barth, Karl, xvi, 4, 5, 15, 19, 24, 28–34, 43–52, 65, 75–77, 86, 98, 99, 105, 111, 114, 119–23, 126, 134, 137, 144, 149, 150, 166–68, 171, 181, 188, 195, 203, 214, 217–20, 226, 228, 230, 233, 234, 236, 237, 239, 240, 264
Barthianism, 22
Basil of Caesarea, 161, 220, 222, 251–52
Bavinck, Herman, 139
Beck, S. D., 182
Begbie, Jeremy, 246
Begg, Richard, 245
Bengel, J. A., 150
Berkeley, George, 64–65, 67
Berkhoff, Louis, 125, 217
Bindley, T. H., 219
Blackie, James, 15
Boece, Hector, 223
Bohr, Neils, 66, 85, 89
Bonar, Andrew, 143
Bonhoeffer, Dietrich, 23, 217–19, 221, 230, 246
Bonn, 30, 122
*Book of Discipline, The Second*, 25
Boston, Thomas, 222
Bouillard, Henri, 218
Brainerd, David, 143
Brewster, David, 88
Brodie, Robin, 245, 246
Bromiley, Geoffrey W., 5
Bronowski, Jacob, 88
Bruce, F. F., 153
Bruce, Robert, 166, 220
Brunner, Emil, 27, 31–32, 181, 217, 218
Buchanan, George, 223
Bultmann, Rudolf, 23, 198
Burnaby, J., 217
Busch, Eberhard, 50, 65, 114, 119

Calvin, John, 4, 15, 20, 31–33, 43, 48, 74, 75, 123, 131, 139, 142, 151, 155, 157, 166, 179, 184, 200, 217, 218, 220, 221, 229–33, 236, 238, 259–61
Calvinism (Federal), xv, 6, 99, 126, 148, 166, 168, 215
Cave, S., 219
Chaffee, Steve, 246
Chalcedon, Council of, 74, 104, 229, 230, 235, 236
Chalmers, Thomas, 120
Cheyne, Alec, 15
Chiarot, Kevin, 162
Chrysostom, John, 252–53
Cicognani, A. G., 46
Cledonius, 161
Clerk Maxwell, James, 7, 66, 85, 89
Cocceius, 223
Columba, x, xi
Constantine, 114
Constantinople, Council of, 74
Copernicus, Copernican, 33, 182
Croall Lectures, 121–22
Crowe, Brendan, 126, 134, 137, 146
Cullman, Oscar, 220
Cyprian of Carthage, 220
Cyril of Jerusalem, 220, 221, 232

Darrow, 83
Dawkins, Richard, 88
Dawson, Gerrit Scott, 13
Deddo, Gary, 243, 244, 246
Dehn, Rudolf, 24
Denney, James, 3, 129, 158
Descartes, Rene, 63–64, 68
Dickson, David, 223
Dionysius of Alexandria, 229
Dodd, C. H., 198
Domitian, 107
Donald, Peter, 243, 244
Dorries, David W., 167
Douglas, Robert, 223
Drygrange Seminary, 33
Duff, Alexander, 120
Duncan, G. S., 122
Duncan, John (Rabbi), 10–11, 126, 175
Duns Scotus, John, 75

Einstein, Albert, 7, 55–63, 66, 67, 84–89, 165, 200
Erskine, Thomas, of Linlathen, 166
Erskine, Thomas, 166, 223
Eugenio, Dick, 243
Evans, Robert F, 220

Fenner, Dudley, 223
Fergusson, David, 9, 243
Ferguson, John, 243
Ferguson, Ron, 14
Ferguson, Sinclair B, 3, 148
Field Theory, 55, 62, 86, 90
Firbush, 6–9, 22, 37, 43, 44, 78, 90, 97, 141–44, 162, 164, 242–47
Floether, Jennifer, 9, 244–47
Forrester, Duncan, 15
Forsyth, Peter T., 3
Forsythe, Alexander, 9, 247
Franks, R. S., 219
Friedrich, Gerhard, 153
Fuller, R. H., 219

Galileo, Galilei, 63
Gifford Lectures, 65, 84, 122
Gingrich, F. Wilbur, 152, 265
Graham, Billy, 26
*Geneva Catechism*, 131, 217
Gödel, Kurt, 64, 84
Grant, Jamie, 80
Green, F. W., 219
Green, Lowell C., 131
Gregory of Nazianzus, 161–63, 221, 228, 250–251, 254
Gregory of Nyssa, 78, 161, 249–50

Habets, Myk, 247
Hamilton, Alan, 245
Hardy, E. R., 219
Harnack, Adolf von, 30, 45, 47, 49, 73, 76, 79, 98–99, 100–124, 146
Hart, Trevor, 246
Hartwell, Herbert, 195
Hegel, Georg W. F., 47
*Heidelberg Catechism*, 138
Heim, Karl, 218
Heisenberg, Werner, 55
Hendry, G. S., 217, 221

# Index

Heron, Alasdair I. C., 13–15, 21, 82, 112
Hewett Lectures, 52
Hick, John, 218, 240
Hilary of Poitiers, 15, 31, 32, 74, 90, 218, 220, 224, 235, 252
Hodgson, L., 218
Horne, Douglas, 17
Hume, David, 64–67, 83, 84

Irenaeus of Lyon, 228, 232
Irving, Edward, 167–68, 223

Jaki, Stanley L., 65, 84
John of Damascus, 234, 238

Kaiser, Christopher, 15, 31, 62, 85
Kant, Immanuel, 33, 65–66, 101, 200, 236
Kelly, Caroline, 9
Kelly, Douglas, 9, 142–45, 242
Kepler, Johannes, 63
Kimber, Peter, 244
Kittel, Gerhard, 153, 264
Knox, John, 6, 11, 120, 223
Kodacsy, Tamas, 9, 247
Kruger, Baxter, 9, 245
Kung, Hans, 220, 221
Kunneth, W., 219

Leibnitz, 200
Lessing, Gotthold E., 104–5
Lett, Jonathan, 245
Livingstone, David, 120
Locke, John, 63
Lonergan, Bernard, 241
Lossky, V., 220
Luther, Martin, 15, 117, 120, 123, 130–32, 196, 229, 262, 268

MacDonald, Joanna, 9, 243
Mackinnon, A., 218
Mackintosh, Hugh Ross, 3, 4, 27, 50, 61, 98, 121, 122, 129, 217, 224
Maclaren, Elizabeth, 12
Macleod, Donald, 3
Macleod, John, 3
MacLeod-Campbell, John, 6, 31, 32, 129, 219, 223, 225, 230, 236

Magruder, Kerry, 247
Major, John, 223
Mascall, E. L., 221
May, Stephen, 246
McConnachie, John, 49–50
McDonnell, Killian, 221
McIntyre, John, 12
McGowan, Andrew T. B., xiii, 6, 9, 164, 242, 243
McGrath, Alister E., xv, 3, 52, 131, 267–68
Melanchthon, Philip, 130–32, 260, 267–68
Melito of Sardis, 228
Meyer, Neil, 245
Miller, John, 243, 244
Milligan, William, 221
Moffat, Robert, x
Mornay, Duplessis, 223
Morrice, Alastair, 204
Morris, Leon, 158
Morrison, Angus, 9, 245, 246
Morrison, Frank, 19
Mozley, J. K., 219
Murray, J. Harris, 153, 266–67

Navarro, Kevin, 244
Needham, Nick, 167
Newbiggin, Leslie, 220, 221
New College, Edinburgh, ix, xv, 3–6, 10–17, 21–26, 30–34, 41, 50, 56, 74–75, 83, 88, 95, 98, 103, 110, 122, 142, 149, 166, 195, 214
Newton, Isaac, Newtonian, 7, 55–58, 63, 65, 84–86, 90, 186–88, 200
Nicaea, Council of, 74, 104, 150, 161, 227, 229, 248
Nigh, Adam, 243
Nissiotis, N. A., 237
Noble, Thomas A., 3, 9, 18, 35, 70, 244–46

Oden, Thomas C., 265
O'Donoghue, Noel, 12
Origen of Alexandria, 28, 221, 228, 230, 232, 248–49
Orr, James, 217
Owen, Huw P., 21 70–71

# Index

Owen, John, 142, 151, 261–63

Pannenberg W, 217, 219
Paul, Iain, 24, 62
Paul of Samosata, 228
Parry, Robin, 9, 244
Peat, William, 24, 27, 62, 70
Perkins, William, 223
Philip, James, xv, 34, 125–28, 136, 140, 148
Platek, Vanessa, 9, 243
Polanyi, Michael, 68–70, 224
Pope Paul VI, 46
Prestige, G. L., 219
Princeton, 51–52

Quantum Theory, 55, 60, 62, 63, 66, 86, 88–90, 165, 187, 215

Radcliff, Jason, 9, 162, 242, 243
Rahner, Karl, 218, 230, 234, 239
Ramsay, Alan, 13
Ramsay, A. M., 220
Rankin, Oliver Shaw, 121
Reid, J. K. S., 5
Reid, Thomas, 68
Relativity Theory, 55, 57, 60, 62, 66, 86, 88, 90, 165, 187, 215
Reymond, Robert L., 265–66
Richardson, C. C., 219
Riddell, John, xv
Ritschl, Albrecht, 100, 105, 108, 114
Robinson, John A. T., 15, 22–23, 42, 79
Rollock, Robert, 223
Rumscheidt, H. Martin, 49, 119, 126
Rutherford, Samuel, 166, 223

Safenwil, 48
Salmond, Charles A., 120
Schillebeeckx, E., 218, 240
Schleiermacher, Friedrich, 45, 47–51, 65, 121, 239
Schweitzer, Albert, 101
*Second Book of Discipline,* 25
Serapion, 220, 221, 231
Shaw, D. W. D., 12
Shedd W. G. T., 151

Sheed, F. J., 30, 217
Sherrard, Joey, 244
Smith, Ronald G., 3, 228
Steele, William, 244
Stewart, Dugald, 68
Still, William, xv, 148–50, 152, 154
Stone, Lance, 70, 246
Stuart, M., 11
Stuart-Lee, Alexandra, 9, 243
Symeon, the New Theologian, 161
Symington, William, 223

Tasker, R. V. G., 153
Taylor, John V., 220
Templeton, Douglas, 12
Tertullian of Carthage, 222, 228, 229, 232, 238
Theodoretus of Cyrus, 254
Theological Students" Fellowship, 22
Thin, James, xvi
Thistlewaite, David, 246
Thomson, G. T., 5, 50
Tillich, Paul, 23, 218
Torrance, Alan, 9, 243, 245
Torrance, Andrew, 9, 44, 245
Torrance, David J, 9, 245
Torrance, David W., 3, 5, 9, 141, 242–47
Torrance, Iain, xvi, 214
Torrance, James B., 3, 9, 11, 13, 14, 21, 26, 33, 47, 64, 70, 98, 101, 104–8, 114–18, 133, 134, 137
Torrance, Margaret, 5, 17
Troeltsch, Ernst, 114

Wainwright, A. W., 217
Wainwright, G., 220
Walker, Donald, 247
Walker, Robert T., ix–xi, xvi, 6–9, 22, 23, 37, 43, 78, 90, 137, 145, 198, 242–47, 258
Walls, Roland, 13–14
Weatherhead, James, 21
Weiss, Johannes, 101
Welch, C., 218
Wellhausen, Julius, 44
Westminster Theological Seminary, 126, 134

# Index

*Westminster Confession of Faith*, xv, 6, 15, 125–28, 132–36, 144, 150, 270, 271
Whaling, Frank, 12
Wilhelm II, Kaiser, 47, 119–21
Wynne, Alistair, 70

Yule, George, 15

Zellweger-Barth, Max, 28
Ziegler, Geordie, 9, 243, 244, 247
Zizoulas, John, 13, 15
Zomba Theological College, 14, 214
Zwingli, Ulrich, 48

www.ingramcontent.com/pod-product-compliance
Lightning Source LLC
Chambersburg PA
CBHW050839230426
43667CB00012B/2074